ECONOMY AND CLASS STRUCTURE

£2
9⊖

17|8.

ECONOMY AND CLASS STRUCTURE

ROSEMARY CROMPTON
and
JON GUBBAY

First edition 1977
Reprinted 1980

Published by
THE MACMILLAN PRESS LTD
London and Basingstoke
Associated companies in Delhi Dublin
Hong Kong Johannesburg Lagos Melbourne
New York Singapore and Tokyo

Printed in Hong Kong

British Library Cataloguing in Publication Data

Crompton, Rosemary
  Economy and class structure.
  1. Capitalism   2. Social classes
  I. Title   II. Gubbay, Jon
  301.44   HT609

  ISBN 0-333-21803-5

Contents

Preface

This book has grown out of our attempts to clarify a number of theoretical issues which arose during six years' teaching together on a second-year course in sociology at the University of East Anglia. Our ideas were stimulated both by the students and colleagues who participated in teaching the course – in particular, Melina Serafetinidis.

We find it difficult to locate the sources of our ideas, but we are conscious that we have been influenced by writings of Miliband, Poulantzas, Carchedi, Cliff, and Urry – although often our conclusions diverge radically from those of these authors.

We would like to thank Bob Blackburn, Geoff Ingham, John Urry, Bryan Heading and Gareth Jones for reading and making comments on earlier drafts – although, of course, we assume full responsibility for the final product.

Our gratitude is also due to Mary Gurteen, who efficiently undertook the bulk of the typing, and Jenny, Anne, Jan and Gerald, who made many involuntary sacrifices during the preparation of this book.

February 1977   R. C.
                                                       J. G.

I

Introduction

An excessive preoccupation with social class and class distinctions is popularly held to be one of the many problems which contributes to the sorry state of 'Britain today'. It is argued that class barriers lead to antagonism between management and work-force, when they should really be pulling together to overcome common economic difficulties, that public schools perpetuate outmoded social distinctions, or that the well-publicised antics of the rich make it more difficult to obtain moderation in pay demands. If only it could be more generally appreciated, runs this view, that 'the colonel's lady and Mary O'Grady are sisters under the skin', then it would be a simpler matter to achieve the sense of harmony and national cooperation essential to the regeneration of Britain.

This kind of approach to 'social class' – which focuses on how money is spent and associated factors such as accent, variations in etiquette, feelings of social superiority and inferiority, and so on – is not a major concern of this book. Nevertheless we do believe that problems associated with social class – as we shall define and use the term – *do* present serious, if not intractable, tensions and antagonisms for modern capitalist societies. Social class in the popular consciousness may be described by the sociological concept of social *status*, that is, a ranking of different groups in society according to the level of esteem or 'status honour' bestowed on a particular group, together with associated lifestyles, patterns of association, and marriage. Status differences do often present important conflicts and difficulties for groups and individuals, and we would in no way wish to underestimate this. However the kinds of tensions and antagonisms to which class conflict gives rise are infinitely more important for the stability of the total society than status group conflicts. For in a capitalist society fundamental class antagonisms are woven into the basic fabric of social life – that is, into relationships of production, distribution and exchange.

In one sense the class theory put forward in this book is not particularly new. The essential insights from which we develop our work were formulated by Marx in the nineteenth century. We believe, however, that it is a worthwhile and necessary exercise to develop these ideas for a number of reasons. First, Marx's basic concepts have been held to be hopelessly outmoded as far as twentieth-century industrial society is concerned – we think that we demonstrate that this is not the case. Second, even if Marx's theoretical insights are accepted as broadly correct, it is argued that the concept of 'social class' in Marxist theory cannot be applied except at the most abstract level – we think the model we develop is capable of empirical application. Last, but by no means least, is the fact that the prevailing tradition of sociological class theory essentially draws its inspiration from Max Weber, rather than Marx.

It has often been considered that Marx and Weber made similar assumptions in their theoretical approaches to social class. Indeed many sociological works supposedly informed by Marxist thinking have assumed, implicitly or explicitly, little difference between the two authors, although the final outcome has more usually been 'neo-Weberian' than 'neo-Marxist'. We argue, on the other hand, that it is a mistake to try to synthesise the concepts of class of these two theorists. In particular the emphasis on distribution and the associated phenomenon of the market in Weberian theory gives only a partial and at times misleading account of the class structure of capitalist industrial societies. In our discussion we follow Marx in grounding the class structure in relationships of production. In order to explain this we have to grapple with the complex structure of economic relationships in advanced capitalist societies.

It is from this relatively simple insight – that class relationships are ultimately located in production relationships – that we develop our model of the class structure. Although we have at all times made efforts to express ourselves clearly and unambiguously, the issues raised are difficult, presenting associated problems of exposition. Here, then, we will take the opportunity of sketching out some of the major arguments that follow.

In the next two chapters we deal more fully with the point we have just raised, setting out the theoretical ideas on social class of Marx and Weber, and illustrating the differences between them. In addition we examine the work of some contemporary class theorists whom we would term 'neo-Weberian': Lockwood, Parkin and Giddens. We argue that Weberian and neo-Weberian class theory is to be found lacking in two very important areas. First, class conflicts are not confined to the gaining and losing of market advantage. Second, that what are apparently major differences in mechanisms of *distribution* do not constitute sufficient grounds on which to argue that a society is no longer *class* stratified. Marxist theory, on the other hand, can be developed so as to deal with both of these problems.

Before we begin this task, however, we discuss in Chapter Four some of the major changes which have occurred given twentieth-century capitalist development, including changes in the occupational structure (in particular the rise of the so-called 'new middle class'), the separation of legal ownership of the enterprise from actual control, and the increasing role played by the modern state in the economy. In addition we consider more closely the account given of the major problems of capitalist industrial societies by Durkheim and Weber.

In Chapter Five we argue that, despite the fact that most firms are no longer run by entrepreneurs, one can still discern 'capital' and 'labour' if these terms are defined by what they do rather than what they appear to be. Capital is a functional complex of roles which exploits labour; that is, appropriates surplus labour and uses it to accumulate capital. Labour also needs to be defined functionally by reference to the co-ordinated tasks carried out at various levels of the enterprise under the direction of capital in order to serve its ends.

In Chapter Six we argue that the dichotomy between control and coordinated labour also holds in state-owned enterprises, both capitals and non-capitals. Non-capitals are conceived of as enterprises which do not accumulate capital themselves but whose purpose is to foster the growth and stability of the overall process of capital accumulation. (Examples include defence, welfare, education, government, and so on.) We analyse the various functions of non-capitals and claim that large capitals, particularly when they are state owned, are pressed into taking on non-capital functions, giving rise to hybrid enterprises which we call quasi-capitals. We further argue that the Eastern states are best understood as quasi-capitals.

Chapter Eight presents our approach to material inequalities. Explaining incomes in terms of how skills and resources are valued on the market begs the question of *why* they are so valued. We show that rewards must therefore be explained both by social market factors and by the particular form that the division of labour takes in *capitalist* enterprises.

In the final chapter we present an overall picture of the class structure of capitalist societies showing the objective bases for alliances and conflicts. Whether the categories so identified will actually pursue their interests is of course a crucial question, and we outline the factors which would need to be taken into account in any specific case.

Academics often claim to be above the petty and sectional interests of political debate. We do not believe such impartiality to be possible, and our own political predilections and value judgements will no doubt become obvious in the course of this book. In common with many other academics, however, we share the belief that the many and complex problems of today's world cannot be explained without recourse to a *social* theory – a theory which explains why appearances assume the form they do, a theory which reveals the underlying factors, or structure, on which are built the complex realities of everyday life. None the less it must always be remembered that abstract theories stand or fall by the illumination they lend to *empirical* material.

2

Marx and Weber

If we preface our analysis of the class structure of contemporary capitalist society with a discussion of the work of Marx and Weber, it is not least because we wish to argue that a class theory derived from Marxist principles is a better analytical tool for the analysis of modern societies than a Weberian or neo-Weberian approach – a conclusion which would be denied by many contemporary class theorists. In this chapter, therefore, besides giving an account of Weber's and Marx's work (which provides essential material for succeeding chapters), we shall also indicate what we think are the more serious limitations of Weberian class theory.

MAX WEBER

Weber's conceptual work on class is limited to two unfinished fragments, with the result that his account is rather confusing and sometimes contradictory.[1] Not surprisingly, therefore, much of the neo-Weberian work on class has attempted to 'tidy up' the original classification. We will examine some of these interpretations later in Chapter Three. For the moment, however, we will confine ourselves to giving an account of Weber's work, bearing in mind the limitations just mentioned.

Central to Weber's conceptualisation of class is the notion of 'life-chances' – i.e., 'the kind of control or lack of it which the individual has over goods or services and existing possibilities of their exploitation for the attainment of receipts within a given economic order.'[2] Put rather more simply, 'life-chance' denotes the opportunity to acquire material and, to some extent, non-material rewards. As the term 'life' implies, such 'chances' are not simply evaluated at one moment in time; incorporated in this measure are the security of existing rewards, and the opportunity to acquire rewards in the future. Individuals with similar life-chances, in so far as they are determined by economic factors, are in the same 'class situation'.

Usually Weber would seem to argue that the notion of 'class' is linked to the existence of a *market*:

> We may speak of a 'class' when (1) a number of people have in common a specific causal component of their life chances, in so far as (2) this component is represented exclusively by economic interests in the possession of goods and opportunities for income, and (3) is represented under the conditions of the commodity or labour markets. . . . But always this is the generic connotation of the concept of class: that the kind of chance in the *market* is the decisive moment which presents a common condition for the individuals' fate. 'Class situation' is, in this sense, ultimately 'market situation'.[3]

Life-chances are mediated through the market, and it is the kind of goods or service brought to the market which determines life-chance and also gives rise to particular class situations. Therefore a group can only be said to be a 'class' in so far as life-chances are decided through the operations of the market, and 'those men whose fate is not determined by the chance of using goods or services for themselves on the market, e.g. slaves, are not, however, a "class" in the technical sense of the term. They are, rather, a "status group".'[4] This apparently simple identification of 'class situation' with 'market situation' is somewhat confused by another strand in Weberian stratification theory. Although Weber only made passing references to 'a talented author'[5] much of Weber's work – and his conceptualisation of class is no exception – constitutes a dialogue with Marx, or rather, as Giddens has pointed out, a dialogue with the vulgar Marxism current in German social thought at the time at which Weber was writing.[6] In this particular debate Weber wished to argue firstly that objective class membership did not invariably lead to common class action and, secondly, that the class structure – in this case, the distribution of life-chances – was by no means wholly determined by economic factors. As far as the latter point is concerned, Weber was explicitly setting out to contradict what he considered to be the 'economic determinism' which he perceived in Marx's work, and this theme is present in much of his writing.[7] As for the first point, this hardly constitutes a criticism of Marx, who clearly recognised the empirical fact that class membership did *not* lead to class action and devoted a considerable amount of effort to explaining this fact.[8] Weber's critique of a supposed 'economic determinism', however, is found in his identification and discussion of 'status' and its relation to 'class situation'.

Unlike classes, which are to be identified according to the objective structure of the market, status groups are to be distinguished according to such essentially subjective criteria as prestige, social honour and so on, which are expressed in a particular 'style of life'. Unlike classes, status groups *are* normally communities, whose members recognise the prestige, lifestyles, etc., they have in common. Status groups for Weber constituted a logically independent dimension of stratification often to be found in conflict with class stratification. For example, status groups will frequently act in such a way as to impede the full development of the market, and thus class stratification. This may be achieved through the monopolisation of particular goods or skills by particular status groups, which is combined with a distaste for 'higgling' or 'bargaining' which is frequently found associated with status honour. Drawing upon this autonomy of class and status stratification, Weber sketched out what we can term a 'cyclical' theory of stratification. That is, in times of rapid economic and technical change such as is characteristic of capitalism, the market, and therefore class stratification will predominate, whereas in more settled epochs status stratification will predominate.[9] In these more settled epochs life-chances will be largely determined not by the disposition of goods and services in a market but according to essentially non-economic, status factors. If we follow through Weber's original, abstract definition of class as 'life-chance', therefore, the term could technically be applied to a status group – as when, for example, Weber defines slaves (in a different context from the one previously mentioned) as a 'negatively privileged property class'.

This point – that life-chances can, according to Weber, be determined either by economic (i.e., market) *and* non-economic factors – serves to confuse the original, apparently unambiguous, linkage of 'class situation' and 'market situation'. This is probably due to the unfinished nature of both of the original writings. However, as Weber's more detailed classification of life-chances is couched in terms which are largely specific to 'market situation', it will be clearer if we continue to identify 'class situation' with 'market situation'.

Weber distinguished three broad types of classes. Firstly, a 'property class', when class status (or life-chances) are 'primarily determined by the differentiation of property holdings', secondly, 'acquisition class', when the class situation of its members is primarily determined by their opportunity for the exploitation of non-property resources such as skills on the market, and thirdly, 'social classes', a 'plurality of class statuses between which an interchange of individuals on a personal basis or in the course of generations is readily possible and typically observable' – that is, a number of groupings whose class situations are sufficiently similar – largely in terms of mobility chances – to justify the aggregate being termed a 'social class'.[10]

Further differentiation occurs within each of these three broad categories. Property classes may be 'positively' and 'negatively' privileged; that is, some groups may own highly profitable property (of various kinds), which brings them substantial rewards in the market, other groups may own no property at all. Similarly, acquisition classes may be positively and negatively privileged, ranging from those whose skills or services enable them to acquire considerable returns, to those who have no skills to offer at all. Social classes will vary across the whole range of class situations, and may be positively or negatively privileged property or acquisition classes. The class structure is composed of this plurality of social classes. Weber's distinction between positively and negatively privileged acquisition and property classes gives rise to the following fourfold table:

	Privilege	
	+	−
Property class	A	B
Acquisition class	C	D

Again, however, this apparently neat classification is confused by Weber's insistence that life-chances, or class situations, are almost never determined by economic factors alone. For example, a status group will characteristically attempt to reserve to itself certain privileges or monopolies – such as land – in which case a status group would also be a property class. Similarly, a social class may combine so as to protect its privileges, when it will closely resemble a status group.[11]

THE MARKET AND THE DEVELOPMENT OF MARX'S THOUGHT

As Nicolaus has noted, Marx and Engels' earlier works were characterised by a preoccupation with, and criticisms of, the market:

All moral bonds in society have been overthrown by the conversion of human values into exchange values; and all hitherto existing laws; even the laws which regulate the birth and death of human beings, have been usurped by the *law of supply and demand*. Humanity itself has become a market commodity.[12]

Labour itself has become objectified, a commodity like any other. In the earlier writings one can detect a sense of humanistic outrage that living, thinking beings can be reduced to the equivalents of bales of cotton or tons of pig iron:

The bourgeoisie, wherever it has got the upper hand . . . has left remaining no other nexus between man and man than naked self-interest, than callous 'cash-payment'. . . . It has resolved personal worth into exchange value.[13]

If Marx's exposition of the nature of classes in a capitalist market society had rested here, then a model of social class grounded in the market, showing, as it does, the asymmetrical creation and application of life-chances, would be a reasonable characterisation of the empirical application of Marx's concept of social class. If we ignored, for analytical purposes, Weber's assertion of the autonomy of status stratification, his conceptualisation of social class would seem to have much in common with Marx.

However, as is demonstrated by Marx's later writings, his researches into the nature of the capitalist system carried him beyond an examination of the vagaries and inequalities engendered by the market. To anticipate the discussion which follows, we have to go 'behind the back of the exchange-process'[14] in order to comprehend the nature of exploitation, and consequent class relations, in a *capitalistic* market society.

In his introduction to the revised edition of *Wage Labour and Capital*,[15] Engels documents this crucial shift in Marx's work. The introductory paragraphs specify the necessary change in terminology:

> In the forties, Marx had not yet finished his critique of political economy. . . . Consequently, his works which appeared before the first part of *A Contribution to the Critique of Political Economy* differ in some points from those written after 1859, and contain expressions and whole sentences which, from the point of view of the later works, appear unfortunate and even incorrect. . . . My alterations all turn on one point. According to the original, the worker sells his *labour* to the capitalist for wages; according to the present text he sells his labour *power*.[16]

As a commodity, labour power is sold on the market like any other, its price arrived at by the laws of supply and demand. As a commodity, however, labour power has unique characteristics which mark off this particular exchange from other exchanges, and provide the key to the dominant mode of exploitation in a capitalist society, for:

In our present-day capitalist society, labour power is a commodity, a commodity like any other, and yet a quite peculiar commodity. It has, namely, the peculiar property of being a value-creating power, a source of value, and, indeed, with suitable treatment, a source of more value than it itself possesses.[17]

The crucial concept of labour power, and its associated concept, surplus value, had clearly been worked out and were applied in the third volume of *Capital* and *Theories of Surplus Value*. In the *Grundrisse*, however, we can trace the evolution of Marx's thought, the jettisoning of the market *itself* as the major variable in the analysis of exploitation, and the development of the concepts of labour power and surplus value.

In a fully developed market society, exchangers approach each other in a single-stranded manner. The relationship is single-stranded because the exchangers only exist for each other as exchangers – there exist no further obligations on either party.

Since they only exist for one another . . . in this way, as equally worthy persons, possessors of equivalent things, who thereby prove their equivalence, they are, as equals, at the same time also indifferent to one another; whatever other individual distinction there may be does not concern them; they are indifferent to all their other individual peculiarities.[18]

Such single-stranded exchange relationships can be contrasted with exchange in non-market, non-capitalist societies. In feudal Europe, for example, the lord directly appropriated use values from his subjects in the form of products. Yet the relationship between lord and subject was not limited to the acqustion of use values by one side and their being given up by the other. The vassal owed the lord other services as well, and these services were customarily defined – he was not free to offer them to the highest bidder. Although the relationship was certainly not one of equality, neither was the lord free of obligation to his vassal, for whom he had to provide security in the violent world of feudal society and protection in times of hardship. Similarly, although the complex ceremonial exchanges amongst the Trobriand islanders certainly result in the exchange of useful objects, such exchanges are constrained and directed by ceremonial/religious and kinship ties – they do not occur in a free market.[19] In such non-market societies exchange relationships are, to borrow a phrase from Polanyi,[20] 'embedded' in social life itself, and exchangers approach each other not simply as exchangers but simultaneously through a network of other social roles. In market societies, on the other hand, the exchange relationship is one of freedom, untrammelled by other considerations. It is also one of equality, each of the subjects is an exchanger, and 'the commodities which they exchange are, as exchange values, equivalent'. The buyer of labour and the seller of labour approach each other, at the level of the market, as equals. Cheating and swindling may occur in the market, but this is not intrinsic to the exchange process itself, but due to *individual* superiority or inferiority – which may apply to either buyer or seller.

Here, apparently, we have a paradox. If one thing is clear in Marx's work, it is that, for Marx, capitalist society is exploitative. Yet, says Marx, the worker as exchanger is not cheated in the exchange process, he receives the full exchange value for his commodity, labour power. Exploitation cannot be successfully maintained through cheating, because in such a situation the one only gains to the extent that the other loses, and therefore the total wealth is not increased at all.

Exploitation, therefore, does not occur at the level of the market. Market relations 'are, in reality, mediated by the deepest antithesis, and represent only one side, in which the full expression of the antithesis is obscured'. For Marx, exchange relations represent only one side of reality, they are 'surface processes' which mask the full expression of the whole. Marx expresses the 'exchange' between capital and labour in two statements which, as he says, 'are not formally but also qualitatively different, and even contradictory'.

(1) The worker sells his commodity, labour, which has a use value, and as a commodity, also a *price*, like all other commodities, for a specific sum of exchange values, specific sum of money, which capital concedes to him.

(2) The capitalist obtains labour itself, labour as value-positing activity, as productive labour; i.e. he obtains the productive force which maintains and multiplies capital, and which thereby becomes the reproductive force, the reproductive force of capital, a force belonging to capital itself.[21]

The first statement summarises the act of exchange, the exchange of equivalents. In this exchange, the worker obtains a sum of values for what his labour is 'worth'; it is fair. The second statement focuses on what is obtained by the capitalist in this act of 'fair' exchange: whilst the worker obtains wages, the capitalist gains control of a commodity of a very particular kind – that is, labour *power*. Labour power, when consumed (i.e., put to work) creates value greater than the exchange value (wages) of labour power.

Labour *power* (rather than just 'labour'), when harnessed to capital, has the unique capacity to *create* values where none existed before; the capitalist, in purchasing labour power, is purchasing this *creative* capacity of labour. Labour power in conjunction with capital is uniquely productive, and the 'surplus value' thus created gives us the key to the nature of exploitation in a capitalist society. When tools, machinery, raw materials, plus the exchange value of labour power have been calculated, the finished product has an exchange value over and above the value which went into its creation – this is surplus value.

If only half a working day is necessary in order to keep one worker alive one whole day, then the surplus value of the product is self-evident, because the capitalist has paid the price of only half a working day but has obtained a whole day objectified in the product; thus has exchanged nothing for the second half of the work day. The only thing which can make him into a capitalist is *not* exchange, but rather a process through which he obtains objectified labour time – i.e. value – without exchange. Half the working day costs capital nothing; it thus obtains a value for which it has given no equivalent. And the multiplications of values can take place only if a value in excess of the equivalent has been obtained, hence *created*.[22]

MARX AND SOCIAL CLASS

As we indicated in the previous section, Marx, unlike Weber, did not perceive class relationships as being structured through a system of market exchange. Rather Marx's analysis directs attention to the unequal social relationship underlying the 'fair' exchange of the market – the process by which the employer obtains labour power, the control of which facilitates the creation of surplus value. Logically, therefore, Marx's analysis focuses upon relationships of *production*, rather than relationships of *exchange*.

We must therefore examine more closely capitalist production relationships if we are to understand Marx's analysis of social class. We can begin by sketching, in very broad outline, the essential features of the capitalist mode of production. This discussion will be deliberately over-simplified, and will be both modified and extended later in this book.

No human society can continue to exist unless its members act upon nature and interact with each other in order to create new products. However the organisation of production and the broader social relationships within which production takes place vary from society to society. In the case of the capitalist mode of production one class of people, the proletariat, have no rights in the means of production (i.e., do not own or control productive property), and are therefore forced to sell their labour power for wages. Those who own/control the means of production, the bourgeoisie, coordinate and direct the labour power that they have purchased in order to carry through the production process. The final product is then the property of the capitalist. The revenue from the sale of this product may be partly consumed by the capitalist, and/or taken off as taxation, but in general a part of this revenue *must* be allocated to renewing the means of production and buying more labour power for the repetition of the cycle.

During a *part* of the time that the worker is engaged in the labour process, he creates new values which are equivalent to the value of the commodities he consumes. The capitalist pays out to the worker wages, which are equivalent in value to this part of the product. The rest of the time worked, however, does not create new values for the workers' consumption, and may be called *surplus labour*. This labour creates new products, which may be called *surplus product*. In the capitalist mode of production, therefore, the capitalist acquires, through the market, surplus labour which creates surplus product. (This process is summarised by Marx in the quotation from the *Grundrisse* on p. 13.)

In other class societies surplus labour may be appropriated directly. For example, in feudalism, the serf may pay his dues to the lord as two days' work each week in the lord's demesne. Again, in feudalism, surplus product may be *directly* appropriated: the serf pays his tithe to the bishop in the form of grain that he produced on his 'own' strip. In this kind of society appropriation is an analytically separable process from the process of production. In many cases they may be empirically observed as distinct processes, as when, for example, the peasant organises his own production and then gives up a fixed proportion to the expropriating authority. In capitalist societies, on the other hand, the production process and the exploitation process are fused together; surplus labour is appropriated through 'free' exchange in the market. Exploitation in a capitalist society, however, does not occur because the worker is swindled in the market. The employer may well pay a perfectly 'fair' market wage, equivalent to that paid for similar work by other employers, yet surplus value will continue to be extracted.

In the discussion so far we have simply stated that the capitalist owns and/or controls the means of production – capital. In order that the capitalist mode of production may continue to function, a continuing supply of new capital must be assured. New capital is acquired through the acquisition of new values – surplus value. The capitalist cannot simply acquire sufficient values for his or her personal needs, but *must* constantly appropriate and accumulate new value through the extraction of surplus value. If the individual capitalist cannot acquire new capital, then he simply goes out of business. Because of the constant pressures toward accumulation, intense competition may occur between productive units which at times might appear to threaten the stability of the capitalist mode of production as a whole – price-cutting wars, for example, or crises of overproduction.

In the *pure* capitalist mode of production Marx's use of class as an *analytical* concept led him to identify the two major classes we have already discussed – bourgeoisie and proletariat. It requires little ingenuity to demonstrate that such a two-class model is inadequate for the *empirical* analysis of modern society. In later chapters we will begin to develop Marx's highly abstract analysis of the capitalist mode of production and associated production relationships so as to take into account both the development and increasing complexity of the capitalist mode of production and the various ways in which the structure has been modified. Such an expansion of Marx's theory will enable us to deal systematically with groups or classes which cannot, at this initial, highly abstract level be incorporated within a bourgeois/proletariat dichotomy (for example, wage labourers who do not create new values, and those who control the labour of others but do not 'own' the means of production in any meaningful sense).

This discussion of Marx's and Weber's approach to the analysis of social class has highlighted the differences between the two theorists. Weberian theory focuses on the way in which societal rewards are *acquired*, and the manner in which patterns of acquisition are determined by the market. Marx's theory focuses on the manner in which new values are *created*, and the social relationships arising out of and sustaining this process. The taxonomy which can be developed out of Weber's work can be utilised to give a reasonably accurate explanation of patterns of distribution in market societies, and the conflicts which arise out of distributive processes. Marx's analysis, except in the broadest sense, indicates little or nothing about distributive patterns. On a more general level Marx saw in the relationship between social classes 'the great law of motion of history . . . according to which all historical struggles, whether they proceed in the political, religious, philosophical or some other ideological domain, are in fact only the more or less clear expression of the struggles of social classes'.[23] Although Weber obviously appreciated that conflicts could arise between social classes (as he defined them), such conflicts were not given this historic role in Weber's analysis; rather Weber identified the major variable in the explanation of social change in modern capitalism as being the increasing rationality and bureaucratisation endemic in modern society.[24]

We have been concerned to emphasise these differences because we feel that the distinction which must be drawn between the two theorists has not been made sufficiently clear in many previous discussions. Besides contrasting Marx and Weber, however, we wish to argue that Marx's theory, even at this very abstract level, gives a better understanding of the class structure of capitalist societies than that of Weber.

As Bottomore has noted: 'For the past eighty years [ninety by now!] Marx's theory has been the object of unrelenting criticism and of tenacious defence.'[25] The defence of Marx we develop in this book is not exactly 'tenacious', as we believe the correct strategy is to build on Marx's original insights, rather than to uncritically accept and defend all that Marx ever wrote; that would be difficult in any case as Marx often contradicted himself!

Our major criticism of the Weberian approach to social class centres on the starting-point of his theoretical analysis of the class structure of capitalist societies – the market. The existence of a market for goods and services is simply taken for granted, rather than treated as a phenomenon that requires explanation. We would not wish to deny that, in Western capitalism, a market *does* exist in what Polanyi termed the 'fictitious' commodities of labour, land and capital, but we would raise the question as to *why* skills and resources have assumed this marketable, commodity-like quality. We would argue that these 'commodities' have emerged *as* commodities because of the development of capitalist relations of production. Such a mode of production requires both freely transferable property and readily available labour. Production relationships logically precede market relationships, and therefore in order to understand the nature of class structures we must direct our attention in the first place to this underlying structure – the capitalist mode of production, and its associated relations of production. Putting the same argument in a slightly different and simpler way, we feel that to study the market without also taking into account the relations of production which underlie the market gives at best an incomplete, and at worst a misleading, account of the class structure.

For example, if, with Weber, we define class in terms of life-chances, which are largely determined by the market, then our account and interpretation of class conflict will centre on the disputes and stratagems through which different groups fight to gain privileged access to the market and the distribution of rewards. Of course such conflicts arise, and can usefully be studied. However, if we have defined class in market terms, our analysis of class conflict will go no further than this, and we will fail to appreciate the even more fundamental conflicts and tensions which, we would argue, are inherent in capitalist relations of production. An analysis of class conflict on the level of the market alone is seriously incomplete.

The Weberian approach assumes that the market and capitalism are synonymous. That is, if there is no market, there cannot therefore be classes, and by implication no capitalism either. In later chapters we will analyse the manner in which the market has been systematically distorted and subject to ever-increasing attempts at control as capitalism has developed. Despite the manipulation of the market, however, access to resources in Western monopoly capitalist societies can be realistically seen as operating through an admittedly imperfect market. In the Eastern bloc 'state socialist' (or, as we will argue, state capitalist) societies, on the other hand, resources are largely allocated not through the market but by central state direction. This difference in the manner of allocation has often been utilised to argue that there are fundamental differences between the societies of the East and West, requiring alternative strategies of analysis.[26] Of course there *are* considerable differences between East and West, differences which must be systematically evaluated – for example, the relatively minor role played by private property in the class structure of the Eastern bloc countries. However, we would argue that once the underlying structure of the capitalist mode of production is properly understood – in particular the compulsive drive for the appropriation of surplus value and its conversion into capital – then it can be seen that the Eastern bloc countries do not constitute a fundamentally different societal type, but a variation on the theme of capitalist development.

In summary, therefore, we would make two major critical points regarding Weberian class analysis. Firstly, because this approach takes the existence of the market for granted our attention is not directed toward, and may even be systematic- ally directed away from, the tensions and antagonisms within relations of *production*, which we would argue are of con- tinuing importance in capitalist societies. Secondly, because the market is taken to be the major element of class differen- tiation and class structure, it has been but a short step to distinguish modern industrial societies on the basis of whether or not life-chances are visibly determined by the *market*. This strategy, again, begs the more basic question as to whether or not *production* relationships are capitalistic. The analysis we will develop, on the other hand, will attempt to demonstrate that capitalist production relationships may coexist with an extremely wide range of market activities, and that a Western-style market is by no means a sufficient basis on which to identify the existence of a capitalist mode of production.

In general our approach to the analysis of social class, as we have already indicated, differs somewhat from those current in British sociology. Other sociologists have either attempted to synthesise the theoretical insights of Marx and Weber – an approach we see as doomed to failure because of the fundamental differences between the two theorists – or have adopted a modified or neo-Weberian position. In the next chapter we will review the work of some contemporary British sociologists, before we begin to develop systematically an alternative Marxist approach.

3

Some Contemporary Class Theorists

In this chapter we will look at the work of three British sociologists who have made major contributions to class theory: Lockwood, Parkin, and Giddens. Each of these writers come to conclusions we would describe as 'neo-Weberian', and our exposition will extend the critique of the Weberian approach which we outlined in the previous chapter. We have not attempted in this chapter to provide a comprehensive summary of contemporary sociological approaches to class, as this can already be found elsewhere.[1]

One of the earliest attempts to synthesise the work of Marx and Weber is to be found in Lockwood's *The Blackcoated Worker*. In this book Lockwood was primarily concerned to explain why clerical workers, despite the fact that they share a common situation of 'propertylessness' with manual workers, had been either apathetic or even hostile to trade unionism. This could be explained, said Lockwood, not by simply arguing that clerks were either 'snobbish' or 'falsely conscious' of their true class position, but by the very real differences between the class situation of clerical and manual workers. Lockwood's definition of 'class position' is worth quoting at some length:

Under 'class position' will be included the following factors. First, 'market situation', that is to say the economic position narrowly conceived, consisting of source and size of income, degree of job-security, and opportunity for upward occupational mobility. Secondly, 'work situation', the set of social relationships in which the individual is involved at work by virtue of his position in the division of labour. And finally, 'status situation' or the position of the individual in the hierarchy of prestige in the society at large. The experiences originating in these three spheres may be seen as the principal determinants of class consciousness. 'Market situation' and 'work situation' comprise what Marx essentially understood as 'class position'; 'status situation' derives from another branch of social stratification theory.[2]

In this passage and in his later work Lockwood is arguing that a total 'class situation' must incorporate consideration of *both* the 'economic' identification to be found in Marx's work, *and* the 'status' hierarchy discussed by Weber. Whether or not the inclusion of the 'status' dimension is justified or not does not concern our discussion at this stage; we will focus instead on Lockwood's assertion that '"market situation" and "work situation" comprise what Marx essentially understood as "class position"'.

As we argued at length in the previous chapter, the development of Marx's work makes it perfectly clear that 'market situation' does not constitute an adequate definition of social class in his terms. 'Market situation' is concerned above all with opportunities to acquire rewards, whereas we have emphasised that an analysis of social class based upon Marx's work must be firmly grounded in relations of *production*. In fact Lockwood's conceptualisation of 'market situation' is obviously very close to Weber's definition of class – the source of income (broadly defined), degree of job security, and opportunities for upward mobility neatly, if briefly, encapsulate 'life-chances'. In general, therefore, this particular dimension of 'class situation' identified by Lockwood has more in common with Weber than Marx.

Lockwood's second dimension – 'work situation' – is a significant departure from the Weberian typology of 'market situation' and 'status situation'. In his comparison of the work situations of clerical and manual workers, Lockwood examines such factors as the extent of discretion and responsibility offered by the work itself, the extent to which workers are physically concentrated (or otherwise) in their work and the nature of authority relationships. In all of these respects Lockwood found considerable variations in the experiences of clerical and manual workers. Such a comparison is interesting and valid, and is certainly an essential part of any attempted explanation of the differing perspectives of white-collar and manual workers. However, does a discussion of the 'work situation' in these terms describe 'what Marx essentially understood by "class position"'? Although the 'work situation' might at first sight appear to encompass production relations, we find that in fact Lockwood simply describes and compares the contemporary conditions of manual and clerical work. Fragmentation, division of labour and the structure of authority relationships are seen as being largely a consequence of increasing size and technical complexity; the question as to why enterprises have grown larger and more complex is not raised in any consistent fashion. Rather as Weber's analysis of 'class situation' takes the existence and structure of the market for granted, so does Lockwood take the structure of work-place relationships for granted. We would argue, on the other hand, that the structure of work-place relationships cannot be treated as unproblematical, but must be systematically derived from the nature and development of specifically *capitalist* production relations. We will extend this point in some detail in our subsequent discussion of the development of the capitalist mode of production.

In summary, our critique of Lockwood has revealed that far from being a synthesis Lockwood's three-dimensional 'class position' is in fact a modified Weberian approach, and therefore is liable to the critical points we have already made in respect of Weber. To 'market situation' and 'status situation' – the original elements of the Weberian taxonomy – is added 'work situation'. However, although the notion of 'work situation' recognises that groups have different experiences of work, these experiences are not themselves related to the structure of capitalist relations of production.

As we will constantly reiterate throughout this book, we consider it to be both a legitimate and useful exercise to analyse the market situation of different occupational groups, and to attempt to assess the effect of the market on attitudes and associated patterns of behaviour. Lockwood's discussion of the work and market situation of clerical workers provides a useful analytical tool with which to approach the study of white-collar unionism; whether or not this approach has proved completely successful is discussed elsewhere.[3]

The adoption of a neo-Weberian approach to class analysis, however, presents certain conceptual problems of which the neo-Weberians are themselves well aware. In particular the grouping of classes according to market situation involves making demarcations within a continuum. With the increasing domination of the capitalist mode of production, practically the whole of the 'gainfully occupied' population participates in the occupational market, giving rise to a very wide range of market situations. This results in a continuum of class positions, making it difficult to determine theoretically justifiable discontinuities. In the previous chapter we demonstrated that Weber's original framework of analysis did not provide a satisfactory answer to this problem.[4] Lockwood's original reconceptualisation of Weber provided no *systematic* guidance on this point, although the possibility of constructing such a classification is certainly enhanced by the identification of work situation as well as market situation. Lockwood, however, did not provide such a systematic classification, largely because his primary concern was with a particular occupational group – clerks – who by 'custom and practice' had long been identified as unambiguously 'middle class'.

Writing some fourteen years after Lockwood, Parkin's initial contribution to class theory indicated that little progress had been made with regard to this particular conceptual problem.[5] Like Lockwood, Parkin assumes that Weber's conceptualisation of social class was not dissimilar to that of Marx: 'Weber's approach thus resulted in a refinement of Marx's model – Weber followed Marx in making classes or strata the main focus of concern.'[6] Parkin then proceeds to develop a 'market model' of class which is, by association, assumed to be close to that of Marx. The 'backbone of the class structure' is the occupational structure, and 'marketable expertise is the most important single determinant of occupational reward'.[7] Parkin recognises the 'demarcation problem' referred to above: 'The picture of the reward system which emerges . . . is one marked out by a *hierarchy* of broad occupational categories each representing a different position in the scale of material and non-material benefits.'[8] However a significant break in the reward hierarchy – significant enough to justify the use of the term 'social class' – occurs along the manual/non-manual divide. Non-manual workers receive better material rewards than manual workers, if not in absolute monetary terms, then in respect of such advantages as sick pay, working hours, holiday time, and so on.[9] This patterned structure of inequality is reinforced by an 'array of social and symbolic elements' which underpin the distribution of material rewards – that is, ensure both their perpetuation and their legitimacy.

Even within the framework which could be developed within the neo-Weberian approach, Parkin's dichotomisation of the reward structure into two unambiguous classes is not satisfactory. The extent of the overlap between manual and non-manual material rewards is probably greater than Parkin suggests,[10] and recent technical developments have made it even more difficult (if it was ever easy) to distinguish between white-collar and manual employment in the first place.[11] These changes have been reflected in official government attitudes, for example, the Prices and Incomes Board firmly rejected the suggestion that non-manual work *in itself* carried with it any entitlement to a high rate of pay.[12]

Parkin's later work clearly recognises that the manual/non-manual distinction is not a sufficient basis upon which to establish social classes.[13] In particular, says Parkin, *all* dichotomous schemes (including the manual/non-manual dichotomy) suffer from problems of mutual exclusivity, and from the associated difficulty of classification of the 'middle strata':

> Current usage requires us to treat collectivities as either manual *or* non-manual, propertied *or* propertyless, subordinate *or* superordinate; it is not logically possible to be partially manual, partially propertyless, or partially subordinate.[14]

These problems can be solved, Parkin suggests, by developing

the Weberian concept of 'social closure', or 'the process by
which social collectivities seek to maximise rewards by restricting access to rewards and opportunities to a limited
circle of eligibles'.[15] Groups typically engage in closure
strategies through exclusion – that is, restricting access to
valued resources to this 'limited circle of eligibles' either on
the basis of inherited characteristics such as race or aristocratic birth, or individual qualifying criteria such as examination certificates, or the possession of certain types of property.
Strategies of exclusion will tend to generate in opposition
solidaristic strategies on the part of the excluded, for example,
political or trade union organisation. Solidaristic closure
invariably aims at usurpation. Therefore, in so far as
solidaristic strategies are successful, excluding groups will
lose their privileges.

The basic line of cleavage in the stratification system
occurs where these two opposing modes of closure, exclusion
and solidarism, meet each other. For example:

> The division between bourgeoisie and proletariat, in its
> classic as well as its modern guise, may be understood as an
> expression of conflict between collectivities defined not
> specifically in relation to their place in the productive
> process but in relation to their prevalent modes of closure,
> exclusion and solidarism.[16]

The advantage of using modes of closure (rather than any
other dichotomy) as a basis for class analysis is that neither
category is logically exhaustive. That is, it is perfectly possible
for groupings (particularly amongst the 'middle strata') to use
both exclusion and solidaristic strategies in maximising their
claims to resources. White-collar workers might at the same
time use 'exclusion devices of a credentialist kind' – insistence
on particular qualifications as a condition for occuaptional
membership – as well as the solidaristic strategy of trade
unionism.

This reconceptualisation might have solved some of the
more obvious difficulties associated with the original, rather
crude, reliance on the manual/nonmanual dichotomy. It does
not, however, represent a fundamental departure from
Parkin's overall strategy of analysis. Classes are still to be

identified according to the rewards which they obtain from the market, a further dimension has been added by pointing to the *'stratagems* by which collectivities lay claim and seek to justify rewards'.[17] The analysis of closure and associated strategies represents a serious attempt to iron out the ambiguities in Weber's initial conceptualisation, to which we referred in the last chapter. Given that Parkin's analysis has not significantly changed, however, it is legitimate to infer that his definition of class conflict is still 'the attempt to gain access to, or control over, those institutions which govern the distribution of symbolic and material advantages.'[18]

In general this approach to class conflict, as we argued in the previous chapter, perceives such conflict as arising solely from the process of *distribution*. *If* some sort of 'fair' allocation of material and symbolic rewards *could* be evolved, would class conflict then be eradicated? Or to approach the problem from a slightly different perspective, *could* a fair allocation of material and symbolic rewards be attained without any change in existing relationships of production? Is it possible to have non-antagonistic distribution patterns coexisting with antagonistic production relationships? Such questions are neither raised nor confronted by Parkin.

These questions assume even greater importance, we would argue, when the class structure of the Eastern bloc or so-called state socialist societies comes under scrutiny. As we have already indicated, Parkin argues that these societies are not class stratified because political rather than market criteria determine *distribution*. The occupational reward structure in Russia and the Eastern bloc countries since the Revolution indicates that 'more egalitarian' and 'less egalitarian' phases have occurred, but overall 'it would be misleading to claim that the market is the governing mechanism of reward allocation'.[19] For example, following the death of Stalin and his subsequent denunciation, trends towards increasing inequality were consciously reversed by the state, the wages of lower paid workers were raised and income tax reforms increased the level of deductions from more highly paid groups.[20] Although a factory manager will still receive a higher income than a manual employee, in all of the Eastern bloc countries skilled manual workers earn higher wages than lower-level white-collar workers. In addition low-level white-collar work is not (as is the case in Western economies) the bottom rung of a ladder which leads to junior managerial positions. For all of these reasons, 'we cannot represent the reward structure of socialist society as a dichotomous class model on exactly the Western pattern, since there is much less of an obvious "break" between manual and non-manual positions'.[21]

Parkin then considers the possibility that even if Eastern bloc countries are not class stratified as in the West the line of class division may be drawn higher in the occupational hierarchy, and the Eastern bloc countries are dominated by a 'new class' of intelligentsia and party intellectuals. Although this stratum does generally receive a higher level of material reward, Parkin doubts that the evidence is sufficient to demonstrate that such a new class is emerging. In the first place, the lack of inheritance in the Eastern bloc countries makes it difficult for this supposed class to hand on its privileges to its descendants, and the available evidence indicates that social mobility into the supposed new class from lower strata is still high. In the second place, the egalitarian ideology espoused by the 'new class' themselves will make it difficult to build in systematic privilege over the long run. To utilise Parkin's subsequent concepts, the 'new class' has not achieved a sufficient measure of 'closure' to warrant the application of the term 'class'.[22] We must conclude, therefore, that although inequalities exist in 'state socialist' societies these are not *class* inequalities in the sense in which Parkin defines class inequalities in the West.

It is not always clear, however, whether or not Parkin would argue that the Eastern bloc countries *are* class stratified. His comparison of the élites of West and East leads him to identify two conflicting élites (termed by Parkin 'classes') in Soviet society.[23] Parkin characterises Western élites as relatively undifferentiated in terms of social background, education and ideologies or 'world views'. Eastern élites, on the other hand, are not homogeneous; in particular there is a significant split between the party hierarchy on the one hand and the intelligentsia on the other. These two élites differ in respect of social background, education and, most important, in their views as to the running of the 'state socialist' economy. (Such splits are sometimes dramatically revealed, as in the events in Czechoslovakia in 1968.) Parkin thus derives what has been termed an 'ingenious but fallacious' two-class model of Eastern European society.[24] However it is difficult to describe this account as a 'two-class' model, as the 'classes' – or élites – represent only a tiny fraction of the population, and the class position of the remainder is not specified.

As in his discussion of Western societies, Parkin's discussion of the class structure of Eastern bloc countries is couched in terms of the distribution of material rewards and access to the levers of distribution. Distributive processes are certainly important, but, as we have already argued, to focus on distribution alone leads to a partial and misleading understanding of reality. Routine white-collar workers in the Eastern bloc countries may be paid relatively less than their Western counterparts, but is this sufficient to preclude discussion of the fact that the organisation of production in the East is broadly similar to that of the West?

As we shall attempt to demonstrate in Chapter Seven, production in the East, as much as production in the West, is geared to capital accumulation. It is true that the manner in which the surplus is allocated is radically different from that of Western monopoly capitalism, although there are some obvious similarities – for example, the arms and space race, and welfare spending. Neither can production for *private* profit be said to dominate in the East, an important difference which we will take up in more detail later. On the other hand the worker in Soviet society has no more control over what he produces or how it is produced than has the worker in the West and, as Lane has said of Soviet society, 'At the bottom, not unlike his Western counterpart, is the worker. He largely regards work as instrumental, as a means to a better life. While he works to promote communism in a ritualistic way, the methods used to motivate him are partly normative but largely utilitarian.'[25] The class analysis we will develop emphasises relations of *production* rather than *distribution*, and has rather different implications for the analysis of the societies of the Eastern bloc. Focusing on production rather than distribution, we would argue that Soviet society *is* a class society, in which it is possible to identify both capital and labour functions. We would look not only at conflicts over distribution and/or the process of social mobility, but at patterns of control and domination as well as the overall process of exploitation. Such evidence may be more difficult to locate, not least because the forces of repression and ideological domination are more firmly established in the Eastern bloc countries than in the West. For example, there are considerable legal impediments to trade union activity in the Eastern bloc and trade unions are formally integrated into the organisation of productive activity, which further inhibits the extent to which they may act as representatives of the labour function.[26] (Interestingly enough, such a role has recently been widely canvassed for trade unions in the West, and attempts – largely unsuccessful so far – have been made to implement such 'reforms' through legislation.)[27]

Parkin's adoption of a neo-Weberian strategy of analysis does not involve an explicit rejection of Marxist theory. Giddens, on the other hand, does examine the Marxist analysis of class before rejecting it in favour of a neo-Weberian model. His reassessment of Marx's analysis commences from a vantage point we will return to later in this book – the increasing complexity of industrial development. As Giddens points out, Marx did not pay much attention to the possible occupational structure, or work allocation, of a future socialist society. The techniques of production developed by the capitalist mode of production make possible the material prosperity on which a socialist order could be built, but, argues Giddens, the complex division of labour and proliferation of authority relationships consequent on the development of sophisticated technique pose serious problems for any classless order which is going to retain these techniques. This is because the complex division of labour, organisation and administration and the work roles thus generated are independent of any particular mode of production. Marx's failure to systematically consider these 'paratechnical' relationships, as Giddens calls them, seriously calls into question an integral part of Marx's class analysis – the labour theory of value and the associated concepts of exploitation and surplus value.

As developed by Marx, says Giddens, the labour theory of value facilitated an easy comparison between exploitation within the feudal and capitalist orders. The nature of exploitation in feudal society is readily comprehensible, a surplus (in the form of use values) is directly appropriated from a mass of near-subsistence producers, and is consumed by a minority who clearly do not produce for themselves. The labour theory of value, by locating the process of exploitation within the process of production (though the extraction of surplus value), 'explains' the manner of exploitation in a capitalist society. Giddens does not criticise the labour theory of value for failing to accurately predict prices or for taking an overly narrow view of value because, as he quite rightly states, these criticisms are only peripheral, rather than central, to the use that Marx made of the theory. Rather he criticises the labour theory of value for failing in its major task – to provide an adequate theory of exploitation. If he is correct, then the whole of Marx's theory of class is suspect.

Giddens summarises the labour theory of value thus:

> Productive labour, that is labour which creates value, depends . . . upon the interplay between nature and human labour power. Those whose work can be described in these terms create the surplus value off which men in 'unproductive' occupations live; in capitalism, this refers to the working class, who produce the commodities which are bought and sold on the market . . . the operations of the market, the circulation of commodities or money, . . . are intrinsically unproductive. Those whose occupations involve the administration of these operations live off the surplus value created by the labourer.[28]

Giddens's summary of the labour theory of value gives rise to two unambiguous groupings: (1) those who create new values (products), the exploited, and (2) those who live off the values (products) created by others, the exploiters.

> Class society is necessarily exploitative in character because the existence of class structure is predicated upon the appropriation of the surplus *product* of the mass of the population by an unproductive minority.[29]

Now, argues Giddens, any complex industrial production, be it capitalist or socialist, will inevitably require for its efficient operation a group of 'non-producers' to administer and organise production and distribution. If, as in Gidden's interpretation of Marx, 'unproductive' labour is seen as being maintained out of surplus value produced by others, then a truly classless society is impossible: '*Any* form of society there-fore, which depends upon the large-scale production and exchange of goods, must necessarily involve, according to the terms of Marx's economic theory, the extraction of surplus value from the producing majority.'[30] Marx's theory of class is therefore fundamentally suspect, and having rejected Marx Giddens goes on to develop a neo-Weberian approach.

From our summary above it can be seen that Giddens's rejection of Marx rests on two crucial points of interpre-tation: (1) that exploitation in class societies invariably takes the form of the appropriation of surplus *product*, and (2) that therefore those who do not produce are 'exploiters'. We will deal with each of these points in turn.

Whilst we would not wish to deny that the appropriation of surplus value *does* involve the appropriation of surplus product, some of which is consumed by non-producers, we would stress that capitalist relationships of production and exploitation involve more than this. If they did not, then the independent artisan who sold his finished product – say shoes – for less than their 'true' market price would be exploited in the same way as an employee in a shoe factory. However, as we argued in the previous chapter, in capitalist societies the production process and the exploitation process are *fused together*; surplus value is appropriated through the control and application of labour power and surplus labour. This distinction has been emphasised by Rowthorn: 'In all but capitalist production, the worker is not paid a wage for his *labour power*, but receives payment for his labour in the shape of a completed *product*.'[31] Therefore, we would argue, the labour theory of value and its concomitant account of exploi-tation can only be properly understood when we realise the capitalist realtionships of production involve the voluntary surrender of *creative capacity*, one result of which is the expro-priation of surplus product in the form of surplus value. It is not simply that the worker has no control over the products of his labour, but that the worker loses any control over labour itself. This surrender of creative capacity – labour power – is as much a part of capitalist relationships of production as is the extraction of surplus value (product) through the application and utilisation of labour power. A one-sided focus on the extraction of surplus product, as is found in Giddens's interpretation, leads to a fundamental misunderstanding of the labour theory of value.

Giddens further argues that the persistence of a class of 'unproductive exploiters' in any complex industrial society implies that if Marx's analysis is taken to its logical conclusion a classless order is impossible – if such an order is to retain the techniques developed by and within the capitalist mode of production. Again we would fundamentally disagree with Giddens's interpretation and subsequent conclusions. Maintenance out of surplus value is a necessary, but hardly a sufficient, criterion for the definition of an 'exploiting' class. For example, any society, capitalist or otherwise, will contain groups – the young, the sick, the old – who are manifestly 'unproductive'. Considerable societal resources must be diverted to support these groups and the personnel who care for them. Although such groupings clearly do not produce and are maintained out of a surplus, no class theory, Marxist or otherwise, has ever suggested that they be classified as 'exploiters'.

However, as Giddens rightly points out, 'workers employed in the "non-productive" occupations, but who are nevertheless propertyless, hold an ambiguous position in marxian theory'.[32] Given that such workers do not create surplus value, they cannot be said to be 'exploited' in the same manner as workers who do; on the other hand as propertyless employees they place their labour power at the disposal of the employer in much the same way as 'productive' workers. It does not follow, however, that this ambiguity will necessarily be carried over into a hypothetical non-capitalist mode of production, as Giddens implies. His critique fails to take into account the fact that within Marx's analysis the extraction of surplus value is specific to the *capitalist* mode of production. Surplus value can only be

created and appropriated given capitalist production relationships, and therefore if they were transcended surplus
value and the associated relationships of domination and
exploitation would simply cease to exist, by definition.

In any case, as we shall argue in later chapters, Marxist
theory can be developed to give a satisfactory account of the
class situation of such employees within the capitalist mode of
production. Giddens's interpretation of Marx focuses entirely
upon the appropriation of surplus *product*, failing to systematically take into account the fact that in the case of the
capitalist mode of production such appropriation takes place
within the labour process through the control of surplus
labour. As we have already indicated, the situation of 'unproductive' workers resembles that of 'productive' workers in so
far as control over their labour has been relinquished – an
essential similarity that will fail to be sufficiently emphasised
if exploitation is simply seen as the appropriation of surplus
product. Although it is true that the labour of 'unproductive'
workers does not create surplus value directly, such labour is
characteristically deployed in order to acquire a *share* of
surplus value produced elsewhere as profits for the employer
of 'unproductive' labour. Of course some of the surplus value
acquired through, say, commercial and financial operations is
allocated as wages to such 'unproductive' employees, and
therefore they are maintained from values which they did not
themselves create. It is difficult, however, to characterise such
employees as members of an 'exploiting' class. They may act
as *agents* of the exploiting class (or the capitalist function), but
the object of the application of their labour is to create profits
for their employer, and such employment is increasingly
subject to the same kinds of constraints and rationalisation as
'productive' work. In addition, many white-collar occupations are not unambiguously 'unproductive'. Given the
complex labour processes characteristic of advanced
capitalism, many elements of the white-collar work role are
an integral part of the production process, and are as 'productive' as manual work.

For these and other reasons 'unproductive' labour can be
satisfactorily located within the framework of Marxist class
analysis. Structurally the class situation of 'unproductive'

workers is frequently ambiguous, but this ambiguity hardly constitutes a sufficient basis on which to reject Marxian class theory.

We can demonstrate, therefore, that Giddens's rejection of Marx rests upon a serious misinterpretation of one of the essential elements of Marx's theory. However, as we wish to argue that Marxist class analysis in fact gives a better understanding of the class structure of capitalist societies than neo-Weberian theories of the kind developed by Giddens, we shall now point out some of the problems raised by the application of neo-Weberian 'market-models'. In the previous chapter we raised two general problems of neo-Weberian theory – the approach to class conflict and the analysis of Eastern bloc societies. Before we consider Giddens's approach to these topics we must first sketch out his model of class analysis.

A class is defined as a social grouping characterised by broadly similar 'life-chances' in the market.[33] Giddens then confronts the conceptual problem common to all such market-models, that of abstracting a manageable range of 'classes' from the infinite variety of 'market situations'. This is dealt with by developing the original Weberian notion of 'social classes'; i.e., 'groupings whose class – or market – situations are sufficiently similar to justify the aggregate being termed a social class'.[34] Giddens's account of this 'structuration' gives rise to three basic social classes in industrial societies, each (broadly) characterised by a particular market capacity or 'mediate' structuration.[35] These are (1) the upper class, distinguished by ownership and control of property, (2) the middle class, distinguished by the possession of technical and educational skills, and (3) the lower class, having only labour to offer on the market. The existence of these three classes is reinforced by 'proximate' sources of structuration – the division of labour, authority relationships, and 'distributive groupings', all structures which feed back into and help to maintain the structuration of class relationships in a three-class model. Class conflict, says Giddens, is endemic in class society, and 'of predominant importance in sociological terms are the types of overt conflict which are linked to oppositions of interest entailed by differing forms of market capacity'.[36] We might therefore expect Giddens's analysis of class conflict to focus upon conflicts between the elements of the 'basic three-class system' of capitalist society.

In fact for the most part this is not the case. Although the nature of class conflict in capitalist societies is fairly extensively discussed, overt conflict would appear to be remarkably absent amongst these three basic classes in the account given by Giddens. He distinguishes between, on the one hand, conflict consciousness, 'where perception of class unity is linked to a recognition of opposition of interest with another class or classes', and on the other, revolutionary class consciousness, which involves 'a recognition of the possibility of an overall reorganisation in the institutional mediation of power, and a belief that such a reorganisation can be brought about through class action'.[37] An important form of class conflict discussed by Giddens is the wage demands articulated by institutions developed by the lower class – the trade unions. Such demands are clearly conflicts which are linked to 'oppositions of interest entailed by differing forms of market capacity', and indeed are considered by Giddens to be expressions of class conflict. Such demands are not, however, expressions of revolutionary consciousness. The institutional separation of economy and polity in 'neo-capitalist' society ensures that 'economistic' demands are limited to just this, and do not fundamentally challenge the 'subordinate control position of the worker in the enterprise in relation to the performance of his task in the division of labour'.[38] In fact in order to explain the existence of struggles over control (or revolutionary consciousness) in capitalist society Giddens is forced to move outside the framework delineated by his original 'market' account of the class structure.

Revolutionary conflict, says Giddens, is more likely to be found in the trade union movements of countries that have experienced 'uneven' capitalist development in the post-feudal rupture. In these cases the advent of capitalist development has been fiercely resisted by a potentially to-be-disadvantaged group – say the peasantry or landholders – and their action provides a focus of resistance to the capitalist order for the emergent industrial working class. If in addition to the unevenness of the post-feudal rupture the legitimate right of the industrial worker to bargain – i.e., develop trade unions – is not recognised, then the stage is set for the development of revolutionary consciousness, the 'will to control' in the working class. Such historical factors are not cultural lags to be overcome with the continuing advance of neo-capitalism, but are 'persisting system[s], highly resistant to major modification'.[39] France and Italy are cited as examples.

One possible explanation of the development of revolutionary class consciousness, therefore, has been located by Giddens in the early history of capitalist development. Another explanation, however, looks to the future development of neo-capitalist society. The rational planning characteristic of the advance of neo-capitalism will increasingly require the direct involvement of the labour unions. In an attempt to control prices and output contracts will have to be negotiated on a long-term basis. The characteristic confinement of class conflict to economism has 'depend[ed] upon the capacity of capitalism to generate a regular increase in money-wages'.[40] If such an increase can no longer be assured, and in addition the cooperation of the unions has to be sought in order to implement long-term planning, the 'result of this is likely to be precisely to stimulate a renewed consciousness of problems of control among the rank-and-file'.[41] This renewed consciousness will possibly create a revolutionary consciousness amongst the working class; conflict, no longer confined by economism, will spill over into the political sphere.

At this stage in the development of our argument we are not particularly concerned to query the validity of Giddens's accounts of the emergence of revolutionary class consciousness – he may or may not be correct that the explanation is to be found in past capitalist development and future neo-capitalist development. We have shown, however, that in order to explain revolutionary consciousness (which is presumably of 'predominant importance in sociological terms') Giddens has clearly moved away from 'oppositions of interest entailed by differing forms of market capacity', and has focused upon the development of capitalist production relationships. It may be argued that such problems have been integrated into the market model by the identification of the division of labour and authority groupings as a 'proximate source of structuration' of market-based class groupings, but we would argue that such features are not 'proximate' but should be systematically integrated into a framework of class analysis derived from relationships of production.

Another form of conflict associated by Giddens with the development of neo-capitalism lies in the development of the 'underclass'. That is, a category of lower-class workers 'heavily concentrated among the lowest-paid occupations . . . chronically unemployed or semi-employed', and often further distinguished by their ethnic origin.[42] Such an underclass is neither assimilated culturally, nor, more importantly, into the prevailing structure of market rewards. They are, as Giddens says, the new 'reserve army' of capitalism, and the highly 'transparent' nature of their systematic exclusion from full participation in the market is and has led to overt conflict between the underclass and more advantageously rewarded groups. Unlike the genesis of revolutionary class conflict discussed above, such underclass conflict is clearly the result of differing forms of market capacity. Here, however, Giddens is not considering conflict amongst the 'three basic classes' of neo-capitalist society, which might have been expected to form the main focus of analysis. In other words, when specifically considering market-derived class conflict, Giddens has extended his original market based typology. It may legitimately be argued that such a strategy is perfectly proper given the flexible procedure inherent in the market model, but it must cast some doubt on the comprehensiveness of the original classification of neo-capitalist society into 'three basic classes' in market terms.

In 'state socialist' societies, argues Giddens, because the economy is subordinated and under the control of the polity the market is not allowed free play and thus 'class structuration' cannot occur. In other words as identifiable groupings cannot be located according to their market capacity, and the market does not determine the distribution of rewards, 'state socialist' societies are not class societies. The absence of class does not imply the absence of tensions and conflicts in 'state socialist' societies, but these are not *class* conflicts. Like Parkin, Giddens considers – and rejects – theories of a 'new

class' in 'state socialist' society – i.e., a stratum whose bureaucratic control and domination of the means of production
places them in a structurally similar class situation to the
bourgeoisie within the capitalist mode of production. This is
because such an élite, given the absence of inheritance or
privileged occupational opportunities, can never become fully
'structurated' into a class. Long-range mobility into senior
positions within the Soviet hierarchy is a continuing feature
of Soviet society, thus it is unlikely that a 'new class' will ever
consolidate its position. The structuration of the middle
classes in 'state socialist' societies is similarly inhibited by
conscious discrimination, in respect of distribution, against
these groups. In this discussion of the existence (or not) of a
'new class' within the Soviet order, the parallels between the
arguments of Giddens and Parkin are very striking, although
the labels – 'closure' and 'structuration' – differ. 'State
socialist' societies are therefore not class societies, but this
does not mean that tensions and conflicts are absent. Conflicts
can arise out of nationalistic pretensions within the variety of
states and nations which make up the Eastern bloc and, even
more significantly, conflicts may arise over rival modes of
administering the industrial order. In particular conflict is
likely to arise out of the possibility of the 'decentralisation' of
economic control resulting from the 'new economic policies
adopted in most of the state socialist countries from the late
1950s onwards'.[43] Such 'decentralisation' has two aspects: (1)
the devolution of economic control to the hands of managers,
and (2) increased responsiveness to price mechanisms. If
greater managerial independence were introduced, together
with an orientation to profits, this would probably meet with
strong resistance from the rank and file – a resistance which
could not be 'absorbed' by meeting 'economistic' demands
(as in capitalist societies), because the integration of economy
and polity in state socialist societies has effectively precluded
the emergence of trade union forms of 'conflict consciousness'
as is found in the West. The only acceptable form of devolution of control, therefore, is one which is 'linked to some
form of workers' self-management'.[44] However any effective
introduction of workers' self-management will be resisted by
the bureaucracy because of the massive threats to the existing

system which the explicit emergence of the 'will to control' would present.[45] In short, 'state socialist' societies, as much as or even more than capitalist societies, are subject to 'occasional, but much more deep rooted eruption[s] of worker antagonism involving an orientation to control'.[46]

In his discussion of capitalist societies Giddens describes these eruptions of the 'will to control' amongst the lower class as forerunners of a potential 'revolutionary class consciousness'. Given his analytical framework, similar conflicts in 'state socialist' societies cannot be described as *class* conflicts, as classes, by definition, do not exist in 'state socialist' societies. Does this therefore imply that 'revolutionary consciousness', as described by Giddens, is not an expression of class conflict or consciousness in capitalist societies? Or does it mean, as we would argue, that Giddens is prohibited by his own framework from correctly analysing the nature of such conflicts in 'state socialist' societies – that they are *class* conflicts arising out of the underlying contradictions of capitalist relationships of production?

In this chapter we have looked at the work of three of the most influential neo-Weberian class theorists in British sociology. We have shown that attempts to synthesise Weberian and Marxist theory have in fact resulted in a modified neo-Weberian scheme. We have shown that attempts to reject Marx's analysis have been derived from fundamental misinterpretations of Marx's work. More important, we have shown that two problems we consider to be central to class analysis – the nature of class conflict and the analysis of the Eastern bloc countries – present considerable problems for neo-Weberian theory which can only be resolved by moving out of the self-imposed market framework of neo-Weberian class analysis. We would reiterate, therefore, our belief that a class analysis derived from Marxian principles is likely to prove a superior theoretical and analytical tool.

We would emphasise, however, that our criticisms of neo-Weberian approaches do *not* imply that such approaches should be discarded. We have argued that they are not so much incorrect as incomplete. Given the dominance of the market, especially in the capitalist societies of the West, it would be futile to deny that much overt conflict is centred round access to the market, or that the sophisticated analyses of 'closure' and 'structuration' give valuable insights into the analysis of such market conflicts. Such insights can still be retained, however, even if class analysis, as we shall suggest, is shifted away from the all-prevailing neo-Weberian orthodoxy of contemporary class theory and towards an analysis grounded in an examination of relationships of production.

4

Capitalism in the Nineteenth Century: Subsequent Developments and Alternative Interpretations

In Chapter Two we outlined in very simple terms the basic elements of Marx's account of the class structure of capitalist society. To recapitulate: in a capitalist society the owner-controllers of the means of production (the bourgeoisie) buy, at or about the market rate, the labour power of the non-owners of the means of production (the proletariat). Labour power and the material means of production are combined, under the control of the entrepreneur, to create new products. The value of the new products is realised in the market, thus enabling the process to be constantly repeated. However the apparently 'fair' exchange between bourgeoisie and proletariat (i.e. labour for wages) masks what is essentially an exploitative class relationship. For the labour power controlled by the entrepreneur as a result of this exchange has the capacity to create values in excess of those reflected in wages – that is, surplus value. This model is, of course, a gross oversimplification both in empirical and theoretical terms. Firstly, it only considers the class situation of those engaged in material production, and in any complex society there will be many who work but are not directly engaged in the production of commodities. Secondly, it assumes that all who *do* engage in commodity production may be unambiguously classified as either 'bourgeoisie' or 'proletariat', which in fact is not the case. These two points indicate that in reality a wide range of class situations are apparent outside of the basic two-class model; in the next chapter we examine this diversity of class situations and show how the complex situation apparent in the modern world relates to the simple model outlined above. Thirdly, the model taken in isolation gives no indication of the *range* of societal issues relevant to Marxist class analysis. Marx considered that the nature of class relationships in capitalist society played a fundamental part in the understanding of conflicts and tensions in society, concerning such issues as the role of the state, the nature of authority relationships, and distributive processes. The development of class relationships, in addition, was essential to the interpretation of present and future social change.

Marx has been described as 'the last and greatest of the classical economists',[1] and the class analysis which we are developing here is derived from Marx's critique of classical political economy as exemplified by the work of Smith, Mill and Ricardo. Marx's critique was developed with empirical reference to a particular society – England – at a particular moment in time – the middle of the nineteenth century. This geographical and temporal location of Marx's work has been extensively cited in various criticisms of Marx. Probably one of the most familiar criticisms is that although Marx's analysis may have had some relevance in the nineteenth century the changed conditions of twentieth-century capitalism are such that (1) the original theoretical framework developed by Marx is no longer relevant, and (2) the *actual* form assumed by modern capitalism has in effect invalidated most of Marx's more important predictions concerning capitalist development – in particular those concerned with class conflict and the eventual overthrow of the capitalist order.

The capitalist mode of production and associated relations of production have both certainly undergone considerable changes since the nineteenth century. What we would question is whether these changes *have* been so fundamental that they render Marx's theory only of limited use. This issue must be squarely faced if we are going to continue to develop the strategy of class analysis suggested in this book. In the first section of this chapter, therefore, we will examine the nature of nineteenth-century capitalism, and in doing so point to some of the more important respects in which twentieth-century capitalism differs from nineteenth-century capitalism. This examination will also provide essential groundwork for the more systematic analysis of the structure of monopoly capitalism and associated class relationships which we develop in subsequent chapters.

In the second section of this chapter we will summarise some of the criticisms which have been made of Marx's work in general. The most common we have referred to above – that is, that Marx's work is simply out of date. It has also been suggested that although much of Marx's analysis may be accepted as broadly correct, as a whole it is *incomplete* in that he failed to identify some of the more important problems of contemporary industrial societies. The failure to identify such problems is often linked with a supposed 'economic determinism' inherent in Marxist analysis. Alternatively it may be held that although Marx correctly identified the problems endemic to industrial capitalism – employer/employee conflict, disputes over distribution, meaninglessness in work, etc. – the root causes of such tensions and conflicts are not those identified by Marx, but lie outside the structure of production relationships and the associated class structure. (In fact Marx's critics do not fall at all neatly into the categories just outlined, many constitute a mixture of all approaches.)

NINETEENTH-CENTURY BRITISH CAPITALISM AND ITS
SUBSEQUENT DEVELOPMENT

The first volume of *Capital* was published in 1867. Marx's intention to complete his critique of political economy was, however, never fulfilled and volumes two and three (the latter unfinished) were posthumously edited and published by Engels. Marx's exposition, therefore, is incomplete, and, although some of the more important of the subsequent developments of capitalist production were anticipated by Marx – for example, the tendency towards monopoly given joint-stock legislation and the extension of credit – the discussion of these developments is far from comprehensive, and his predictions sometimes inaccurate.

Britain was the most industrially advanced capitalist country in the nineteenth century. The capitalist mode of production has obviously developed considerably since then, and countries which have subsequently undergone the capitalist industrial transformation have not necessarily followed the same path. In mid-nineteenth-century England, although factory production was firmly established in some industries (for example, cotton and iron), the scale of productive units was small. Much industrial production was carried out in small workshops in which, although the organisation could be described as capitalist (i.e., the bulk of the work was carried out by propertyless work-force), the owner worked alongside his employees.[2] Technological innovations accompanying the industrial revolution had been considerable, but by the mid-nineteenth century their effect had largely been to 'deskill' manual craft work – to reduce the skill element within the labour process. Further technical developments have eventually led to the emergence of a stratum of 'white-collar' technicians, but this occupational group has really only achieved significance in the twentieth century. Clerical work within manufacturing industry was still largely the province of the entrepreneur or his closest associates. The occupational structure of manufacturing industry was therefore relatively undifferentiated in terms of both skill and status, a majority of manual workers were serviced by a small 'managerial' stratum which overlapped to a considerable extent with the owner/entrepreneur and his family connections. Although industrial production dominated the British economy by the 1850s, a substantial minority of the occupied population was still engaged in agriculture; in the 1840s, for example, more than a quarter of the working population in Great Britain was located in the agricultural sector.[3] Outside agriculture and manufacturing 36 per cent of the occupied population were employed in the 'service' sector.[4] The size of this sector does not, however, indicate the existence of a large 'middle-class' stratum outside manufacturing; 1·3 million of the 3·3 million comprising this 36 per cent were domestic servants, and this percentage also includes transport, defence, the police and independent artisan services as well as the more usual middle class categories such as finance, education and other professional services.

All of these features – the tiny managerial stratum, the relatively high levels of employment in agriculture and the low status of much service employment – indicate that one of the major features of modern capitalism, the presence of a skilled or educationally qualified, propertyless, employed middle class, was not a major element in the occupational structure of mid-nineteenth-century capitalism in Britain, or in other countries in the earlier stages of capitalist industrialisation.

Until the advent of limited liability legislation in 1856 the owners of the enterprise (industrial or otherwise) were directly responsible for ensuring its viability. Before 1856 the fact that owners were responsible for any debts incurred by the enterprise had both acted as a brake on the size of the enterprise and ensured a relatively high level of entrepreneurial involvement. The development of joint-stock legislation and the extension of credit were both recognised as potentially important by Marx, but the features associated with these phenomena – the extension of 'ownership without control' and the development of large, multinational corporations – had not assumed the fundamental importance which they have today in respect of contemporary monopoly capitalism.

Finally, and with particular importance for our subsequent analysis, we would draw attention to the nature of state involvement in the mid-nineteenth century as compared to today. The state's part in the development of capitalist industrialism should not be underestimated, despite the prevalence of laissez-faire ideologies at the time. The state's role, however, especially in England, was largely indirect, and bore no resemblance to the direct intervention increasingly characteristic of the modern state. State activities in England during industrialisation have been described as 'negative intervention' – that is, the state played an active role in dismantling many pre-capitalist, pre-industrial restrictions, thus facilitating the full and free development of market activity.[5] The state has historically provided 'externalities' during the process of industrialisation, that is, the provision of services such as transport, or technical education. These services are essential to the industrialisation process, but often have not yielded a high enough return on capital invested to be sufficiently advantageous to the capitalist entrepreneur. In fact the availability of private capital in England meant that such externalities were largely provided by private enterprise rather than the state: the railways, for example, were wholly developed by private enterprise in England, whereas the provision of a rail network in other European countries was only achieved with varying levels of state finance and support.[6]

Our summary of the nature of capitalism in nineteenth-century England – the template from which Marx drew his critique of political economy – has stressed three features which differ from modern monopoly capitalism. Firstly, the occupational structure of contemporary capitalist societies is very different from that of the nineteenth century. The range of occupations has greatly increased, and considerable differentiation and specialisation has occurred within occupations: today's equivalent of the great engineer Brunel, for example, would probably be a medium to large-sized engineering firm, with access to computers, market researchers, accountants, and so on. Particularly significant for Marx's analysis (and predictions) has been the emergence of the middle class stratum, a heterogeneous group of occupations including managers, higher and lower professionals, civil servants, technicians, clerks, etc. Characterisitically these groups draw better material rewards than manual workers, but these rewards are not usually derived from property rights but from the real or supposed value of the work or services performed. In Chapter Three we noted the difficulties which the emergence of the middle class presents for Marxist class analysis.[7]

Secondly, contemporary capitalism is dominated by large national or multinational corporations, usually administered by managers who do not legally 'own' the vast resources of these corporations. Thirdly, in every capitalist society of today the state plays an increasingly direct role in the economy, directing investment, providing or withholding resources, and in some cases (recently in the United Kingdom for example) directly installing new management.

In later chapters we will be developing our own version of an up-to-date Marxist analysis which accommodates these features of modern capitalism. However, given the importance of these developments for his analysis, it would have been surprising if Marx had been completely unaware of these possibilities, and indeed we find that Marx did give some consideration to each of the three features we have discussed above, albeit in a rather sketchy and often ambiguous fashion.

That Marx was aware of the possibilities of 'middle-class' expansion is evident in this extract from *Theories of Surplus Value*, in which he points out that Ricardo forgets to emphasise

> the constant increase of the middle classes, who stand in the middle between the workers on one side and the capitalists and landed proprietors on the other side, who are for the most part supported directly by revenue, who rest as a burden on the labouring foundation, and who increase the social security and the power of the upper ten thousand.[8]

This quotation is frequently triumphantly presented by Marx's defenders in order to demonstrate that Marx *had* anticipated one of the major criticisms of his theory and predictions. Unfortunately Marx's defenders less often engage in the logical follow-through – what are the implications of this for Marx's theory and predictions as a whole?

In Marx's writings two major groups of 'white-collar' workers can be unambiguously identified. Firstly, the 'service class' – that is, personal servants, who, as we have already seen, were a substantial proportion (1·3 million) of an occupied population of only 9·7 million. In addition it is clear that Marx considered security services – the police, the army – a part of this service class:

> What a beautiful arrangement, where a factory girl sweats in the shop for 12 long hours so that the factory owner can use a part of her unpaid labour to take her sister as maid, her brother as groom, and her cousin as policeman or soldier into his personal service.[9]

Marx saw the increase in the numbers of this service class as being a reflection of the increasing prosperity of the bourgeoisie given the immense productivity of the capitalist mode of production. Such workers are maintained out of revenue, they do not produce any new value, but the services they perform and the wages they receive must be paid for out of surplus value (or revenue) raised elsewhere.

The presence of the second major group of white-collar workers discussed in some detail by Marx, commercial wage-workers, is also associated with the rising mass of surplus which is generated as capitalist production becomes ever better established:

> as the scale of production is extended, commercial opera-tions required constantly for the circulation of industrial capital, in order to sell the product existing as commodity-capital, to reconvert the money so received into means of production, and to keep account of the whole process, multiply accordingly. Calculation of prices, book-keeping, managing funds, correspondence – all belong under this head, . . . This necessitates the employment of commercial wage-workers.[10]

Unlike the service workers just discussed, commercial wage-workers do not represent capitalist 'consumption' as such: commercial labour-power 'is not bought for private service, but for the purpose of expanding the value of capital advanced for it.'[11] The use of commercial labour power enables the commercial capitalist to *acquire* a share of surplus value actually created elsewhere; and activities in the sphere of circulation (which includes commercial capital) are an essential part of the *total* process of the *realisation* of surplus value, but no new values are *created* in this sphere. Like service workers, therefore, commercial wageworkers are unproduc-tive in that they do not create surplus value.

Marx's discussion of groups such as domestic servants and commercial wageworkers clearly indicates that he was aware of the probable increase in middle-class or white-collar occupations. However it is equally clear that the actual range of white-collar occupations which comprise the middle-class

stratum of today was not anticipated by Marx. The importance of domestic servants as an occupational group has
declined dramatically, and their place has been taken by a
variety of services, such as restaurants, hairdressers, dry-
cleaners, and so on, *organised along capitalist principles*.
Commercial wageworkers have certainly continued to increase
in numbers, augmented by market researchers, sales analysts,
advertising personnel and many more, the like of which Marx
never envisaged. The state (in the majority of advanced
capitalist countries) now provides a range of services such as
health, education, and social welfare, which has vastly increased the tiny professional class existing in Marx's day, and,
as already mentioned, the process of production itself
increasingly involves white-collar employees as technical and
managerial experts.

Some writers, Nicolaus in particular, have argued that it is
legitimate to infer from Marx's writings on the subject that
the development of the middle class is a logical corollary to
his account of the development of the capitalist mode of
production.[12] Such a class (labelled the 'surplus class' by
Nicolaus) is described as necessary both to administer the
ever-rising surpluses generated by capitalist production, and
also to *consume* the surplus, thus helping to maintain the
stability of the capitalist system as a whole by regulating or
avoiding crises of overproduction. Such a functionalist
account may be superficially attractive, but lacks the
explanatory power of the rest of Marx's work. Therefore
Marx's writings on the growth of the middle class cannot
simply be discussed as evidence of 'the remarkable prescience
of a man whose insights not infrequently broke the bounds of
the theoretical formulations whereby he sought to discipline
them'.[13] On the other hand neither can Marx be argued to
have laid firm foundations for a 'theory' of the middle class,
as Nicolaus argues. In this important respect, therefore,
Marx's theory must be developed in order to take into
account the changed conditions of modern capitalism.

The second broad feature of capitalist development which
we have identified as necessitating further elaboration of
Marx's original theory is the development of national and
multinational corporations, together with associated features

such as the separation of *de jure* ownership from *de facto* control (the supposed 'managerial revolution'), and increasing domination and manipulation of the market by such corporations. Again, we find that Marx did consider these possibilities, albeit only briefly, and his discussion is a mixture of inaccurate prediction and penetrating insights.

For Marx the development of joint-stock legislation and the extension of credit had a double aspect. On the one hand he argued that limited liability could be seen as a transitional stage towards the development of fully social production. Capitalist production had socialised (made cooperative) the *labour* process, joint ownership through shareholding marked the beginnings of social *ownership*, as manifested, for example, in cooperative factories. To quote directly, 'It is the abolition of capital as private property within the framework of capitalist production itself.'[14]

An enthusiastic addition by Engels points to the increasing rationalisation and concentration of the chemical industry in England after Marx's death, thus 'the road has been paved, most gratifyingly, for future expropriation by the whole of society, the nation,'[15] and this massive (by the standards of the time) organisation could more easily be taken into public ownership.

On the other hand, says Marx, joint-stock legislation and the extension of credit raises the level of exploitation to even greater heights. Limitation of personal liability means that the operation of capital is no longer constrained by considerations as to the extent of *personal* loss.

> What the speculating wholesale merchant risks is social property, not *his own*. Equally sordid becomes the phase relating the origin of capital to savings, for what he demands is that *others* should save for him.[16]

Freely available credit means that capitalist production can become world-wide, it 'raises the material foundations of (capitalism) to a certain degree of perfection'. However, although the extension of credit raised the capitalist mode of production to this 'certain degree of perfection', the lack of constraint which results from the ready availability of credit leads to constant crises of overproduction and over-speculation. These crises can only be temporarily resolved by increasing industrial and financial concentration and demands for state aid in the protection of monopolies. In this process small to middling capitalists lose out heavily, 'the little fish are swallowed by the sharks and the lambs by the stock exchange wolves.'[17]

Marx therefore clearly anticipated the increasing concentration and centralisation which is so striking a feature of today's monopoly capitalism. However some of the more important features of these developments were not anticipated by Marx, and in addition some specific predictions have proved misleading. Although the formation of joint-stock companies is logically a move towards social ownership, historically, this has not proved to be the case. 'Mere managers', these 'functionaries without capital', have for a variety of reasons continued to carry out the capitalist function *as capitalists*; there is no doubt that Marx made too much of the importance of *personal* wealth in determining the operations of the capitalist system as a whole.[18] Additionally Marx seriously underestimated the extent to which crises of overproduction and overspeculation can be 'managed' (and sometimes avoided) through the national and international control of credit, and state and large corporation manipulation.[19] In general Marx's discussion of these issues failed to anticipated the increasing level of direct state intervention in the economy, although he did note that the state had a role to play in the protection of monopolies.

The nature of the modern state, as compared to the mid-nineteenth-century state, is the third major area of difference which we have selected for emphasis in our comparison of nineteenth- and twentieth-century capitalism. Marx's (and Marxist) theories of the state have recently attracted much critical attention, and we will not go into much detail at this point in our argument.[20]

In volume one of *Capital*, Marx discusses at some length the role of the state in 'so-called primitive accumulation' – the process by which large fortunes are amassed on the one hand, and labour is separated from the means of production on the other. In the English case, Marx argues, the state played a direct role in this process. The enclosures consolidated ever larger landholdings, at the same time expropriating the rural population. This population was forced into wage labour through successively severe penalties against vagabondage, and wage rates themselves were forcibly held at low levels through direct state legislation. Capitalist development was further encouraged by the extension of public credit – the National Debt – an essential prerequisite for the development of finance capital. State indebtedness required taxation, which itself raised the level of expropriation of the working classes. Finally, the state played a direct role in the process of colonisation, the opening up of new territories under the jurisdiction of the State. Colonisation acquired massive wealth for the 'home' capitalist, to say nothing of new markets, and, on occasion, a tractable (i.e., slave) labour force as well.

> The different momenta of primitive accumulation . . . arrive at a systematical combination, embracing the colonies, the national debt, the modern mode of taxation, and the protectionist system. These methods depend in part on brute force . . . but they all employ the power of the State, the concentrated and organised force of society, to hasten, hothouse fashion, the process of transformation of the feudal mode of production into the capitalist mode, and to shorten the transition.[21]

Thus the state played a direct *economic* part in the early stages of capitalist development, not only in dismantling barriers to expansion, but in such details as legislating on wage rates and the movement of labour. What was the case for England in the earlier stages of development, was also the case for the 'developing' capitalist countries in the nineteenth century: Marx contrasts, for example, French industry's need for state protection with the demand of the English bourgeoisie for free trade.[22] It is noteworthy, however, that in his detailed discussion of *developed* capitalism – the English case – the state, for Marx, no longer plays this direct role. To be sure, state aid is still necessary in the protection of monopoly, and of course the state's part in colonial and imperial expansion can never be less than direct, but in these and other respects the state *facilitated* continuing capitalist development, rather than only pursuing such a course through direct intervention.[23]

In modern monopoly capitalism, however, we find that the modern state again plays a directly interventionist role in the economy. This feature of modern capitalism was not anticipated by Marx. Indeed one of the major criticisms of Marx's analysis is that he failed to see how the intervention of the state could ameliorate the grosser excesses of capitalism, so as to not only avert capitalist crises but also modify the structure of capitalist society to such an extent that the label 'post-capitalist' is now claimed to be appropriate.[24] This issue will be taken up in greater detail in Chapter Six; for the moment we will simply indicate state activity as an important area in respect of which Marx's original account will have to be extended.

CRITICISMS OF MARX

As we indicated in our introduction to this chapter, many of the changes in the structure of capitalism we have been discussing have been used to argue the case that although Marx may have been broadly correct in his analysis of nineteenth-century capitalism, the development of capitalism since then has had the effect of invalidating both his theoretical analysis and specific predictions. Many versions of this argument have been put forward – the range covered includes both the 'ownership and control' and 'post-industrial society' debates. We will only give a short summary of such arguments here, more detailed versions can be found in the work of such authors as Kerr et al., Galbraith, Dahrendorf, Marshall and Kaysen.[25]

Our strategy will be to simply present criticisms of Marx's work as cogently as possible. We shall not engage in detailed refutations at this stage, as the discussion we shall be developing from Chapter Five onwards should effectively counter these arguments.

We can begin our summary of the general critique of Marx with what is perhaps the most famous and oft-quoted of Marx's political predictions:

> Our epoch, the epoch of the bourgeoisie, possesses, how-
> ever, this distinctive feature: it has simplified the class
> antagonisms. Society as a whole is more and more splitting
> up into two great hostile camps, into two great classes
> directly facing each other: Bourgeoisie and Proletariat.[26]

In the majority of the advanced capitalist countries in the
world, however, this polarisation has failed to occur, and, in
addition, the mass of the industrial proletariat has shown a
marked reluctance to act as the 'grave-diggers' of the bourgeoisie, and thus of capitalism itself. This failure of Marx's
predictions forms the basic starting point of the wide area
covered by the whole 'post-capitalist' society debate. A
simplified version of the argument would run thus: The class
polarisation expected in mature capitalist societies has
simply not happened, and indeed, in all cases of mature
capitalism (or 'industrial society'), an 'intermediate stratum'
(or middle class) has emerged, standing between the bourgeoisie on the one hand and the proletariat on the other.
These middle classes have not only (historically) been politically conservative, but have also afforded a valuable safety
valve for the worker, who can see an immediate means of
bettering himself (through upward occupational mobility)
rather than through class conflict leading to revolution.
Therefore not only has polarisation not occurred, but in
addition the working class has failed to develop any consciousness of its historic role. This is partly due to opportunities for advancement, as noted above, but also due to the
fact that the 'immiseration' of the working class (another of
Marx's predictions) has not happened either. The state has
constantly intervened in order to improve the lot of the
working man, culminating in the development of the modern
welfare state. Additionally, the separation of ownership from
control and the administration of capitalism by a managerial
stratum who no longer have a *personal* interest in maximising
profits and raising the level of exploitation have led to a
generally more humane approach to the production process,
which has also benefited the worker. This more benign
management, alternatively pressured by, and cooperating
with, the modern *industrial* (rather than capitalist) state, has

evolved techniques which limit the worst excesses of the market, thus avoiding periodic crises which have adverse social consequences such as mass unemployment or widespread poverty. In short the contradictions of nineteenth-century capitalism, which indeed at times seemed capable of tearing society apart, have been largely resolved (if not totally overcome) within the framework of twentieth-century capitalism, without the necessity for any revolutionary change.

The kinds of criticism summarised above largely accept the validity of Marx's analysis of nineteenth-century capitalism, but argue that the accuracy of his predictions has been invalidated because of the changed conditions of mid-twentieth-century capitalism. We now turn to those critics who have challenged his original analysis of nineteenth-century capitalism, arguing that it was either incomplete, or gave an inaccurate explanation of the source of the manifest conflicts and tensions in industrial society. Although many contemporary authors have made these kinds of criticisms,[27] we shall use the work of Weber as an example of the former critical stance, and Durkheim as an example of the latter. This is not least because much contemporary criticism of Marx's work has its intellectual origins in the work of these two writers.

We have already looked at Weber's theory of class in some detail, and in so doing have detached his class theory from the rest of his work. In a way, to take Weber's class analysis in isolation is perfectly legitimate given his professed approach to the study of the social sciences (including sociology) in general. Weber argued that it was not the task of the social sciences to construct universal 'systems' which (illegitimately) 'explain reality' and subsequently indicate what men 'ought' to do. For example, Weber considered Marx's theoretical framework as an example of a series of 'ideal types' – that is, a series of purely *analytical* constructs and concepts developed in order to gain a better understanding of social life. On this level Weber accepted the validity of Marx's work. However, argued Weber, such theories are not 'real' in themselves, must never be taken for *objective* reality – and certainly cannot be used as an indication of what action 'ought' to be taken.

Marxian 'laws' and developmental constructs in so far as they are theoretically sound – are ideal types. The eminent, indeed unique, *heuristic* significance of these ideal types when they are used for the *assessment* of reality is known to everyone who has ever employed Marxian concepts and hypotheses. Similarly, their perniciousness, as soon as they are thought of as empirically valid or as real . . . 'effective forces', 'tendencies', etc., is likewise known to those who have used them.[28]

However, although Weber consciously set his face against descriptions of reality that purported to be 'objective', it is difficult, in taking an overall view of Weber's work, to avoid the conclusion that like Marx he identified certain features of modern society which not only explained reality but also indicated the *universal* development of this reality; this is particularly evident in his work on bureaucracy. As far as social classes were concerned, Weber considered their identification as important constructs in the explanation and understanding of contemporary capitalist society, also he thought class conflict to be highly likely, if not inevitable. For Weber, however, the explication of the class structure was not of *central* importance in explaining the nature of capitalist society, neither did the relationship between social classes 'explain' anything about the past or future development of capitalist society, as it did for Marx.

It can be argued that in Weber's political, as opposed to his sociological, writings class analysis was always of central importance. 'Only a class analysis was adequate to elucidate . . . power and the striving for power in *particular* societies.'[29] However it is equally clear from his sociological and political writings that he thought that class divisions and conflicts *could* be to a large extent resolved *within* the capitalist system. If the different classes could only throw off the blinkers of the narrow pursuit of economic gain, they would realise that a liberal, well-ordered capitalist system could operate for the benefit of *all* classes, combining as it did the opportunity for enhanced material wealth with the freedom of the individual.[30]

From our previous discussion of market-based approaches

to social class we can see that such a belief in the possible resolution of class conflict within capitalism is in fact entirely logical. If the only tensions and inequalities generated by the class structure are those of the market, it is not impossible, given goodwill and understanding on all sides, to overcome these tensions with rational planning and explanation – plus a bit of inspired intervention on the part of entrepreneurs and political leaders.

Such a positively desirable state of affairs could be severely inhibited, or even fail to develop, Weber argued, because of *the* great problem facing the modern industrial world – bureaucracy. In his sociological writings Weber's conception of the 'Janus-faced' nature of bureaucracy is entirely evident. On the one hand the *technical* efficiency of bureaucracy could not be bettered as a formally rational instrument for achieving the necessary goals of complex administration, themselves an integral part of modern life. On the other hand there is a constant danger that the bureaucratic machine – in particular, the state bureaucracy – will outstep its limits, will abrogate to itself the power and decision making which by right belong to the democratically elected political leadership.[31] For bureaucracy, once established, is *permanent*. Once the bureaucratic means of administration have been firmly established, they can only be overthrown given the total collapse of the whole society, as is demonstrated by the examples of the ancient Egyptian and Roman bureaucratic empires. In his own time Weber thought that the Prussian bureaucratic machine, apparently so efficient, had hampered the development of an independent spirit in the German entrepreneurial class, and had even thwarted the German war effort in the First World War.[32] Socialism, said Weber, provided no answers to the bureaucratic problem. For the advent of socialism would only bring into being an even more terrible and powerful bureaucratic structure, crushing out individuality, and before which the individual worker would be powerless.[33] Indeed a major element in Weber's defence of capitalism against socialism was that a properly developed entrepreneurial class would provide counter-bureaucracies to the overwhelming power of the state.[34]

In his discussion of bureaucracy, therefore, Weber is clearly making assumptions, both about the *real* nature of the social world, and also about the future development of industrial societies and, by implication, what *ought* to be done about present or future perils. Bureaucracy is inevitable; given a certain level of complexity it must be established, and the modern industrial order simply cannot develop under alternative modes of administration or authority, for 'rationality' is essential for the development of industrial capitalism.[35] Bureaucracy is also permanent, but, once alerted to the dangers inherent in bureaucratic administration, modern man *can* avoid its more terrible aspects. Despite his methodological protestations, therefore, Weber was, as much as Marx, both theorist and prophet of the modern social order, but his analysis led him to identify both different problems and different cures.

Durkheim did not actively participate in political life; with some exaggeration it could be said that for Durkheim the new science of sociology, rather than political man-oeuvring, was the most hopeful avenue to the solution of the problems of the modern industrial world. For Durkheim, unlike Weber, argued that the role to be assumed by the scientist was not one of 'value neutrality', disinterestedly proffering explanations as to the nature of the world, but one of active engagement, confronting real problems and through scientific analysis offering workable and hopefully successful solutions: 'The progress of a science is proven by the pro-gress toward solution of the problems it treats.'[36] Although not overtly 'political', therefore, much of Durkheim's work must be seen in the light of his belief in sociology as a practical science, and in this wider sense his work is pro-foundly political. It has been pointed out, for example, that for Durkheim, 'ideally, socialism could in the future become the application of the remedies proposed by sociology. It would then become "the social and political art which complemented the social and political science constituted by sociology".'[37] Although Durkheim, unlike Weber, did not consciously formulate his sociological analysis as a reply (at least in part) to the work of Marx, the framework of analysis he developed provides a cogent alternative explanation of the problems which Marx identified as endemic in capitalist society. There are also clear links between Durkheim's work and that of contemporary theorists – Parsons in particular – who have taken an overtly critical stance *vis-à-vis* Marx's work.[38] Durkheim, like Marx, thought that the explanation for social behaviour should be located in the structures of the society in which individuals and groups were located: however he argued correctly that the adoption of this perspective in no way implied that the particular conclusions Marx came to should therefore be accepted.[39]

For Durkheim the source of the majority of the problems and tensions of modern society – problems he identified as ranging from the increasing rates of crime and suicide to class and industrial conflict – lay in the lack of *societal* regulation in contemporary industrial society. Industrial capitalism and the accompanying division of labour had broken the restraining bonds of feudal dependence, guild and church, but as yet no institutions had arisen to take their place and perform the function of 'binding' the individual to society. Both individuals and society as a whole, therefore, were and are in a profound state of *anomie*, or de-regulation. Discussions of anomie are to be found in two of Durkheim's major works: *The Division of Labour in Society* and *Suicide*.

The increased division of labour, argued Durkheim, is a 'normal' feature of all societies where human density is increasing (i.e., population concentration). The increasing division of labour breaks down older, 'mechanical' forms of solidarity, that is, a solidarity based upon the essential *likeness* of the societal components. Although mechanical solidarity leaves little scope for individuality, the individual is bound to society through sets of rules and customs which all must follow. Such 'solidarity through likeness' collapses with increasing differentiation and division of labour, but is replaced by a new form of solidarity, 'organic' solidarity. In highly differentiated societies, no one individual or part can do without the other (as in, for example, the complex organism) and thus, through a consciousness of this interdependence, organic solidarity emerges. There is therefore nothing pathological about the division of labour as such, and organic solidarity is its 'normal' counterpart.

Although, however, the association of the complex division

of labour and organic solidarity is 'normal', in modern society, the division of labour is manifest in 'abnormal' forms. Two major abnormal forms are identified by Durkheim as characteristic in modern industrial society – the 'anomic' and the 'forced' division of labour. The anomic division of labour occurs when the parts are insufficiently well articulated with each other, when producer is too far separated from consumer, employer from work-force, and is manifested by outward occurrences such as business crises and industrial conflict. The individual or part *fails* to perceive the essential solidarity of society as a whole, lacks any real goals or sense of regulation, and therefore any sense of direction. Lacking regulation, individual wants are limitless and ever unsatisfied. The anomic division of labour, however, cannot be overcome either by demonstrating the interdependence of the whole to the individual (say, through better education) or through a more systematic set of rules. This is because of the problems associated with the forced division of labour, which coexists with the anomic division of labour.

Organic solidarity only arises when the division of labour is 'spontaneous', that is, when every individual, through the process of differentiation of tasks and responsibilities, performs a task which reflects his or her natural capacities. Because of the manifest inequalities in the modern world – of birth, wealth, etc. – natural abilities are only rarely reflected in the allocation of tasks, responsibilities, and rewards. Contracts, supposedly between 'equals', can never be so if they are located within a structure of social inequality.

> If one class of society is obliged, in order to live, to take any price for its services, while another can abstain from such action thanks to resources at its disposal which, however, are not necessarily due to any social superiority, the second has an unjust advantage over the first at law. In other words, there cannot be rich and poor at birth without there being unjust contracts.[40]

Such a division of labour in an unequal society is hardly spontaneous, but 'forced'. The lack of system integration and regulation characteristic of the anomic division of labour could not be overcome unless the forced division of labour was modified as well. Durkheim's proposed solutions to the forced division of labour were radical. All inequalities, including inheritance, which masked the expression of natural inequalities of talent should be abolished, for 'labour is divided spontaneously only if society is constituted in such a way that social inequalities exactly express natural inequalities.'[41]

Although equality of opportunity and social justice provide a suitable framework within which the problems of anomie may be tackled, they do not in themselves actually *solve* the problem of anomie. In *Suicide* Durkheim again returns to the problem of anomie in complex industrial society, identifying anomie as one of the four major causes and categories of suicide – a phenomenon which, as shown by its rapid rate of increase, was assuming pathological proportions in contemporary society. Durkheim's practical proposals for dealing with anomie centred on the occupational group. (After all, as we have seen, in both the *Division of Labour* and *Suicide* anomie has been linked with the disturbances of modern business life.) Corporate activity is a 'natural' source for the re-emergence of social groupings which will bind and regulate the individual to and in society in a meaningful way. For, given the extensive division of labour in industrial society, almost everyone works, and therefore it is at this point that men naturally participate in society as a *whole*.[42]

Durkheim therefore identified as one of the major problems facing industrial society that of creating a new *moral* order to replace that which had been swept away during the process of industrial transition. It would be misleading to dismiss such preoccupations as conservative, for as we have seen Durkheim argued that such a moral order could only be constructed within a framework of fairness and equality. Nevertheless it is justifiable to characterise the overall strategy of Durkheim's approach as one of the analysis of 'system strain', and his prescriptions are prescriptions which, if successful, will lead to a greater level of system integration. If we followed Durkheim's analysis, class or industrial conflict could be seen as stemming from two sources: firstly, the manifest inequality and essential *unfairness* of the existing allocation of rewards, and secondly, from the insufficient integration and regulative function of the differentiated elements of modern industrial society – or anomie.

> The prevalence of class conflicts in contemporary societies is symptomatic of the *malaise* of the modern world, but not its root cause. Class conflict derives from a disorder which has its origins elsewhere. 'From which it follows', in Durkheim's view, 'That the economic transformations which have been produced during the course of this century, the changeover from small to large-scale industry, do not necessitate an upheaval and radical reorganisation of the social order.'[43]

In the work of Weber and Durkheim we have the example of two late nineteenth-century social theorists actively attempting to identify the major problems of complex industrial society; although both indeed saw that there were serious conflicts and tensions in society, the *source* of the conflicts identified by Weber and Durkheim was very different from that identified by Marx. Increasing bureaucratic rationality on the one hand and anomie on the other were alleged to be the source of the problems facing industrial society. Neither excessive bureaucratic rationality nor anomie were held to be a *necessary* feature of capitalist relations of production. Because Weber and Durkheim identified different sources of tension, it naturally follows that their prescriptions for the alleviation of problems were very different from those of Marx as well. In particular both Weber and Durkheim thought that they could be solved to a large extent within the framework of the existing society, and by implication within the framework of the capitalist mode of production.

In this chapter we have simply reviewed various criticisms of Marx's work as a whole, without any attempt at refutation. The case we will make to support the general validity of Marx's analysis will be built up in the chapters that follow. We believe, however, that the correct strategy is not to attempt to counter Marx's critics through a close textual analysis of Marx's writings, although a considerable Marx industry has been developed using this technique. Rather we will develop Marx's original framework so as to take into account the changed conditions of modern monopoly capitalism. In the next chapter we will examine the debate on the separation of ownership from control in some detail. Although we would willingly concede that the large corporation of today bears little resemblance to the nineteenth-century firm controlled by the owner-entrepreneur we shall argue, nevertheless, that it is possible to unambiguously identify capital and labour functions within the modern corporation. An examination of the techniques which have been developed in order to raise the rate of extraction of surplus value, and thus maintain or raise the level of capitalist accumulation, will indicate that increasing differentiation and division of labour is not simply the natural outcome of an increase in human density, as Durkheim would argue, but an inevitable outcome of intensified capitalist development. Indeed we shall suggest that the 'forced' and 'anomic' division of labour, as described by Durkheim, are not simply 'abnormal forms', but are entirely *normal* given the constraints imposed by capitalist production relationships. An analysis of the complex process of the generation and allocation of surplus value will enable us to locate more precisely in the class structure the 'middle stratum' which has been so important in the rejection of Marx's polarisation prediction. As our argument will make clear, it is misleading to view such groupings as a buffer zone; within the so-called middle class we find considerable tensions and heightening ambiguities.

In Chapter Six we will examine the nature of the modern state, and its role in the capitalist economy. We will directly challenge the view of the state as 'neutral arbiter', and will argue that the state is an integral feature of modern capitalism: indeed that monopoly capitalism cannot hope to survive without continuing state involvement. In short, the state bureaucracy has not so much thwarted capitalist entrepreneurial development and enterprise as Weber would argue, as come to constitute a necessary ingredient for its continuing existence. (Interestingly enough, Weber's fears as to the crushing nature of the state bureaucracy find their contemporary echo in some variants of modern conservatism.)[44] In countering the criticisms of Marx which have been raised in this chapter we do not believe that we will thereby entirely dispose of them. Rather we hope to demonstrate that it is possible, indeed necessary, to accept some of these criticisms, but at the same time we do not think that they undermine the validity of Marx's thesis as a whole.

5

Economy and Class Structure in the West

In our account of nineteenth-century British capitalism in the last chapter, we noted that in the initial stages of capitalist development each company's owner or owners typically supervised the work of their employees and directed the overall operation of the enterprise. However this clearly is not an adequate description of the modern corporation, as we indicated. The analysis of the entrepreneurial firm demonstrates that surplus value is generated by the employees and appropriated by the employers (capitalists), but we cannot simply assert by analogy that similar processes take place in the modern corporation, for it is far from obvious that the entrepreneurial firm is relevantly similar for the analogy to hold. There have been fundamental changes in the size, structure, ownership and environment of the firm so that any valid attempt to discern a surplus value producing process must not start by abstracting from these changes but recognise that they have taken place and that their significance requires careful analysis. Even in highly industrialised capitalist societies there are very many small firms, particularly in personal services, agriculture and retailing, but they are increasingly exposed to competition from big firms and are dependent on them for supplies or demand.[1]

We recognise that there are still a significant proportion of firms, including some very large ones, where ownership is concentrated among fairly close kin and most of the senior managers are drawn from this group; and indeed there are some sizeable corporations owned and controlled by a single 'tycoon' or partnership.[2] However it is readily admitted that such cases constitute a small minority; the typical large firm of the twentieth century is a joint-stock limited liability company with a large number of shareholders who have no managerial position in the company. An important qualification to this typification is that in some cases a small number of the shareholders, particularly those with large holdings, do occupy top positions in the company. Furthermore many top managers do own shares in the company. In spite of these caveats, in the typical corporation the groups of shareholders and managers are far from identical.[3] Dahrendorf extends the argument in the following terms:

> Joint-stock companies differ from capitalist enterprises in the structure of their leading positions. In the sphere with which we are here concerned, the process of transition from capitalist enterprise to join-stock companies can be described as a process of role differentiation. The roles of owner and manager, originally combined in the position of capitalist, have been separated and distributed over two positions, those of stockholder and executive.[4]

While we would not dispute that there has been a powerful tendency to such role differentiation, it would be logically invalid to conclude on this basis alone that the characteristic capitalist function of extracting surplus value ceases to be performed by the combination of manager and shareholder. What is required is an analysis of the links between the two roles and the consequent effects on their incumbents' behaviour. The evidence of similarities in social class background,[5] educational experiences and social relations between managers and shareholders suggests that even though there may be some characteristic areas of difference or conflict of outlook there are likely to be common general beliefs and attitudes. The two groups are equally wedded to the instrumental and moral value of company profitability and the principle of production for profit as such, together with an associated corpus of conservative ideas. A number of authors[6] have advanced views to the effect that managers may have other aspirations than profitability, such as company growth, job security, esteem by the public, a desire for socially responsible company policy, and so on. While not denying that managers may genuinely see their goals in such terms, the argument is unconvincing unless it can be shown that managers characteristically sacrifice profitability where there is conflict with these goals. Failing such a demonstration and recognising ever present competition between firms, it is apparent that managers' central goal is the pursuit of profit, even if this is 'only' a necessary means to other goals that are positively embraced.[7] We certainly do not wish to suggest by this that the managers of the modern corporation simply select that policy which yields the best short-term profit. Rather, long-term profits are characteristically sought, which requires an extremely complex evaluation of alternatives, using partial and inadequate calculative techniques applied to imperfect knowledge of a situation which is only subject to limited control by the firm. In deciding between alternatives, it may be that share-holders favour a different choice from managers – a possibility that a valid theory of the firm should not deny *a priori* – but it should also be rembered that any such conflict is *within* a consensus about the supreme importance of long-term profitability. The possibility of effective long-term profit is enhanced by the creation of corps of experts in the firm and procedures for checking and pooling their evaluations, which is in turn facilitated by the development of a body of theory and techniques prescribing rational managerial decision making. From the point of view of management there are threats to profitability from a number of different directions; price and quality competition in the product market, price rises in the factor market – particularly for labour – availability and cost of credit or share yield demand in the capital market, and danger of take-over or forced merger. The best way to cope with these threats to *profitability as such* is to plan, calculate and organise methodically to *maximise* long-term profit; the controllers of the modern corporation are characteristically devoted to that cause.

Although there are a very large number of shareholders in most joint-stock companies, it is often the case that a small number of major shareholders dominate the rest, even where their holdings constitute quite a low proportion of total shares.[8] While it may be plausibly argued that the managers cannot be directly controlled by the large number of dispersed and unorganised shareholders as a whole, it is clear that they constantly have to bear in mind the interests of the shareholders, especially the major ones. Where many shareholders, even if only relatively small ones, do not approve of company policy generally or profitability prospects in particular, they may sell some of their shares; this possibility puts a considerable constraint upon the managers since any significant wave of selling tends to lower share prices, reducing capital gains, making it more difficult to obtain loans or float new share issues and exposing the firm to the danger of take-over. Where, as in many large corporations, a considerable proportion of all shares are held by investment trusts, insurance companies, pension funds and similar institutions, their natural concern for stability and long-term profitability reinforces management's motivations towards such goals.[9] Those cases where shareholders cannot be seen to intervene in policy making may simply indicate that managers are doing what shareholders wish anyway because of constant pressures of the market to maximise long-term profit.

In our view it is a misunderstanding to regard such role differentiation as has taken place between owners and managers as evidence of the 'decomposition of capital.'[10] We argue that the whole manager/owner complex constitutes a functionally definable element, which we refer to as global capital, and which is related in characteristic ways to the market and means of production. The case for such a view will be initially stated in this chapter and expanded later in the book. If the capitalist mode of production is to be sustained, it goes without saying that capital enters into a definite relationship with labour. Marx nicely characterises the way in which work is caught up in the relation between labour and capital, by contrast to a person working on his own behalf:

The labour-process, turned into the process by which the

capitalist consumes labour-power, exhibits two characteristic phenomena. First, the labourer works under the
control of the capitalist to whom his labour belongs; the
capitalist taking good care that the work is done in a proper
manner, and that the means of production are used with
intelligence, so that there is no unnecessary waste of raw
material, and no wear and tear of the implements beyond
what is necessarily caused by the work.

Secondly, the product is the property of the capitalist
and not that of the labourer, its immediate producer.
Suppose that a capitalist pays for a day's labour-power at
its value; then the right to use that power for a day belongs
to him, just as much as the right to use any other commodity, such as a horse that he has hired for the day. To
the purchaser of a commodity belongs its use, and the
seller of labour-power, by giving his labour, does no
more, in reality, than part with the use-value which he has
sold. From the instant he steps into the workshop, the use-
value of labour power, and therefore its use, which is
labour, belongs to the capitalist. . . . The labour process
is a process between things that the capitalist has purchased,
things that have become his property. The product of the
process belongs, therefore, to him. . . . [11]

It will be convenient for our argument to adapt the above
definition of the relationship between labour and capital
by removing Marx's restriction to industry[12] and adding, as
does Marx himself, the stipulation that capital's overriding
goal is capital accumulation. Firstly, capital pays labour
according to a fixed system of payment, by time or piece,
at the market rate for the job. Secondly, capital supervises
labour with regard to speed and quality of task execution.
Thirdly, capital systematically reviews alternative methods
of work and, in the light of calculations of costs and benefits,
makes appropriate changes, with consequent effects on task
definition and employment of labour, as we shall shortly
see. Fourthly, capital weighs costs and benefits of alternative
policies according to how they contribute or detract from
the accumulation of capital.

In this formulation we can identify the nineteenth-century

entrepreneur with 'capital' and the employee with 'labour';
such identifications do violence to phenomena like partner-
ships, family firms and salaried works superintendents, but
it is still a good approximation and thus an appropriate
model. However, in applying this formulation to modern
capitalism, it will be impossible to identify 'labour' and
'capital' with persons; rather we shall need to discern
functional complexes.

Capital in the modern firm should not be conceived of
as a set of people, top managers and major shareholders,
but a complex structure of roles defined in functional terms.
The functions include exchanges in factor and product
markets for labour, goods and capital and the supervision
of labour, all of which are subject to monitoring, evaluation,
directions to innovate, planning and control for the purpose
of achieving accumulation of capital. Such functional
elements would include personnel management, purchasing
management, stock control, plant management, market
research and analysis, quality control, investment management, marketing, research and development, design
management and so on; these functions are coordinated and
controlled by financial and general management according
to company strategy as determined by major shareholders
and top managers. These various functions are organised in
different ways in different firms. In one firm personnel
management may be organised from the centre along uniform
lines and responsible to general management, whereas in
another corporation there is a separate personnel management system in each work-place, which is answerable to the
plant manager. Financial control may be strongly centralised or delegated to local, regional or national offices.
In some companies market research is most closely linked
to design while in others it is associated with marketing.
And so we could go on pointing out the complex and various
organisational arrangements by which the functional
elements are related to each other.[13] For the purposes of
our general argument we can abstract from all this variety
by simply noting that the elements must be interrelated in
such a way as to further capital accumulation; we use the
term 'global capital' to refer to the abstract system for

achieving this goal. (For ease of exposition we often use the term 'capital' where it is clear that it refers to the functional system.) Capital in this sense embraces the full role specification of top managers and major shareholders but only some aspects of the roles of lower participants, those aspects which regulate labour in accordance with sub-goals stipulated at each level of the managerial heirarchy as contributions to the overall goal of capital accumulation.[14]

The labour function is the carrying out, under the control of capital, of tasks specified by capital. It should be clear that the labour function is not defined simply as task execution but by the social relations in which tasks are embedded. It is quite true that in capitalist society many jobs are highly routine and mechanical, but this is not so much an inherent quality of labour as the way labour is divided and organised.[15] Whether labourers like or loathe their tasks and appreciate or abhor their product is irrelevant for capital, except in so far as such feelings may affect capital's main concern for labour – that it is cheap, disciplined and efficient. Although labour frequently has no element of 'problem solving', there are a significant proportion of cases where this is present – but it is then capital which poses the problem and determines the acceptability of solutions. Braverman stresses that with the development of the capitalistically organised enterprise labour is forced to submit to managerial authority:

It thus becomes essential for the capitalist that control over the labour process pass from the hands of the worker into his own. This transition presents itself in history as the *progressive alienation of the process of production* from the worker; to the capitalist, it presents itself as the problem of management.[16]

The labour process in the modern firm characteristically demands coordinated activities. As summarised above, the capitalist mode of production presupposes that labour, through the freely negotiated contract of employment, places itself under the control of the global capitalist, in this case managerial control. The overriding goal of the global capitalist must be to maintain or increase the appropriation of surplus value with a view to accumulating capital. In the early stages of capitalist development labour, although at the capitalist's disposal, employed tools and techniques in a work process which had been developed within the pre-capitalist modes of production. Early 'factory' production often took the form of an aggregate of artisans carrying out similar task performances under the same roof. The necessity of raising the mass of surplus value, however, has led to far-reaching modifications of the work process, and given rise to the problem of 'management'.

The simplest way of raising the mass of surplus value is to make the available work-force work more consistently, and for longer hours. If 'necessary labour time' – the time taken by the worker to create new values equivalent to the value he receives as wages – remains constant, then the extension of the working day will increase surplus labour time and thus raise the mass of absolute surplus value. In the early stages of capitalist development in Britain sustained efforts were made by employers first to guarantee the length of the working week and subsequently to extend it, attempts which met with considerable resistance from a refractory proletariat unused to capitalist work discipline.[17] Beyond a certain point, however, it is physically impossible to continue to raise the mass of absolute surplus value, although this point may take a long time to be reached if there is a labour surplus and a relatively docile work-force. When this point is arrived at, it is still possible to increase the rate of extraction of surplus value if necessary labour time can *itself* be reduced. That is, if necessary labour time is reduced, but the length of the working day remains constant, then surplus labour time is increased *relatively* – thus *relative* surplus value.[18] Raising the mass of relative surplus value therefore means setting the available labour force to work more efficiently. Increased efficiency can be achieved with new tools, machinery and working techniques, and above all through the rational, systematic division of labour and fragmentation of the work process. The production of any commodity – say a pair of shoes, or butchering a carcass – can be systematically broken down into a number of inter-dependent parts, the different parts being carried out by different groups of workers.[19] Such a detailed division of labour enormously increases the productivity of labour power. Another result of this division of labour is to reduce labour costs overall; differential rates are paid to workers concerned with different tasks within the fragmented work task as a whole. The rates for such unskilled or semi-skilled labour work out considerably less expensive than the employment of skilled artisan labour to complete the total, undifferentiated work process.[20] We would argue, therefore, that the division of labour is not simply a consequence of increasing complexity of production and distribution, as Durkheim suggests, but that the form it takes is decisively affected by the fact that these changes take place in a *capitalist* society. The manner in which labour is divided is a direct consequence of the need in a capitalist society to continually raise the mass of relative surplus value; the resulting lack of moral commitment to work and endemic industrial conflict flow not from the development of industry as such, as Durkheim claims, but specifically from capitalistically organised industry.

Breaking jobs down into small elements carried out by different workers increases the possibility of measuring and controlling labour, but it also accentuates the need for effectively combining these tasks into an integrated whole. In order to stress that to fulfil the function of labour, labour must be coordinated, we shall use the term 'collective worker'. Beyond rudimentary collective tasks, coordinated labour requires specialised personnel – that is, the collective worker must be functionally differentiated into operatives and coordinators, though the extent of such differentiation varies considerably.

Many parts of the management structure will be responsible for this coordination in order to ensure completion of tasks stipulated by capital, thereby contributing to the function of the collective worker. On the other hand, in so far as management controls labour in order to further the accumulation of capital, it carries out the function of global capital. As discussed earlier, there are enormous practical and conceptual difficulties in reckoning the extent to which any particular manager performs the functions of

capital and labour since the elements of control and
coordination are generally fused in their role specification.
There will thus be important ambiguities in the class situation
of managers,[21] but this fact is quite consistent with the central
analytic distinction we have established by functional
definitions between labour and capital.[22]

Our attempt so far to identify labour and capital in the
modern corporation was made crucially dependent on the
supposed drive to accumulate capital. The pressures of the
market force each unit of capital to accumulate, or else
it suffers a loss of competitiveness and inevitably loses its
autonomy as a unit of capital – by bankruptcy, take-over
or forced merger. (We should make it clear that we use
the term 'accumulation of capital' to refer to the processes
of investing in new plant and equipment, hiring and training
labour, acquiring other companies or shares in them, and
so on, with the aim of reducing costs, expanding the business
and attaining more security in the various markets in which
the firm is involved.)

Accumulation is accumulation of capital when its goal
is the expansion of *capital as such*, rather than, say, increasing
the means to future consumption or reducing hours of work.
The sources for investments are loans, receipts from the
issuance of shares and profits from the previous period; from
the point of view of the firm dividends reduce the funds
available for expanding its capital, although it may well
result in accumulation of other capital. Since the total of
capital for accumulation derives mainly, though not entirely,
from surplus value we cannot properly understand this
process without seeing how surplus value is created and
appropriated. Capital is always necessary for appropriating
surplus value but we do need to distinguish cases where
surplus value is *created* under the aegis of units of capital, in
those sectors which we will shortly identify as industry and
capitalistically organised services, from those cases where
capital *acquires* surplus value generated elsewhere, in those
sectors which we shall identify as commerce, finance, property
and some cases of services. In making these distinctions we
shall utilise the categories, initially developed by Adam Smith
and modified by Marx, of productive and unproductive

labour.[23] A capitalist employing a productive worker lays out some of his money capital to buy the commodity labour power, which he 'consumes', thereby creating value – socially necessary value equivalent to the worker's wages and surplus value which is appropriated by the capitalist.

Following Marx, rather than Adam Smith, we do not stipulate that productive labour necessarily involves creation or alteration of material objects; transport, storage and services may be productive. We also follow Marx in allowing that productive labour may be socially useless or even harmful from the point of view of the observer's values or vision of an alternative society. It is sufficient that the good or service produced actually finds a buyer.

Unproductive labour, on the other hand, does not create surplus value, although in all other respects it may assume the characteristics of wage labour, as we briefly discussed in Chapter Three. Indeed, as our following discussion will make clear, 'unproductive' labour plays a vital role in the overall process of realising and distributing surplus value in the complex structure of today's monopoly capitalism. However, unlike productive workers, unproductive labour is not exchanged directly with capital, but is paid for out of surplus value. The distinction between productive and unproductive labour refers neither to the usefulness of the product nor the type of work required, but to the social relations in which the wage labour is embedded, either paid to create surplus value or paid out of surplus value. Although the distinction between productive and unproductive labour is important for us since we wish to classify class situations with reference to their role in the creation and allocation of surplus value, we make no presumption at this stage that these categories have a characteristic status, income or consciousness. There will be people whose labour is partly productive and partly unproductive, but we are not concerned to quantify 'ratios' (although we shall be interested in such possible ambiguities in class situation); the distinction will be employed as an analytical device for understanding the flows of surplus value in the total system.

Much of the discussion so far in this book has concentrated

on the process through which surplus value is created, the major and most characteristic productive sphere being industry; by which we mean the transformation of raw materials by the application of labour using fixed capital to make a new product or alter its location. The functions of global capitalist and collective worker and their relationship in the process of surplus value creation have been broadly identified, giving a general understanding of the class situation of both – the function of global capitalist corresponding to the bourgeoisie and that of collective worker to the proletariat in classical Marxist theory. However, as our discussion of productive and unproductive labour has just demonstrated, not all labour, even within industry, is productive. In addition much labour is employed outside industry. Therefore if we are to understand the class situation of unproductive workers in industry, as well as that of non-industrial workers, we have to examine the manner in which surplus value flows through the system as a whole, and how different groups of workers are related to this system.

Surplus value is created by capitalistically organised *industry* and *services* – in the latter case the commodities are non-material. The process of selling a commodity may be undertaken by a different capital from the one organising its production. We refer to capitals carrying out the buying and selling of commodities as *commerce*; these activities do not alter the nature of location of the commodities and do not change their value. Surplus value, therefore, is not created in commerce, although the commercial capitalists acquire a share of the surplus value generated in industrial or service sectors. Although the initial capital for setting in motion the surplus value *generating* process is, in a developed capitalist system, ultimately derived from surplus value,[24] this does not mean that this initial capital is invariably that which has been produced by the original firm. The time span of production and time spent on difficulties in marketing the product (even via the commercial capitalist) are but two reasons why a firm may have to acquire capital well in advance of the realisation of the surplus value it is in the process of creating. In short it requires a loan. Such loans are provided by the sector we shall discuss under the heading of *finance* capital: as our discussion will make clear, the activities of finance capital go far beyond simple loan provision, but finance capital's role as creditor provides the clearest way of understanding its articulation in the total flow of surplus value. In repayment for such a loan the industrial or service capital pays interest,[25] that is, a proportion of surplus value generated is diverted to the finance capitalist. As with commerce, therefore, no surplus value is created in the sphere of finance. The final sector we will discuss in our analysis of the flow of surplus value is that of *property (rentier)*, that is, the hiring out of property of all kinds – land, buildings, and machinery. Where such property is hired out to capitalists in productive sectors, the rent paid to the *rentier* constitutes a share of surplus value.[26] When property is hired out to either a commercial or financial capitalist, the rent received is a share of the surplus value acquired by these 'unproductive' sectors. In either case it is clear that the property capitalist, like the commercial or financial capitalist, does not organise the creation of surplus value but acquires a share of surplus value generated in the productive sectors.

This sketch has served to illustrate, in very general terms, how surplus value is generated and acquired in the various sectors of *private* capital. In the following discussion we will examine in greater detail the operations of and inter-relationships between each of the sectors we have identified above. Having analysed the system more fully, the way is then open to make some preliminary statements about the class situation of the workers engaged in the various sectors. Even after we have done this, however, our discussion of the flow of surplus value and the structure of class relationships. is far from complete. In this chapter we deal only with private capital, whereas in modern monopoly capitalism, as we indicated in the previous chapter, the state is an integral part of the economy and thus of the total system of surplus value generation, allocation and capital accumulation. In the next chapter, therefore, we will examine the articulation of the state in the economy, and the class situation of state employees, in some detail.

INDUSTRY

The core process of industrial production is represented in Figure 1. L, representing labour, is combined with the means

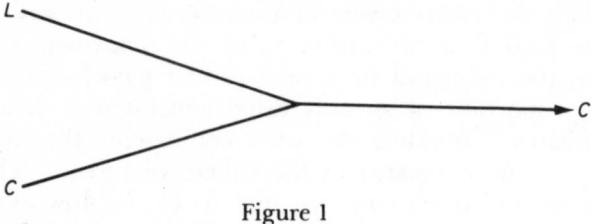

Figure 1

of production C to result in the product C' with all the labour and means of production thereby expended. We use the notation C and C', standing for 'commodity', to emphasise that raw materials, tools, and the product are all goods available in the market. For the purposes of simplicity at this stage of the argument, we are assuming that the means of production; plant, raw materials, machinery, vehicles, etc., are acquired afresh with each circuit of investment, production and sale; the accounts of industrial firms do indeed show depreciation on 'fixed capital'.[27] Labour, as 'variable capital', relates to capital *as if* it were simply another factor of production like tools and raw materials, but as this certainly does not exhaust the character of the relationship we show labour separated from other means of production.

In the process of production, symbolised by Figure 1, surplus value is created as labour is directed and supervised by capital in pursuit of the latter's goals. However the nature of these goals can only be properly understood by seeing how the production process is embedded in the full circuit of three phases, investment, production and realisation; this is set out diagrammatically in Figure 2.

The industrial capital may be conceived as having a sum of money M available at the start of a circuit, of which M_1 is used to purchase labour power and M_2 to buy means of production. As discussed earlier, capital directs and controls coordinated labour so that a new product C' is made, which is sold for a sum of money M'. The difference between the sum M' and M is defined as the money form of surplus value; this surplus value is created by the application of labour to means of production and is thus theoretically measurable as labour time – hours of unpaid labour.[28]

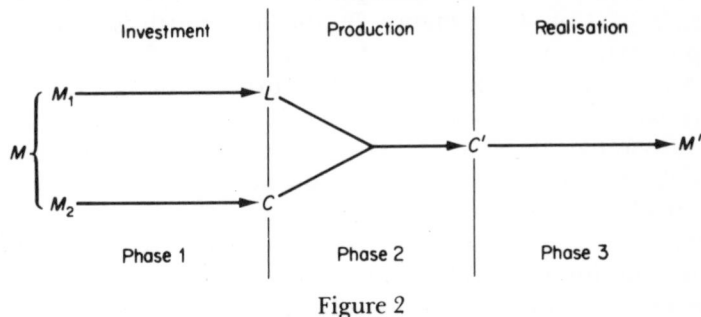

Figure 2

We briefly consider surplus value as reckoned by labour time in an appendix, but at this stage of the analysis it will be convenient to employ the money form $M' - M$. It is crucial for our argument that although surplus value is here expressed as money, surplus value is not generated by exchange as such but by utilisation of labour power, that unique commodity which is capable of creating more than its own value when consumed.

The three-phase division of the capitalist production process into investment, production and realisation makes it easier to grasp conceptually the fact that surplus value is only actually *created* in the second phase – the core production process. Any labour performed in this phase must therefore, according to the distinction previously introduced, be productive. In our earlier discussion we distinguished between managerial control (a function of global capital) and managerial coordination (a function of the collective worker). Combining together the productive/unproductive and control/coordination distinctions, we can see that managerial coordination in the second phase, production proper, is both productive labour and a function of the collective worker. A part of managerial remuneration (that for coordination) is for productive labour as collective worker, and another part (that for control) is paid for out of surplus value. We recognise that the distinction between coordination and control is analytical, so that many managers carry out both functions jointly. In practice it would obviously be extremely difficult to distinguish how much of any particular manager's pay is as collective worker (i.e., a part of M_1 in Figure 2), and how much is as global capitalist (i.e., a part of $M' - (M_1 + M_2)$ in Figure 2).

Although we have located the process of creation of surplus value in phase 2 (see Figure 2), it is obvious that a substantial amount of labour is expended in phases 1 and 3 and managers spend a good deal of time and effort controlling and coordinating these phases. However, although these phases are vital for capital accumulation, and thus for the *capitalist* production process as a whole, as surplus value is not actually created in these phases, work performed in these phases is not productive. Nevertheless it does *not* follow from this that work carried out in phases 1 and 3 is wholly that of the global function of capital. For in each of these phases capital still 'regulates labour in accordance with sub-goals stipulated at each level of the managerial hierarchy as contributions to the overall goal of capital accumulation',[29] and labour carries out, under the control of capital, tasks specified by capital. In short, in order to carry out the function of the collective worker, it is not necessary that labour is 'productive' as defined above.[30] Within phases 1 and 3, therefore, and within sectors of the total structure associated with these phases, we can locate the functions of global capital and collective worker, although the collective worker function will not be productive.

Some of the surplus value created in the production process proper (phase 2) will therefore be allocated to labour employed in phases 1 and 3. However, as we have stressed before (see Chapter Three), the fact that such workers are maintained out of surplus value does not automatically place them in an antagonistic class relationship *viv-à-vis* productive workers. As Wright has recently emphasised, the distinction between productive and unproductive labour does not mean that these workers have fundamentally divergent class interests at the economic level. 'In both cases, the capitalist will try to keep the wage bill as low as possible;

in both cases, the capitalist will try to increase productivity by getting workers to work harder; in both cases, workers will be dispossessed of control over their labour process'.[31] Another part of surplus value, as we have indicated above, is allocated to the remuneration of managers,[32] both as global capitalist in all phases and as collective worker in phases 1 and 3. A varying, and often substantial proportion of surplus value is siphoned off by other units of capital. Yet more is appropriated by the state as taxation; we shall examine this phenomenon in the next chapter. The remainder, which is retained by the company, is distributed between payments to owners, savings and capital accumulation. The latter two categories of allocation are essential to maintain the competitive strength of the firm but they are also indirectly beneficial to the owners in that they tend to increase the profitability of the company and thus the value of each share held. However, payments to owners normally take the form of a dividend paid on each share[33] – the distributed profits of the company. By now it should be obvious that total profits and *a fortiori* distributed profits only constitute a *share* of the surplus value; it is a serious analytical mistake to treat profits as if they were synonymous with surplus value in its entirety. Surplus value may still be created even though all of it is accounted for in interest payments, tax, and rent so that profits are nil.

SERVICES

In defining industry we stipulated that a material object was made available for sale either by actually forming it as such or by moving it to a location where it could be purchased. Thus industry includes extraction, agriculture, manufacture and transport. However, services are differentiated from industry in that no material object is made available for sale; rather the service capital hires labour power and directs it to carry out work for a client. The 'commodities' generated by the service industry – a haircut, a clean hotel room, an education – clearly do not involve the production of material objects for sale; rather the service capitalist hires labour power and directs labour to carry out work for a client. Labour power does not exchange with the fee paid by the client, for that is taken by the service capitalist, but it does exchange with the service capitalist's capital. The service capitalist may provide fixed capital, a fully equipped hairdressing salon, cleaning material, schools and teaching materials, etc., but not raw materials. (For simplicity of exposition we ignore fixed capital in the following discussion; the argument is not significantly altered by incorporating it into the analysis.) Service capital may be represented as in Figure 3.

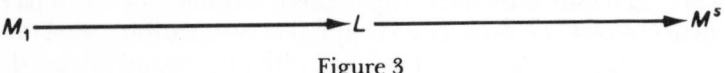

$$M_1 \longrightarrow L \longrightarrow M^s$$

Figure 3

As in the case of industrial capital, the excess $M^s - M_1$ will be distributed externally to other units of capital and the state, and internally to shareholders, for saving and for accumulation. Those cases where the client is a consumer rather than a capital[34] are analogous to industry, only in this case the 'product' is non-material; thus the excess $M^s - M_1$ is surplus value and the service worker is productive. In a well-known passage Marx puts this argument very forcefully:

> If we may take an example from outside the sphere of production of material objects, a schoolmaster is a productive labourer, when, in addition to belabouring the heads of his scholars, he works like a horse to enrich the school proprietor. That the latter has laid out his capital in a teaching factory, instead of a sausage factory, does not alter this relation.[35]

It is of course essential to Marx's argument that the service is capitalistically organised – that labour is hired and supervised to carry out a service which is sold in the market; it is not teaching as such which is productive but only where the teacher is hired by a capitalist who markets teaching services. Whether it is teaching, catering, hairdressing, entertainment or legal advice, we do not analyse it as service capital where it is organised as a family business, partnership, fee-taking professionals or jobbing artisans. In such cases it is the individual who sells his services to the client rather than the capitalist. Clearly, in those cases, capitalist relations of production do not hold and no surplus value is created or acquired. Such activities exist outside the capitalist mode of production.

In those cases where the client is another unit of capital there are alternative ways of analysing the creation and appropriation of surplus value, but the most reasonable view is that the service worker is productive where the client is an industrial capital but not where it is a unit of another sort of capital.

Figure 4 shows how services and industry may be articulated. Arrows with dotted lines indicate flows of labour, money and commodities between firms. Arrows with solid lines indicate idealised time sequences of labour, money and commodities under the ownership and control of a firm.

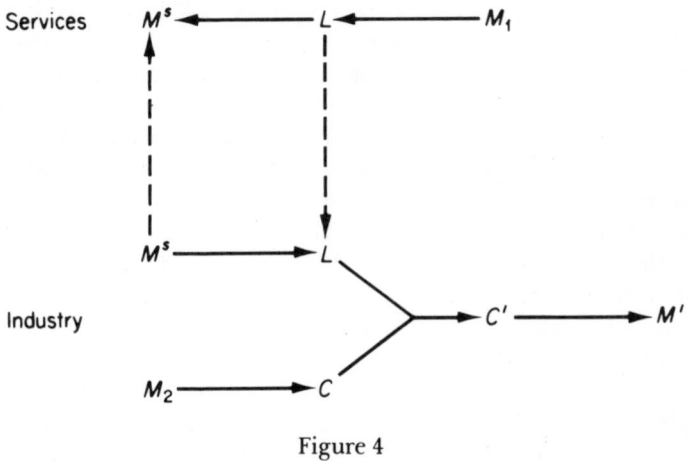

Figure 4

M_1 in Figure 4 corresponds to M_1 in our 'key' Figure 2. It is easier to grasp the relationship between industrial and service capital if we assume that the industrial capitalist obtains all of its labour via the service capitalist. Here, therefore, the total of surplus value is $M' - (M_1 + M_2)$ of which the service capital initially appropriates $M^s - M_1$

while the industrial capital gets $M' - (M^s + M_2)$. Comparing Figures 2 and 4, it may appear that the industrial capital simply loses $M^s - M_1$ of potential profit by establishing this relationship with the service firm. However there may be significant advantages for the industrial capital such as reductions in indirect labour costs (pension provision, insurance, redundancy payments, and so on), greater control of labour costs in circumstances of fluctuating labour requirements and possibly more rapid turnover of capital, thus increasing *annual* surplus value created.

Where the service firm contracts labour to a non-industrial capital, part of the surplus value that capital initially appropriated from elsewhere is siphoned off and shared between service worker and service capital. Although in such cases both capital and labour 'live off' surplus value, the bases for conflict of interest between them will still exist. (This point will be clearer after we have discussed the commercial and financial sectors.)

The overall profit-making enterprise of hiring and disposing of labour power itself involves differentiated functions where the lower participants are characteristically engaged in routine administration, functions of the collective worker. But note that such employees may be in a different class situation from the service workers proper as analysed above; they are only productive in so far as coordinating the labour of the service workers, to the extent that they do this, they may be regarded as the 'coordinative part' of the collective service worker.

As with all other capital, service capital is driven to accumulation, which may involve hiring more labour or increasing the productivity of labour by training it or hiring skilled labour. In concrete cases, as distinct from our analytical model, service capital is usually found in combination with other forms of capital so that investment need not be restricted to the rather narrow categories mentioned above.[36]

Having discussed industry and services we now turn to those forms of capital which are incapable of generating surplus value but are nevertheless able to appropriate shares of it – commerce, finance and property. We shall claim that there are great similarities in the relation between collective worker and global capitalist in these three types but that their different functions and articulations with other capital give rise to distinctive class situations. In these three types the collective worker is unproductive, which means that it enables its capital to obtain part of the surplus value created under another capital. The amount of surplus value appropriated by such non-productive capital will be related to its size rather than the wages of the collective worker, but other things being equal wages and profits vary inversely.[37] In so far as unproductive labour is paid at market rates, skill for skill as for productive labour, we may consider by analogy that part of the labour of unproductive workers is unpaid; to the extent that this is so, profits are enhanced. The fact that both labour and capital are paid out of surplus value does not in any way make their class situations similar for, just as with productive labour and capital, there are conflicts of interest over wages, conditions of employment and disposal of surplus value appropriated by capital.

COMMERCE

Let us now examine how the relations between labour and capital are associated with the flows of surplus value. In commerce the firm buys products and sells them at a higher price without altering their nature or transporting them. Figure 5 represents this situation.

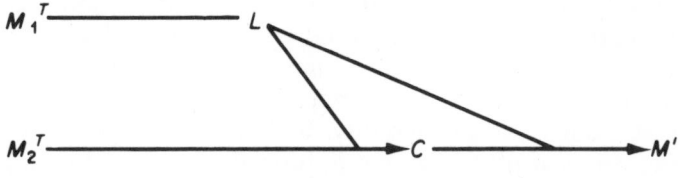

Figure 5

The excess obtained is $M' - (M_1{}^T + M_2{}^T)$, which is initially appropriated as the commercial capital's profit, but there may well be deductions from this such as tax and interest on loans. The diagram shows labour purchased for $M_1{}^T$ carrying out the functions of buying and selling commodity

C. The source of the surplus value can be seen when we show Figure 6 representing the commercial firm buying and selling the product of an industrial firm.

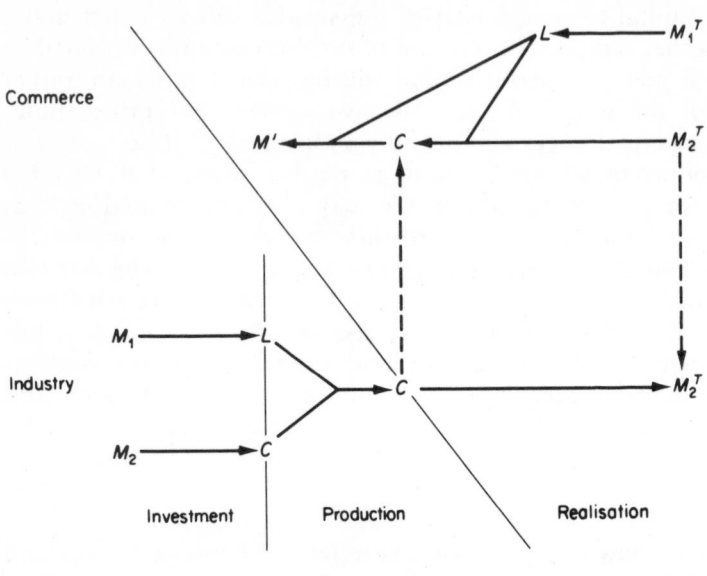

Figure 6

Of the total surplus value created, $M' - (M_1 + M_2)$, the industrial capital acquires $M_2^T - (M_1 + M_2)$ while the commercial worker gets M_1^T and the commercial capital $M' - (M_1^T + M_2^T)$. Comparing this situation with Figure 2 it appears that the industrial capital loses $M' - M_2^T$ by entering into such a relationship with commercial capital. Although in each circuit of capital commercial costs and profits tend to reduce industrial profitability, there are also very great advantages. In particular the industrial capital is able to get payment as soon as the products are made without having to wait until a final consumer eventually buys them;[38] early payment allows early investment in the next cycle of production so that the speedier turnover of capital results in a larger total surplus value for the year. For many products the cost to industrial capital of setting up a marketing apparatus would be exorbitant, but they could easily be incorporated into the range of commodities sold by a commercial firm. Certainly this differentiation between industry and commerce, by which commerce takes over the third phase of the industrial circuit, greatly enhances each industrial capital's capacity to accumulate capital.[39]

FINANCE

As we shall see, finance capital is quite as important as commerce in facilitating the accumulation of capital, and is crucial in its own right for centralising and mobilising capital.[40] The core process of finance may be defined formally as the provision of loans and their repayment with interest, a process which does not create new value but merely transfers the interest from the hands of the debtor to the financier. Figure 7 shows the basic elements of finance capital:

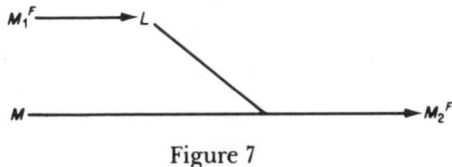

Figure 7

Here the finance capitalist makes a loan of M and at a later time this is repaid with interest as the sum $M_2{}^F$. Where the wages of the finance workers total $M_1{}^F$, the profit initially appropriated by the finance capital is thus $M_2{}^F - (M + M_1{}^F)$. Where loans are made to workers in order to enable them to maintain the customary standard of living for such workers the interest they pay is a portion of total surplus value, the situation being as if the capitals employing them hand over surplus value directly to finance capital. Interest on mortgages and hire purchase may be viewed ideologically as a peculiarly naked form of exploitation of workers' weak economic position or conversely as a justifiable payment for avoiding the effort of saving; from our point of view it is just one among a number of institutional arrangements by which capital appropriates surplus value.[41]

However, the main significance of finance capital is not how it relates to individual consumers but how it articulates with other capital and in doing so obtains, although possibly indirectly, a share of surplus value. Let us start by considering finance for industry (Figure 8). We shall assume for simplicity that all the industrial capital's outlay is initially provided by a loan.[42]

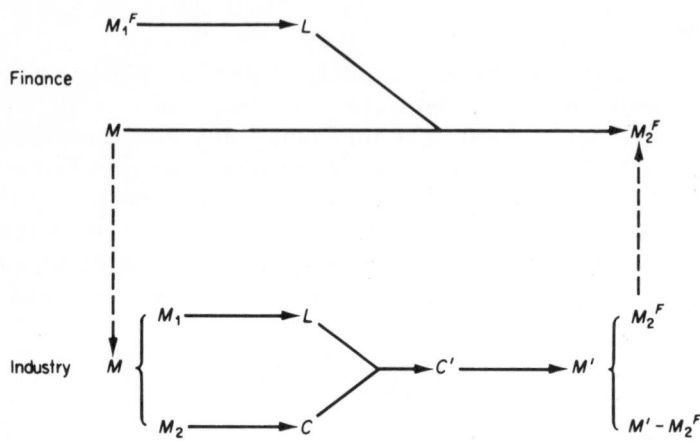

Figure 8

The total of surplus value is $M' - M$, of which the industrial capital gets $M' - M_2^F$ and pays out $M_2^F - M$ as interest; this interest is divided between the finance worker, M_1^F, and the finance capital, $M_2^F - (M_1^F + M)$. In paying out interest industrial capital suffers a loss in the surplus value generated during the circuit, but there are advantages which more than compensate for this. The availability of credit enables a new circuit to begin before the previous circuit has been completed and indeed before even phase 1 is completed, thus enormously speeding the turnover of capital and thereby annual creation of surplus value. Credit allows the industrial capital to purchase very expensive means of production and yet pay for them over a long period and to phase investments to take advantage of fluctuations in price and demand for factors and products. In this nexus between finance and industrial capital the latter borrows, rather than saves, in order to invest.[43] Finance capital thus allows industrial capital to continue and expand production without recourse to its share-holders for additional outlays, and thus further divorces the global function of capital from personal ownership.

Finance capital similarly facilitates the operation of commercial capital and is particularly crucial where there is likely to be a long delay between the buying and selling of the product.[44] Without credit the commercial capitalist's stock would have to be sold before money would be available to buy more, but finance capital obviates such delay and thus increases turnover of capital – and therefore potential profit. By financing trade finance capital obtains a share of the surplus value that the commercial capital initially appropriated in its dealings with industry.[45]

So far we have identified finance capital by the function of making credit available to others, but in fact it is also a recipient of loans. Other units of capital may have funds which cannot be profitably invested at that time, so rather than leave them standing 'idle' they are loaned to a finance capital where they will 'earn' interest. Individuals may also make loans to finance capital. In short each finance capital is at the centre of a flow of loans and borrowings from numerous agents with different rates of interest varying with the periods of the loans; finance capital is a mobiliser and centraliser of capital.

The class situation of finance workers is coloured by the specific functions of finance capital but they share with other sorts of wage labour the fact that they are hired and con-trolled for the purpose of capital accumulation and thus, as discussed previously,[46] the sources of antagonistic interests will make themselves felt. Just as with the commercial worker, conflict of interest with capital is not destroyed by the fact that finance workers are unproductive.

PROPERTY

The final type of capital we distinguish is property capital. Property capital lets others use property it owns for a given period in return for payment, rent.[47] At the end of the period the property returns to the hands of the property capital together with the tenant's rent, no new value having been

created by these transactions. Where workers pay rent to maintain customary living standards it constitutes a share of
surplus value which can be envisaged as being transferred
from the capitals employing them to the property capitals.
In the case of a rented house, for example, the only part
of tenant's payments which can be reckoned as a deduction
from wages is a proportionate share, according to the length
of time he or she is a resident, of the cost of building and
maintaining the house over its expected life: the rest is rent
proper.[48] In the case of housing, whether state or privately
owned, a large proportion of the surplus value initially
obtained by the *rentier* is often paid out in interest to finance
capitals.

Where property is hired out to services or industry as means
of production, the rent, after allowing for depreciation, is
the property capital's share of the surplus value created by
the workers employed by those capitals.

Property capital as defined above is not restricted to land
and buildings, though in fact these make up the bulk of
property capital in the societies we are considering. Land
is not a true commodity in that it is given by nature rather
than produced by labour, but it may come to be treated
as a commodity, being saleable at a market price or being
available for hire at market rent.

Whatever the type of property or nature of the tenant,
property workers are unproductive, and while their class
situation will be affected by these factors[49] it will also be
moulded by conflicts of interest with their employers.

The above scheme is designed to analyse the sources and
flows of surplus value to functionally defined agents in the
economic system – global capital and collective worker
in industry, services, commerce, finance and property. In
concrete reality capitals are bound together in structured
relations of mutual dependency and indeed carry out a
number of functions jointly. For example, a firm may both
produce goods and market them,[50] thus being both an
industrial and commercial capital. The conflict between
separate units of commercial and industrial capital over the
price at which the product changes hands is thus transformed
into a problem for the joint capital of the relation between

production and selling costs; such problems are frequently manifested in the firm's organisational structure, with separate divisions responsible for marketing and production and top management resolving differences between them or, more positively, designing an overall strategy within which the divisions have to operate. While some parts of management may be unequivocally identified as either carrying out the commercial or the industrial function of capital, they are subordinated to top management, which harnesses them to the goal of maximising the *total* of surplus value that they appropriate. The organisational structure of the firm may well indicate which are industrial and which are commercial workers; assembly line workers can be clearly contrasted with salesmen. Differences between commercial, industrial and 'joint commercial/industrial' workers may correspond to differences in pay and conditions, work situation, union organisation and consciousness. These differences may well lead to conflicts within the same broad class grouping. Functional differentiation within the organisation is an important secondary structural factor enhancing ambiguities of some class situations. This point is fully discussed in the final chapter.

There are a number of different patterns of commercial/industrial enterprise ranging from mainly commercial firms, which manufacture part of their range of goods or are engaged in transporting them, to mainly industrial firms, which also put some of their resources into selling, though not necessarily to final customers.

Industrial, commercial, service and financial enterprises generally own substantial fixed assets, which may be analysed as property capital.[51] Some firms do indeed operate a separate property division or even a subsidiary company to control the firm's property; in such cases we will have a good indication of which managers and workers are carrying out the functions of the property global capital and the property collective worker respectively, and which are operating in the sphere of other types of capital. In many firms the cost of providing fixed assets is carefully reckoned and compared with the rent that would have to be paid if those assets had been hired from an independent property firm on the market. Such calculations may be the basis for a nominal rent which the firm 'charges itself' and which may be used as a measure of the efficiency of its property operations. In some cases the firm will consistently review the advantages and disadvantages of actually selling part of its property – for example, a factory on an expensive city centre site – and for such considerations it will need to look at such assets *as property*, not just as means of production. Some companies characteristically hire out their property from time to time and thus have to operate separate property functions; for example, an oil company may own a shipping company which transports oil for the company and hires out its ships to other firms when not needed by the oil company. The conclusion of this argument is simply that property capital is frequently fused with other sorts of capital, thus creating ambiguities and complications in the class situations of workers and managers in such firms.

Where a capital's non-financial activities have resulted in a temporary excess or shortage of cash it can lend or borrow from other capitals via finance capital, thus establishing a network of relationships with other capital. Indeed a single finance capital, or a linked group of them, may effectively bring a number of other capitals together as a unitary capital with a common strategy. The intimate links between finance and other types of capital may allow the creation of a corporate empire acquired through growth, merger, take-over and joint venture; in some cases this involves expansion around a single line of business but there are also giant firms, the so-called conglomerates, engaged in very diverse activities.[52]

Finance capital was earlier characterised as making credit available in return for interest but this core function is found in reality in association with a whole range of other functions – accepting loans, money changing, share dealing, insurance etc. – which bring it into intimate contact with many other types of capital, thereby coordinating them to some extent.

The increasing centralisation of capital is indeed a crucial and apparently inevitable tendency in capitalism, thus transforming the free market economy of nineteenth-century Britain.[53] There are many different ways whereby capital can be effectively concentrated or coordinated, ranging from the single unified corporation to the 'gentleman's understanding'.

A holding company is a company which owns all or most of the shares in a number of subsidiary companies. For example, the Japanese *zaibatsu*, such as Mitsui and Mitsubishi, owned more than two hundred subsidiaries each, which were engaged in coal, steel, electrical equipment, shipbuilding, shipping, trade, banking, and soon. Holding companies vary in the extent to which they are centrally controlled and the operations of the subsidiaries coordinated.

Concentration of capital may also be achieved by long- or medium-term agreements between companies, even though the parties to the agreement are otherwise independent. There are many varieties of such agreements including agreement on minimum prices, agreement on standard prices, and agreement on areas of a country, or indeed of the world, as to which corporation should market its goods free from competition. Also firms may trade through a 'joint' buying or selling company.

A firm may coordinate the pricing and quality of a large number of small companies through franchise, agency or tenancy. Franchise means that companies are allowed to use the trade name, for a fee, subject to price and quality control. Agents are companies which enter on exclusive contract with the central company in exchange for preferential pricing of the company's products. Tenancies occur where the agent is operating from premises owned by the central company, which naturally constrains the tenant to obedience to the company's 'requests'.

Finally, it is worth noting that coordination between units of capital may occur without any formal agreement, and in particular a general awareness of the dangers of price wars may be sufficient to keep corporate pricing policies mutually adjusted. Where, as is often the case, one corporation is considerably larger than other big corporations in that line of business, a change in its prices will generally be followed by similar changes by other companies.

Our analysis of the generation and allocation of surplus value within the private sector has revealed an extremely complex structure, notwithstanding the fact that for the purposes of exposition we have not as yet analysed in any detail the economic role of the state or taken account of the international nature of the capitalist mode of production as a whole. Any account of the class structure we derive from this analysis will therefore reveal a similarly complex structure of class positions. In the course of our analysis we have made some preliminary remarks as to the class position of all of the various elements in the structure, but here we will present in summary form some of the major points concerning the class structure which we would draw from our preceding analysis.

Firstly, despite the admitted complexity of the monopoly capitalist mode of production, it is still possible to identify two dominant functions within this mode: those of the global capitalist on the one hand and the collective worker on the other. These two functions are at the root of the social relationships engendered by the capitalist mode of production. For, notwithstanding the many attempts to argue otherwise, the relationship between these two functions is fundamentally exploitative and therefore antagonistic. In order to maintain the process of accumulation (the overriding task of global capital) the global capitalist must operate in a manner calculated either to raise the rate of generation of relative or absolute surplus value (in the productive sector), or increase and/or maintain the rate of acquisition of surplus value (in the unproductive sector). Commitment to this overriding goal (which, as we have made clear, is not simply a matter of 'choice), means that labour – the collective worker – *must* be organised as efficiently and in as disciplined a fashion as possible, with as little regard for the interests of labour (whether expressed or latent) as is consistent with the need to maintain the overall tractability and minimum level of commitment of labour which is necessary for system stability (although this stability, we would emphasise, is often illusory and fragile).

The fact that we have identified these two dominant functions, however, does not mean that we are advocating a simple two-class model of monopoly capitalist society as a whole. Even *if* it were possible to apply such a rigid distinction within capitalist society, such a model would still be inadequate as it would fail to take into account those areas of the economy (and associated employment) which exist outside the dominant capitalist mode, although they will of course be significantly affected by capitalism. We refer here to small family firms, independent artisans or professionals and so on, who sell their goods and services directly to the consumer. Although, with some oversimplification, the fundamental conflicts within the capitalist mode of production can be said to arise out of the antagonisms endemic to this most basic relationship, the distinction between global capitalist and collective worker is not clearcut, even to the extent of individual work roles. Particularly in the lower levels of what may be loosely termed the 'managerial hierarchy' individual work roles and task specifications contain elements of both the global capitalist and collective worker functions. For example, the foreman – traditionally in industry the front line of managerial authority – has to coordinate work tasks, ensure the provision of tools and raw materials in the right place and at the right time, even work alongside his subordinates in an emergency. All of these aspects of the foreman's work role may properly be ascribed to the function of the collective worker. At the same time the foreman has to exert control over and discipline the work-force in order to ensure that labour power is properly organised towards its end – the creation of surplus value. In carrying out these duties, the foreman is fulfilling an aspect of the global function of capital.[54] The class situation of employees such as the foreman is therefore structurally ambiguous. Many other work roles beside that of the foreman manifest this structural ambiguity to a greater or lesser extent: we would mention lower-level management, testing and inspection, and much of technicians's work. This ambiguity can be seen to be clearly reflected in the attitudes and behaviour of such groups and individuals. As Wright has argued, 'it is the contradictory determination [i.e. structural ambiguity] of class at the economic level which itself determines the extent to which political and ideological relations act as determinants of class position'.[55] That is, the more ambiguous a given class situation the more important will be the effect of political and ideological factors in determining the overall class position. We shall discuss such secondary structural factors in the last chapter.

We would argue that the distinction we have been emphasising between global capital and collective worker overrides the distinction between productive and unproductive labour. If we look at the generation and allocation of surplus value as a *whole*, as we have tried to do in this chapter, it is clear that the 'unproductive' sectors are necessary to maintain the viability of the structure as a *capitalist* structure. Within these sectors, however, we can still identify the functions of global capitalist and collective worker, and the class situation of the unproductive collective worker parallels that of the productive collective worker. Labour in the unproductive sectors of the economy is as rationally organised, with as much of an eye to 'efficiency' rather than the interests of the labour force, as it is in the productive sectors. Therefore the fact that the global capitalist and the unproductive collective worker are both maintained out of surplus value does not lead to a mutuality of class interests between global capitalist and collective worker in unproductive sectors. Within commercial, financial and property sectors the requirements of a complex organisational structure will give rise to work roles which combine the functions of global capitalist and collective worker, as described above, and such class situations will be similarly ambiguous. However, although we have argued that class situations within productive and unproductive spheres are basically similar, it is still the case that the fact that work *is* unproductive *does* complicate the class situation of the unproductive worker. For example, the fact that labour and capital do derive their income from the same source in these sectors *may* be convincingly exploited to argue for a mutuality of interest. Secondly, and this is probably more important, although 'unproductive' work is undeniably necessary to the functioning of the system as a whole, it is still the case that resources allocated to maintain unproductive workers divert resources from the overall process of accumulation of surplus value. If the total amount of resources allocated to such workers appears to threaten investment in productive spheres, or if it is a time of economic recession (the two often occur simultaneously), there will be considerable pressure to either lower the rate of allocation or reduce the level of employment in the unproductive sectors. An attempt at such a 'shake-out' was clearly behind the introduction of Selective Employment Tax in 1966 and the present Industrial Strategy (1977) where raising industrial investment is elevated to a national crusade. Although campaigns against particular groups of unproductive workers might have the effect of emphasising the basic similarities of class situation between the productive and unproductive collective worker, it is more likely, given the nature of the media and the tenor of public debate, that a further wedge will be driven between productive and unproductive workers – that is, productive workers will believe that they are competing for resources with unproductive workers (which is a fallacy), and therefore that their class interests are antagonistic.

This summary has given an indication of how the detailed analysis of the flow of surplus value through the system as a whole can illuminate our understanding of the class structure, class relationships and the many ambiguities of class situation. We have not attempted to construct a universally applicable two-, three-, or four-class model of advanced capitalist societies, beyond pointing to the basic dichotomy between global capitalist and collective worker. We consider that in the long run it will be more useful and relevant to analyse particular class situations in some detail, with reference to the basic model we have suggested. Neither have we described, in any systematic fashion, the manner in which the location in the class structure is reflected in the consciousness of particular groups. We will make some suggestions concerning this topic in Chapter Nine, but for the moment we will willingly concede that there are likely to be no easy answers: the particular structure of the labour market, the dominant ideology and short-term historical circumstances will all tend to act as intervening variables in the description and explanation of objective location in the class structure and the consciousness, attitudes and behaviour of the groups so located.

6

State and Economy in the West

In the previous chapter we focused on what is commonly termed the 'private sector' of the Western mixed economies, and no serious attention was given to the state sector or the state's role in the economy. Similarly, in our analysis of the class structure, we have so far only paid attention to those engaged in the private sector. However, as we indicated in Chapter Four, the state plays an increasingly important role in today's monopoly capitalism, and this is reflected in the ever-increasing proportion of state employees in the modern work-force. For example, in 1973 20 per cent of the employed population of the United Kingdom were employed by national or local government, and a further 8 per cent in state-owned enterprises such as coal, steel, gas, electricity, the post office, and so on.[1]

At first sight the class situation of state employees might seem to give rise to analytical difficulties. Those employed in administration – national and local civil servants – can in no sense be said to make a profit for their employer; the same is true of the many employed in state services such as health and education (enterprises which we refer to as non-capitals). Even in the case of state-owned enterprises which supposedly charge an economic rate for their goods and services – the post office, the railways, the steel industry, coal, gas, electricity and so on – we often find they operate (either short-term or long-term) at losses which could not be sustained by private industry.[2] Since the majority of state workers are not employed for material gain or profit, how can they possibly be said to be exploited? In the previous chapter we demonstrated that managers, administrators and white-collar workers in private productive spheres fulfil, to varying extents, the function of global capitalist *and* collective worker, and their class situation can be understood in these terms. This is also true, as we have shown, of those engaged in unproductive areas within the private sector – commerce, finance, property and some services. Unproductive these activities may be in the formal, analytical sense, but they nevertheless perform a necessary function in the total circuit of creation and realisation of surplus value and thus accumulation.

But can the class situation of state employees be analysed within this framework? As we have already noted, the vast majority of state employees are not employed to create a profit, unlike unproductive workers in commerce, finance, and so on. Can the state be legitimately portrayed as having anything to do with private sector accumulation at all – are not the state's many and varied activities carried out on behalf of the community at large? Our answer to these rhetorical questions would be 'yes' in both cases: the class situation of state employees *can* be analysed within the general framework we have been developing and, in the circumstances of modern monopoly capitalism, the state *is* an integral part of the capitalist accumulation process. In this chapter, therefore, we shall examine the role of the state in the capitalist economy, and the resulting class situation of state employees.

The nature of the modern state has been the subject of much recent work in politics, economics and sociology; we would mention the work of Poulantzas, Miliband, Gamble and Walton, and O'Connor amongst others. In this chapter we do not claim to develop a comprehensive theory of the modern state in all of its aspects, rather we shall concentrate on some of its characteristic economic activities in order to develop further our model of capitalist economy and the associated class structure.

With the growth of monopoly capitalism the stability of the system comes to depend ever more crucially upon regulation of the relations between capitals, and between capital and labour. Although such functions are exercised in part by each capital and by combinations of capital,[3] they are increasingly centralised in the state. As Miliband writes:

> Capitalist enterprise . . . *depends* to an even greater extent on the bounties and direct support of the state, and can only preserve its 'private' character on the basis of such public help. State intervention in economic life *means* intervention for the purpose of helping capitalist enterprise. . . . Governments may be solely concerned with the better running of 'the economy'. But the description of the system as 'the economy' is part of the idiom of ideology, and obscures the real process. For what is being improved is a *capitalist* economy; and this ensures that whoever may gain or not gain capitalist interests are at least likely to lose.[4]

These quotations emphasise that the state provides necessary conditions for the accumulation of capital, but this does not imply that 'private capitalism' and 'the state' are distinct systems, with latter 'intervening' in the former. The modern capitalist state does not influence the economy 'from the outside', but is an integral and necessary part of the system it regulates.

In laissez-faire capitalism governments did not control the means of production although of course they furthered the accumulation of capital by fostering the free play of the market. More abstractly we may say that while the economy constrained the polity, these two systems were structurally *separated*. By contrast, as we argue in the next chapter, in a directively planned state capitalist society, those who govern also control the means of production; polity and economy are *fused*. However in contemporary Western capitalism the government controls some of the means of production and, in order to further the accumulation of capitals it does not control as well as those it does, it has to intervene in the economy as a regulator of market relations and as an agent promoting the restructuring of capital; therefore polity and economy *overlap*.

Another feature of laissez-faire capitalism is that all capitalistically organised production is production for the market, production of commodities. But in contemporary monopoly capitalism some production is contracted for at administered prices, with the state or between corporations (which may be state or privately owned). Strictly speaking, as these products are not 'marketed', the corporations involved, whether privately or state owned, do not obtain surplus value. However, as we argue later in the chapter, the mechanisms by which they are driven to appropriate surplus product are similar to the mechanisms which drive capitals to appropriate surplus value as analysed in Chapters Three and Five. Where we particularly wish to emphasise that an enterprise does not appropriate surplus value but seeks surplus product *as if* it were surplus value, we use the term 'quasi-capital'.[5]

The political and economic functions of the modern state in the West have been summarised thus:

> The State, then, acts almost as a national Managing Director, supervising a series of subsidiaries which stand in varying relationships to it. Private industry needs the protective shell of the state to ensure stable production and defence against foreign competition. State welfare services smooth some of the effects of economic change in order to safeguard social stability. Finally, international competition prompts the state to seek to focus all national effort on the foreign field, rather than permitting efforts to be dissipated in domestic competition and conflict.[6]

There are, however, profound limitations to the state's ability to achieve these objectives. While the general function of the state is necessarily the promotion of continuing capital accumulation overall, each particular policy is moulded by diverse pressures, sectional interests competing with one another within a 'biased'[7] social order – conflicting groups of capitals, the need to contain possible lower-class discontent, strains internal to the state itself and the exigencies of the international environment. Among capitals there will typically be a whole series of cross-cutting divisions of interest, such as between finance and industry, big and small firms, exporters and producers for the home market and firms which do or do not contract with the state; they may dispute such matters as high or low interest rates, weak or strong anti-monopoly legislation, low or high tariffs and expansion or reduction of state expenditure.[8] The state will also be pressed by trade unions and political parties, particularly those dependent on working-class electoral support, to enforce concessions to some or all sections of labour at the expense, at least in the short run, of some or all capitals; a failure to respond to lower class discontents weakens the basis for 'non-political' trade unionism and reformist, usually social democratic, political parties. It goes without saying that employers' organisations and right-wing political parties simultaneously press the state to limit 'concessions' to the working class and curtail certain types of state expenditure.[9] Since the state apparatus is a very complex amalgam of organisations engaged in a wide variety of activities, sometimes conflicting with each other, and since state employees are not passive cogs in a machine but have their own various interests, indeed *class* interests, there are severe internal limits on what the state can do.[10] State policy is also profoundly constrained by the country's situation in the world economy; the terms of trade, flows of capital, acceptability of the currency and availability of foreign credits are all factors which may force the state to bring about more or less radical changes in the economic and political systems. The international political/military alliances also restrict economic policy and compel each state to ensure that a substantial part of the social product is expended on arms.

It follows from the above discussion that it is as crude to conceive of the state as a machine controlled by a group of 'conspiratorial politicians and bureaucrats' as of 'agents of the capitalist class'. What is true is that in monopoly capitalist societies, unless the state efficiently carries out certain public functions, which we try to specify in this chapter, the accumulation process could not continue – the economy would collapse. Evidently many capitalist economies are and have been very inadequately regulated, as we can see by the evidence of mass unemployment, widespread bankruptcies and industrial conflict, and we make no presumption that any battery of regulative policies could be sufficient to create order in a particular economy. The purpose of the functional analysis of the state that we give here is to distinguish necessary conditions for successful regulation of monopoly capitalism, but we do not fall into an objectionable functionalist methodology since we do not assume that these conditions are either achievable or sufficient.

Our analysis will concentrate on the economic functions of the state. We shall review such functions under two broad headings: firstly, state regulation of demand, and secondly, the direct role played by the state in production relations and the restructuring of capital. Both of these functions have as their ultimate objective the maintenance of the rate of accumulation; although we can draw a distinction between these two major state economic functions for analytical purposes, in practice, as our discussion will demonstrate, they will tend to overlap with each other – policies explicitly formulated to regulate demand will often effectively restructure capital and vice versa. Furthermore, as we stated in the introduction to this chapter, the political/ideological functions of the state overlap with the economic functions.

REGULATION OF DEMAND

As Keynes insisted, there is no market mechanism ensuring that all goods produced are purchased at full employment; there are certain to be serious disruptive consequences if there is too low a level of effective demand.[11] With inadequate demand, Keynes argued, unemployment, idle fixed capital and low profits reinforce each other. As in the 1930s, particular capitals may expand by merger or take-over but there is no overall capital accumulation, and for the workers there is mass unemployment, insecurity, a weakening of trade unionism and intensified political and ideological divisions. However, if inadequate demand were the cause of economic depression, then as Keynes claimed the state has the opportunity and potential to ensure continuing accumulation and full employment by intervening in the market to stimulate demand.

Control of credit and money supply is one possible stratagem of demand management. Banks, hire purchase companies, building societies and other financial institutions make credit available at varying interest rates according to the reliability of the customer and the period of the loan, but since the state bank is generally the 'lender in the last resort' these rates tend to rise and fall in line with its interest rates; thus the price of credit throughout the economy can be manipulated by altering the state bank's interest rates. The state can also change the total amount of money available for loans by imposing or relaxing restrictions on bank lending. Since interest rates constitute only one of a number of factors affecting investment decisions, and frequently not the most important or immediate consideration (especially in firms which generate their investment funds out of profits), credit and monetary control make a rather blunt instrument for fine-tuning demand. It is nevertheless true that over a period of time a plentiful supply of cheap credit does tend to promote investment but there is no guarantee that it will be placed in productive spheres and, even if this did happen, that it would increase employment. Although the state, through the state bank, controls the general level of interest rates, its decisions are constrained by the constant need to attract new loans. High interest rates may also be necessary to encourage holdings of the national currency, particularly if there are fears that it might devalue. Unless the currency is sound and exports are steadily increasing, a cheap money policy tends to result in bottlenecks and shortages, including labour shortages, thus promoting inflation. But high interest rates and restrictions on lending increase the burden of mortgage and hire purchase repayments on the workers as well as reducing production and employment and, as servicing the National Debt becomes more costly, the state comes under pressure to raise taxation and cut public expenditure. Market and production relations on an international as well as a national level put bounds on the state's room to manoeuvre on credit and monetary policy, this situation leading variously to inflation, rising unemployment, cuts in public expenditure, increasing tax burdens, increased financial exploitation.[12]

In combination taxation and state expenditure provide another means of market regulation, stimulating production and employment when the former aggregate is less than the latter. Employment can be increased directly by taking on people in local and national government, state corporations and firms contracting with the state, the resulting rises in spending power feeding demand and thereby tending to further raise production and employment. Tax relief and cash payments also increase demand – unless they are saved (which is often true of interest on the National Debt, but rarely the case for welfare benefits). Grants and tax concessions to private capitals are often tied to levels of investment, regional investment, the rate at which old fixed capital is scrapped and numbers employed. Direct aid to capital accumulation, socialisation of capital's costs and increased consumption (within limits) all promote fuller use of productive capacity, but since the latter two are a drain on surplus value the first has to take priority when state and national capitals come under severe strain.[13] In Britain there has been a pronounced trend in recent years for taxes on earned income and expenditure to rise proportionately as well as absolutely, such that taxation is itself a major cause of poverty,[14] while the 'social wage' is being cut and subsidies to private capital stepped up. Where the capitals in a nation state begin to lose out in international competition, deficit financing becomes self-defeating, resulting in increased money supply and state indebtedness and thus boosting inflation and building up pressures for a reversal of Keynesian demand management – reducing real wages, raising taxation, cutting state expenditure in welfare, education, environment and administration and allowing unemployment to rise.

Regulation at the level of the market may be relatively successful where the world economy is expanding, as in the first twenty years after the war – but the current situation is very different for Western capitalism's sickest nations, notably Ireland, Italy and Britain.

As Gamble and Walton have written of Britain:

The post-war role of the state in the capitalist economy was of major importance in assisting accumulation to get under way again. After a time, however, the implications of its new role brought an increasing conflict between prosperity and accumulation. The costs of maintaining the latter began to loom too large. Inflation was the direct result. Governments kept pumping their own spending into the economy and aiding the expansion of private debt and credit to maintain demand. This meant that the money supply kept on outrunning output. To raise output meant raising profits and increasing productivity. This obliged governments to intervene much more directly in the economy – helping to restructure capital into larger units, redistributing income to companies through the tax system, and confronting trade-union claims for more pay and better conditions directly.[15]

PRODUCTION RELATIONS AND THE RESTRUCTURING OF CAPITAL

In contemporary Western capitalism state intervention does more than simply regulate the relations between existing capitals; the state promotes new combinations of capital, takes control of particular capitals and reorganises relations between capitals and between capitals and labour.

We begin our discussion of state involvement in production relations by seeking to clarify the role of state enterprises. In our view some state enterprises are *capitals* in their own right, operating in competition with other capitals and compelled, like them, to appropriate as much surplus product as possible.[16] It is certainly true that many activities of the state, although making charges to the public (such as, for example, the health service) cannot be regarded as capitals or even quasi-capitals; they carry out other state functions that we review in this chapter.[17] Conversely, although no state enterprise is entirely independent of the government, many of them act primarily as capitals. (Incidentally, no large corporation can be entirely independent of the state either.) There are no owners of state enterprises who are enriched by its profits but, as we argued in Chapter Five, shareholders' dividends are only one possible source of motivation for the appropriation of surplus product, and are, if anything, a detraction from that defining property of capital – capital accumulation. It is also the case that state

enterprises have a different relation to money markets than
do private capitals, loans being obtained from the market
or government rather than shares being issued to the 'public',
but this fact does not necessarily lessen their freedom to
respond to competitive relations with other capitals. Many
state enterprises have a legal obligation to act 'commercially'[18] and others can in fact only maintain themselves as
ongoing organisations if they seek to maximise their
appropriation of surplus product and capitalise it. But, as
we argued in the last chapter, a compulsive drive to capital
accumulation is necessarily associated with a characteristic
form of the division of labour – a hierarchy of authority
separating coordinated labour from control, dichotomising
collective worker and global capitalist. We are arguing,
then, that state enterprises which operate, directly or indirectly, in the market may be state capitals. However, some
authors discount this very possibility:

> those in charge of the nationalised industries cannot but
> be aware that their primary duty is to make the best possible
> use of the national assets entrusted to them, and in this
> way promote the welfare of the community in general
> and of their customers and employees in particular. This
> follows from the fact that the industries are owned by
> the nation and that their shareholders and the community
> are one and the same. In this situation, profit maximisation
> is no longer a credible objective, because it is clearly
> ridiculous to make the highest possible profit one can
> on behalf of the nation as shareholders if it is earned
> at the expense of these same shareholders in the guise
> of consumers or employees.[19]

Besides the major premise that 'the welfare of the community' is unproblematic, which this whole book attempts
to challenge, the above argument assumes that 'popular'
control is actually exercised with the result that state-owned
enterprises adopt a 'social services orientation'.[20] In fact many
of them are not at all closely controlled even by ministers,
most obviously where state ownership takes the form of a
partial or total shareholding in a limited liability company

and where, as in 'public corporations' in Britain, the government deliberately abjures interference in their day-to-day management. In some cases where the enterprise is a department of a ministry, the minister has only limited capacity to direct its affairs in detail. We are not denying that political leaders have considerable powers over the long-term general policies of state enterprises by informal pressures, appointments to boards of directors, sanctioning of capital expenditures, limiting access to credit, settling profitability targets, and so on, but it must also be recognised that such political controls are themselves constrained.

Economic constraints are most evident where the enterprise is producing goods or services for a competitive market, a good example being nationalised vehicle manufacturers. Such a firm can only sell its products if it matches them in price and quality with its competitors, so unless it makes lower profits than them it must adopt similar investment policies, pay similar wages and obtain similar levels of labour productivity. Since economic competition occurs on a world scale state enterprises like the British Airways Corporation and the British Steel Corporation, which are engaged in exporting or are not protected in home markets, have to adopt policies and organisation congruent with their competitors. Even state enterprises which have a 'natural' home monopoly, such as state-owned transport undertakings and power supply, may face competitive pressures by producers of substitutable goods or services, an example being competition between state-owned railways and private road hauliers; indeed unless there is ministerial coordination there may be competition between state enterprises, such as gas and electricity supply. It is important to recognise that the logic of market relations is symmetrical, a state enterprise as much forcing other capitals, private or state owned, to accumulate capital as it is being compelled by them to do the same. The implication of these arguments is that state enterprises may be autonomous capitals, their controllers being compelled to appropriate and capitalise surplus *value*.

However, in so far as state enterprises are subsidised, cartelised and coordinated, their prices are determined to that extent by central authority rather than the market; since each enterprise's products are not pure commodities, surplus labour is not appropriated entirely as surplus value.

Where a number of state enterprises cooperate in certain areas,[21] with or without ministerial instruction, they are *to that extent* released from mutual competition. But as a conglomerate whole they may still have to respond to the market, competition having been shifted to a new plane. Each enterprise is a quasi-capital as we have defined the term in the introduction to this chapter. However, given the constraints of its commitments to specific areas of cooperation, its relations with other enterprises, privately or state owned, compel it to operate essentially like any other capital, separating control from coordinated labour and accumulating capital.

In so far as the state systematically subsidises a state enterprise,[22] controls its prices or instructs it to act in certain respects 'non-commercially' for the sake of other state functions, surplus labour is not registered in the market as surplus value; but the enterprise retains its character as a capital (more strictly, a quasi-capital) if within these restrictions it is compelled to separate coordinated labour from control with the latter appropriating and capitalising the surplus product generated by the former; it is *as if* the enterprise sought surplus value. The state itself becomes a part of a conglomerate capital[23] which faces competition at a different level, above all internationally.

It may seem that the government has a wide range of choice over the price levels and profit targets set for nationalised industries. Prices, and therefore profits, could be set high by establishment of a legal monopoly, in which case the government could acquire large funds for the exchequer or the enterprise could accumulate capital at a particularly rapid rate. Conversely government subsidy could allow the state enterprise to sell its products cheaply. However there are limitations to the range of choice available to the government. On the one hand other capitals are concerned that the price of products of state enterprises which are inputs for their own production should be kept low. On the other hand a subsidised state enterprise has to be financed out of borrowing or taxation, in both cases leading, at least in the long run, to either directly decreasing surplus value available to capitals or reducing net wages thereby encouraging workers to demand wage rises. Moreover, from the point of view of private capitals, state enterprises, with the immense resources of the state behind them, could be extremely powerful competitors; this dangerous possibility could be avoided if state capitals made no more than average rates of profit, profitable firms were never nationalised and state firms were prevented from moving into new profitable spheres of activity. It is clear then that private capitals have a very strong interest in securing systematic discrimination against state capitals and in favour of private capitals. Although many or even most private capitals may oppose the encroachment of state capital, usually but not always with considerable success, there are definitely situations where more state involvement in production is the only possible way to stimulate overall accumulation.[24] Total capital accumulation by some state and private capitals may be furthered by new combinations of capital with an increased weight of state capital, the state being compelled by world economic and military/political pressures to bring about such a capital restructuring, even in spite of some private capitals' resistance. Since the state's core function is the promotion of *overall* capital accumulation, any state (quasi-) capital, because it is a *state* capital, is bound to be pressed into the service of this total function. However both national and international competition require that state (quasi-) capitals do not depart far from their character as capitals since it is impossible to make rational decisions about investment and allocation unless price relativities approximate to those in international markets.

For all the reasons discussed above we can see that state capitals and quasi-capitals operate as *capitals*, whatever the degree of market distortion resulting from these activities being carried out under the aegis of the state. Much or most of the kinds of state economic activity discussed above have the important economic function of socialising costs, thus furthering capital accumulation. Such costs are socialised as the state takes on an increasing responsibility for maintaining the two basic categories of input for capital, that is, labour and means of production. Other agents may also bear costs of these inputs, particularly that of labour – for example, families, churches, and charitable agencies – but it is the state's contribution that we focus on here. Adapting O'Connor's terminology, we shall refer to such 'projects and services that lower the reproduction costs of labour'[25] as 'socialised variable capital' and state 'projects and services that increase the productivity of a given amount of labour power'[26] – the maintenance of an infrastructure, aid in technical development, etc. – as 'socialised constant capital'. Both of these kinds of state input, other things being equal, increase the surplus value capitals are able to appropriate.

As capitals, both privately and state owned, become more dependent on the socialisation of constant and variable capital through the state, the state becomes an even more integral element in total production relations, thus directly reorganising relations between capitals and between workers and capitals.

State provision of education and training is a clear example of the cost of a pool of suitably skilled labour being met socially. A whole range of items, which are often regarded solely as welfare, also contribute to socialised variable capital: family allowances, income tax allowances on children, the state health services, social security, sewage disposal and state subsidies for passenger transport and urban housing – all these serve to ensure a continuing work-force and keep it able and fit. In the past a large proportion of the costs of training, sickness and unemployment was borne by family and kin, but as these costs are increasingly shouldered by the state, other things being equal, the socially necessary wage would tend to fall. Of course other things are not equal for the very development of the system generates new needs, but it remains true that capitals are relieved by the state of part of the costs of the reproduction of labour.

Socialised constant capital has enormously increased in scale and significance in recent years. Tax reliefs, subsidised industrial estates and cash grants encourage investment generally, but may also be contrived to aid 'key' capitals or industries whose health promotes overall capital accumulation. The state may aid capitals by providing loans at lower than the market rate of interest or, more radically, purchasing shares in the company, in larger quantities and at higher prices than the 'public' would be willing to do; such measures do not merely prop up an existing capital but bring it into an organic relationship with the state, even to the extent of partial or total state ownership. The state may also provide a physical infrastructure which is available for common use but which, in particular, reduces capitals' costs, notable examples being the road system and disposal of industrial wastes. State-owned firms also contribute to social constant capital in so far as the government deliberately restricts their profitability by controlling the prices of their products or services to other capitals; it is not, as such, the state ownership of basic industries and services like post, telecommunications, railways, buses, gas, electricity, water, coal and steel that constitutes socialised constant capital but the circumstances that they are directed by the government to make a profit less than the 'normal' rate. It is of course significant that firms producing goods and services necessary for a very wide range of other enterprises should be state owned, for state capital in physical infrastructure provides a guarantee of supply and, where it is subsidised, a convenient means of enhancing productivity in the capitals concerned, thus enabling them to compete better in international markets.

State demand for the products of capitals may provide an effective subsidy to them as well as regulating the market. A guaranteed market on a 'cost-plus' basis means that the state is effectively paying capitals' 'risk' costs – a socialisation of economic uncertainty. Such forms of social investment are very important in industries where development costs of a new product are very high and unpredictable, such as aircraft manufacture, atomic energy and computers. Where a significant proportion of a capital's output is contracted to the state it begins to lose its autonomy as a capital. Its profitability and investment plans are dependent upon the state, so that it may be roughly described as a semi-autonomous semi-nationalised capital. Just as we have argued for state enterprises, such private enterprises are quasi-capitals, essentially similar to other capitals in so far as they are forced to separate control from coordinated labour and constantly seek means of increasing labour productivity. The possibility that the state may not renew the contract when it expires, if the government believes it has been overcharged or other firms can offer a more favourable deal, makes it *as if* the firm were competing in a market as far as its internal organisation and goals are concerned. In 'cost-plus' contracts state procurement agencies have access to the company's accounts and are able to carry out a sophisticated auditing, comparing costs in each phase of production as far as possible with those in other firms. Contracts often build in inducements to the firm to reduce costs, in particular by raising labour productivity.[27]

In the case of armaments production, the costs and benefits of any particular contract cannot be calculated in purely economic terms, even in principle, since arms have no value for consumption or as means of production, but even here the manufacturers may properly be regarded as capitals (or quasi-capitals). Arms are usually exchanged in the context of inter-state treaties and political/military alliances, so they are not pure commodities, but this fact does not detract from the intense international competition over quality and prices. It remains true that a large proportion of all arms are retained for 'use' by the state in which they are produced, but the fact that they have to match potential enemy states' arms in quantity and sophistication imposes cost constraints *as if* they were to be exchanged. Inter-state military competition, like inter-capital market competition, compels each group of controllers to raise labour productivity, which means appropriating and capitalising surplus product.

POLITICAL/IDEOLOGICAL FUNCTIONS OF THE STATE

We now turn to a brief analysis of political and ideological functions of the capitalist state, emphasising their economic implications. We would argue that the consciousness of the subordinate classes is a crucial factor for stability (or otherwise) in all class societies, including capitalism, but 'acceptance' of a social order varies from enforced submission, through habitual conformity, to self-conscious commitment. The essential political/ideological function of the state is the creation of grounds for obedience, resting at one end of the continuum on the threat or use of force, and at the other on persuasion that those who issue commands have the right to do so.

Miliband outlines this latter problem of legitimation:

> the whole structure of economic and political domination . . . depends, in Western-type political regimes, on the support or at least the acquiescence of those who are subjected to it. The subordinate classes in these regimes, and 'intermediary' classes as well, have to be persuaded to accept the existing social order and to confine their demands and aspirations within its limits.[28]

To a considerable extent the state achieves such legitimation directly, through its controls on those institutions which are specialised for communicating ideas, notably the media and educational systems. State-controlled media may prevent unorthodox views being heard publicly and, in thus creating the appearance of consensus, make those ideas seem natural and reasonable while dissidents' opinions, if they are known at all, come to seem esoteric or immoral. However, state control of the media may ultimately exacerbate instability caused by other factors, for the appearance of 'real' debate deflects discontent from the state itself onto the current government. In many capitalist societies educational curricula are not directly controlled by the central state authorities and the teaching is avowedly 'non-political' (in the sense of being unbiased as between political parties). This appearance of political and ideological neutrality is a source of stability since it seems to refute any suggestion of indoctrination, but in the broader sense in which we have used the terms education is profoundly political and ideological, generating overwhelmingly positive attitudes to the prevailing social order, submission to established authority, respect for authority and commitment to work as a wage labourer. But since education can also stimulate questioning and criticism it is hardly surprising that some governments have been tempted, or forced, to seek direct control over educational content, preventing the imparting of 'dangerous' knowledge.

As these remarks suggest, there are considerable variations from society to society in the ways in which legitimation is promoted, but we would claim that no capitalist society could persist unless there were mechanisms, in which the state plays a major role, to create and re-create consent. It is noteworthy that in societies where coercion plays a major role in sustaining the social order there is characteristically *also* an enormous propaganda effort.

Legitimation of a social order is achieved to the extent it is not only by control of the content of education and media but also by social benefits to the population at large, and in particular to workers and their families. State expenditures on social benefits, the 'social wage', are a *necessary* expense from the point of view of capitals overall, although since this is a deduction from surplus value it is also a potential threat to capital accumulation. The very development of capitalism generates new needs which can only be met if they are met socially by the state, but where the state and private national capitals are faced with particularly severe international competition there is strong pressure to reduce such expenses. However, since they are a component of working-class living standards, this retrenchment provokes widespread opposition. For capitals as a whole, the Welfare State is an unfortunate necessity, the levels and nature of such state expenditure being a focus for class conflict. [29]

The benefits to the working class of the Welfare State are very real and certainly soften the rigours of the market, thereby sustaining a sense of national community, a feeling that the state will help individuals and families in times of trouble. However, it should be recognised that these expenses are often inextricably tied up with other functions of the state. Education not only benefits its recipients but trains them for the labour market, that is, it is social variable capital. Unemployment and sickness benefit protects those people that capitals profitably employ at a particular time, but it also makes available a pool of labour when it is needed. Free or subsidised health services also cheapen the cost of reproducing labour as well as benefiting those who obtain treatment. Subsidised housing, while being an undoubted benefit to the workers, also facilitates their availability for work at locations where capitals wish to employ them; this can be seen particularly clearly when, in pursuit of regional industrial location policy, the state induces firms to move to particular areas with promises that there will be sufficient houses for their workers at low prices or rents. Subsidised transport firms and, even more, state provision of highways directly reduce the constant capital each enterprise lays out and make workers more 'available' for local labour markets. This is not in any way a denial of the fact that such expenditures also constitute a significant benefit for workers. State pensions may appear to be a clear case of social service without regard to other state functions but it should be recognised that these payments reduce the portion of their wages that workers would otherwise have to devote to savings for retirement or looking after aged parents. Even geriatric hospitals, in caring for those who will never work, release the families of the elderly for the labour market. Where industrial capitalism tends to weaken the multi-generation family there are new needs created for social (i.e. state) provision of help for the sick and aged. Urbanisation, which seems inseparable from capitalist development, also generates needs – for recreation, sewage disposal, pollution control, urban renewal and town planning and so on – which the state has to meet in order to secure workers' health and popular acceptability of urban living conditions; failure to do so results in early deaths and tends to encourage people to move out of the big conurbations (providing, of course, that there are jobs and houses in smaller towns); it should also be recognised that political discontent among the urban masses imposes a major threat to property and social order generally.

Doubtless many of those who participate in welfare policy formation and implementation view it as an expression of the national community helping to satisfy the people's needs *rather* than serving vested interests, but in our view welfare is both a genuine benefit to labour and a cost to capitals which it is in their interests to pay.

Acquiescence of the subordinate classes depends on

coercion as well as legitimation, and this requires a body of law and a 'repressive state apparatus' of police, courts and prisons. It is important for our analysis to recognise that the legal system does not simply enforce orderly economic relations in the abstract, but particular, capitalist, economic relations; the major part of law and law enforcement is concerned with property and contract. Law regulates relations between employer and employee, landlord and tenant, capital and capital, the state and capital, the state and worker, the shareholder and the manager, the property owner and all others, and so on.

Laws relating employer and employee govern rights of hiring and firing, statutory holidays, safety at work and in some cases minimum wages. Tenants and landlords are subject to law in respect of levels of rent, security of tenure and damage to property. Capitals relate to each other under laws regarding price and terms of contracts and prohibition or permission to form cartels and other combinations. The state relates to capitals and workers subject to law in the collection of taxes and disposal of benefits and allowances. Laws protect shareholders against individuals, including managers, who might improperly attempt to use corporate wealth for private gain.

EXTERNAL FUNCTIONS

Characteristically the state's functions in managing external affairs are simultaneously economic, political and ideological. Each national society exists in an arena containing political/military blocs and is caught up in a complex web of credit, trade and investment relationships; this environment severely constrains decisions of national capitals and the state.

Military power may enable a state to protect foreign markets, sources of raw materials and investments, both in the overseas country concerned and from third parties. Defence of territorial integrity – which in times of peace may involve, say, fishing rights – whether from immediate dangers or only long-term potential threats, also requires a military capacity. The military effort is frequently associated with internal political/ideological functions: defence of the 'nation' or a 'way of life', or even militarisation of society as a guarantee of 'order'. These circumstances give rise to a system of more or less stable alliances, where partners urge 'appropriate' levels of arming on each other as contributions to deterring the common 'enemy'. Each bloc is compelled by the military preparations of the others to do likewise, thus sustaining an arms race that no one party controls; just as markets force capitals to acquire exchange values, military competition compels states to seek use values (in means of destruction) which are comparable in quantity and quality with their competitor states.[30]

Capitals trading or investing overseas seek free access to markets abroad, freedom to move capital and invest in the most profitable areas, guarantees against expropriation and freedom to pay wages at local market rates. Besides military threats there are many 'peaceful' methods by which a state can promote its national capitals' overseas interests – subsidies on exports, aid or loans with 'strings', state-sponsored international cartels, promises to encourage investment and so on. States may also seek to defend home markets against foreign imports by means of tariffs and quotas, whether through formal interstate agreements or in a war of competitive protectionism.

Foreign investments initially strengthen the balance of payments, foster employment and tend to develop the means of production but they can only be encouraged by granting freedoms to foreign capital which may ultimately frustrate the state's capacity to coordinate and direct economic growth. Foreign capitals may enter a national market by direct investment in enterprises within its territorial boundaries, controlling as well as owning them; multinational corporations' policies are designed in the light of their world operations, taking due account of variations in wages, prices, interest rates and taxation from country to country.[31]

It is clear then that states exist in an unplanned world economic environment which they cannot control but are forced to adapt to, in so far as they are able, in ways which protect the interests of their national capitals. This 'system' is structured in complex relationships of alliance, antagonism, dependence and domination. States may combine, in an attempt to bring some order to the international economy, by establishing supra-national regulative bodies and multilateral trade agreements (for example Bretton Woods and GATT) but they only seem to be effective during periods of relatively stable growth. In any case, international agreements are rarely, if ever, world wide, and those such as NATO, the Warsaw pact, or the Common Market, often project inter-state conflict into conflict between blocs of states. This conflict can be overtly military (NATO), or economic (EEC).

THE CLASS SITUATION OF STATE EMPLOYEES

We have seen that state regulation of the market and involvement in production relations is essential to overall capital accumulation, not least in the role played by the state in socialising the costs of constant and variable capital. Many of these activities, however, although certainly *necessary* to capitalist accumulation, do constitute a drain on accumulation as 'unproductive' activities are thus maintained. In addition the process of capitalist accumulation also requires the fulfilment of political/ideological conditions entailing expenses which are a deduction from the surplus product. Surplus product is generated within (state and private) capitals in the productive spheres and appropriated by them and by (state and private) capitals in non-productive spheres, much of it being capitalised. The state also appropriates surplus product which is used for general administration, defence, internal law and order, welfare and socialisation of capital costs. We can analyse the class situation of the various categories of state employees by identifying the parts they play in the flows of surplus product.

The case of employees in state capitals (and quasi-capitals) is very similar to corresponding class situations in privately owned firms, there being a functional separation between control and coordinated labour. In state industrial and (some) service capitals the collective worker creates surplus product, while in the non-productive spheres it enables its capital to appropriate surplus product originating in production. In both cases there is conflict over the terms and conditions of the labour contract, in productive spheres over the amount of surplus product the worker creates and in unproductive spheres over the share of surplus product obtained.

Where the state capital is more or less autonomous (that is, more a 'true' than a 'quasi-' capital) the surplus product tends to take the form of surplus value so that the controllers can in principle make an accurate reckoning of comparative labour productivity and workers' contributions to profitability – thus providing a 'rational' basis for choosing between such alternatives as imposing new work norms, changing work organisation, introducing new machinery, making workers redundant, and so on. As we have remarked, no state capital can ever be entirely free from pressure to respond to other state functions. The legitimation function may be exemplified in the tendency for state enterprises to be model employers, typically in such respects as trade union recognition, pension provision, job security or the 'humane' implementation of redundancies. On the other hand the government, with its constant problem of financing the total state budget and subject as it is to the pressure of capitals not to bid up the price of labour, may attempt to restrain wages in state capitals. Government incomes policy is likely to be enforced more scrupulously in state-owned firms than in privately-owned ones. Although the class situation of employees in state industries is essentially congruent with that of employees in private capitals, conflict may be generated between these two broad categories of workers on the grounds that state workers are a cost to the tax-paying 'private' employee.

Where state enterprises depart systematically from autonomous capital ambiguities in the class position of their employees are intensified. As the quasi-capital is forced to carry out functions of market regulation, socialisation of capital costs and legitimation, its employees become agents redistributing resources between capitals, between capital and labour and between workers. Difficulties in their class position arise over the questions 'Who benefits at whose expense?' and 'Are their expenses necessary and, if so, for whose interests?' These questions are reflected in debates as to whether or not state firms are efficient or feather-bedded and whether they should be a social service or a commercial business. They also bear upon the possibility of alliances and conflicts with employees in other state and private capitals. A state quasi-capital operates, subject to definite 'political' constraints, as a capital on the market, so that the particular characteristics of state quasi-capitals are an important set of secondary factors which overlay the characteristic class positions we have analysed for capitals generally. (We return to this important topic in our final chapter.)

In state non-capitals (that is, parts of the state which obtain only a small proportion, if any, of their income from the market) all employment is a drain on surplus product. In addition – and this is an important point of difference between state and private unproductive workers – these employees in no sense create a *profit* for their employer, thus their 'unproductive' status is further underlined in everyday perceptions. Bacon and Eltis argue, for example, that workers in private finance capital are productive because their services are marketed, unlike their counterparts in the state sector.[32] The twin questions 'Who benefits at whose expense?' and 'Are their expenses necessary and, if so, for whose interests?' now dominate any attempt to characterise these employees, imparting profound tensions at all levels of the organisation. For example, in the state health service, the functions of legitimation (welfare) and socialised variable capital conflict, producing characteristic tensions (e.g. cost efficiency or the inherent sacredness of human life? Preventative or curative medicine? Personal service or rational, impersonal efficiency?). In state education the same dual functions generate a conflict between the goals of education as 'personal self-expansion' or 'investment in human capital' (i.e., job training). Social security officials carry out both a welfare and a repression function, helping all, but only, the 'deserving' people in need. Furthermore tensions between state non-productive workers and all other employees may be exacerbated by the characterisation of state non-productive workers as 'useless bureaucrats' or a drain on the community as a whole. Such activities are seen as luxury expenditure by the community at large because of the manifest absence of any profit in these spheres, and overt and obvious maintenance from taxation.

It is clear then that these factors generate a complex pattern of potential alliances and tensions between workers in non-capital spheres of the state and workers elsewhere. The tensions are perhaps least pronounced among the least specialised (often least skilled) employees in state non-capitals since they appear in the same labour market as others who are similarly qualified, and are able to move from one sector to the other. Many state employees, particularly in non-capital spheres, have jobs which require specialised skills not required in other sectors in large numbers (e.g., nursing, teaching, police) so restricting their movement to alternative employers. Systems of promotion and seniority, pension schemes, contracts of employment and special housing provision may tie state employees to their jobs, an extreme case being the armed forces. Wage labour may be a necessary condition for rational evaluation of the contribution an employee makes to an organisation's goals, but it is not sufficient since, in non-capital state sectors at least, goals are often insufficiently specific or capable of entering into calculations. Of course there is variation from one type of activity to another. In some non-capital state spheres 'scientific management' is possible and may be vigorously applied – exact job descriptions, detailed division of labour, measurement of performance and constant attempts to improve as measured by indices of achievement. However, other activities are simply not susceptible to these types of management at a given level of technology, although attempts may be made from time to time to introduce new measures of performance.

Given this variation, it remains clear that state non-capital employees are in profoundly complex and ambiguous class situations, where the influence of authority relations and trade union organisation is likely to be of decisive independent importance in determining consciousness and action.

7

Economy and Class Structure in the East

In all class societies, by definition, one or more classes carry out surplus labour, thereby creating surplus product which is appropriated by the dominant class or classes. However, what is distinctive about capitalism is that this process is organised in autonomous units, while overall order in the economy results from the mutual relations between these units rather than central external authority. Units can only survive in such an environment if accumulation is their major priority. Capitalist society requires that there be differentiated role complexes for control and coordinated labour, complexes that we have identified in Chapter Five as the global function of capital and the collective worker. (We shall further develop this point in Chapter Nine.) This differentiation ensures that each unit can respond to system pressures, whilst hindrance from labour is kept within fairly narrow confines. The classic exemplification of this model is the free market society, where entrepreneurs are compelled to direct their employees towards goals determined by market relations, creation and appropriation of surplus value and its conversion into capital. As we have seen, the situation is significantly modified by the concentration of capital, and the increasingly important role played by the state in the restructuring of capital (which is partially achieved through state ownership) and the regulation of the market; however the effect of these changes is not to erode competitive relations as such but to transform them into new patterns of rivalry, military and political as well as economic, involving states and giant corporations at the international level. While there is a more complex division of labour, we can still distinguish the functions of collective worker and global capitalist.

In this chapter we shall argue that this definition of capitalism applies to the East[1] as well as the West, and that the class structure of those societies can be understood in these terms. Just like any other capital, state capitals in the East are constrained by the international environment and, as in the West, there is a disjunction between coordinated labour and control. It is true, as many observers have pointed out, that market relations *within* some of the Eastern societies are very different from those in Western societies, but we would argue that once due account is taken of the international context the relations of production can be seen to be basically the same.

In Weberian analysis, as we have pointed out in Chapters Two and Three, the existence of classes hinges upon whether or not there is a stable pattern of inequalities sustained by market mechanisms; failure to identify such stability and mechanisms, or explaining patterns of inequality by reference to non-economic factors such as political decisions, then warrants rejection of the view that they are class societies. On the contrary we would argue that the appropriate criterion for class-divided societies is not the presence or absence of inequalities sustained through a market, but whether or not there are fundamental differences in relations to the means of production – although of course we do recognise that patterns of inequality *may* flow from class divisions and indeed help to sustain them. (This point will be extensively discussed in Chapter Eight.) In this chapter we argue that all the Eastern societies are, by this criterion, class-divided societies, in fact capitalist societies. Certainly this argument demands clarification of what differences in relations to the means of production should properly be regarded as 'fundamental'.

In discussing the Eastern countries together we would certainly not wish to deny that there are substantial differences between them any more than we would make the absurd claim that, for example, France, Spain and the United States have identical economies and class structures. Russia, East Germany and Czechoslovakia are considerably more industrially developed than other Eastern countries; Poland and Yugoslavia have larger private sectors than the other countries, particularly in agriculture; Yugoslavia and Hungary have price systems which are less centrally regulated than in the other Eastern countries; there are very different levels of trade with the West and variations in the extent to which internal prices are allowed to reflect world prices. Many other dimensions of variation could be stated and there have also been major changes over time, but there are also striking similarities: state or collective ownership of most industrial, commercial and financial enterprises; more economic coordination than is current in the West and in some cases a very high degree of central planning; suppression of organised dissent, in particular of political parties other than 'official' ones; the absence of democratic trade unions and a merging, particularly at higher levels, of 'trade unions',[2] the party and the state; and an international environment which in some cases severely restricts available options for the enterprises and in general profoundly constrains the priorities of national planning. To present our position we will outline two polar types of economy – directive planning and guided market. These are ideal types in that they have never occurred in the pure form sketched out below but they are intended to highlight the theoretical problems of understanding the dynamics of actual societies which are a blend, in varying proportions, of the two types.[3]

In a system of directive planning the overall plan is devised by central agencies for approval and modification by the highest political authorities.[4] Information for constructing plans comes from surveys, statistical analyses and returns from ministries, local authorities, enterprise managers, inspectors and so on. There will be a number of related central plans over different time scales, any of which may be revised in the light of experience or as the outcome of political changes. Plans will cover the whole scope of economic activity – manpower requirements and availability, investment in each industry, physical inputs and outputs from industry, credit, taxation, prices, wages, total consumption, the composition of state expenditure, and so on. Central plans are refined by successive specialised agencies on a sectoral and territorial basis, where the task of such lower-level planners is to decide how the targets assigned to their sphere are to be realised. Eventually each enterprise will be set a battery of goals such as minimal targets for physical output, labour productivity and accounting profit,[5] maximal limits on the use of raw materials and total wages, improvements in productivity and output, and so on. The state bank, at which enterprises obtain loans and keep their accounts, is able to check on the achievement of such goals, but there may also be specialised control agencies. Corrupt or unsuccessful managers may be punished or dismissed by the authorities. There is a hierarchical system of authority within the enterprise which is buttressed by the 'responsibility' of the 'trade union' and local party to fulfil the plan targets by trying to ensure labour discipline and promoting 'appropriate' work norms. Wage scales and prices are laid down by central authorities. There may be both restrictions on geographical mobility and job changes.

In a system of directive planning there is no competition between enterprises nor free contract between them. The allocation of total labour time in various activities is determined by the central authorities, as is the mix of products made in the society; imbalances of supply and demand for a product at a particular price affects neither pricing policy nor the pattern of future production – unless the planners choose to take account of such occurrences. Prices do not necessarily reflect costs of production;[6] although the authorities may attempt such a correspondence for some products, others may be kept at prices quite out of proportion to the labour time expended on them. Since there is effectively only one employer, there is no genuine market for labour.

Considered as an isolated system, although it is evidently a type of class-divided society, the process of creating and appropriating surplus product is not organised in autonomous units and overall order in the economy results from central external authority rather than the mutual relations between enterprises – it is not a capitalist society. But the

premise for this argument, that there is an *isolated* system
of directive planning, has not been realised. It remains to
consider the possibility that, considered in the international military, political and economic environment, a
system of directive planning constitutes a single national
capital with a division of labour akin to that of any other
large complex capital.

We shall return to these considerations later, but first we
outline the guided market system, elements of which operate
in some of the Eastern countries.

National plans are considerably less detailed than in a
directive planning system: a forecast of likely economic
developments, a statement of the government's intentions on
major constructions, regional development, fiscal and
budgetary policy, and a guide to lower-level economic
management. Considerable scope for decision making is
devolved to regional and municipal authorities and, most
significantly, to the enterprises. Enterprise managers have an
area of freedom within which they can modify prices and
adjust investment in the light of shifting demand. A representative body for enterprise employees is able to influence
managers' policies with regard to individual complaints and
indeed the general level of wages and working conditions.
The employees may even be able to dismiss their managers
and appoint new ones. Some enterprises are owned by the
state or local authorities but many others have ownership formally vested in the employees, although without them
having rights to dispose of or realise any of the assets. There
are no restrictions on job mobility and wages will be significantly affected by labour surpluses or shortages. There
may be some direct instructions or targets imposed upon
the enterprises by central or local authorities, and the banks,
through their credit policy, will encourage them to keep
in line with the plan; but the major impetus to overall
integration and control of the economy derives from a
complex system of inducements. Improvements in productivity, increases in output, declines in use of materials, rises
in profits and so on, all result in funds being made available
for bonus payments to managers and workers. Good performance may also allow an enterprise to invest extra sums

in plant and equipment, thus improving the chances that it can perform well in future years.

In a guided market system there is competition between enterprises and they can freely enter into contracts. There is a free market in labour, although no collective bargaining as we know it in the West; strikes are suppressed. In theory the planners' objectives are realised, in spite of decentralised decision making, by utilising market forces and constructing 'rules of the game' which make it in managers' own interests to act in such a way as to further the achievement of the plan. The workers equally wish to obtain the bonuses made available for high output, productivity, profitability, and so on, and are thus concerned about management's ability to achieve these goals which in turn impels them to comply with managerial authority. Both the party and the 'trade unions' promote hostility to inefficient managers and submission to competent ones.[7] While it is true that the central authorities lay down the proportions of different products to be made and the allocation of total labour time between broad areas of activity, the reality of autonomous enterprises powerfully constrains the design of the plan and investment tends to flow into potentially profitable spheres, whether or not this is stipulated by the plan.

In a guided market society surplus product does take the form of surplus value; each enterprise is compelled by its relation to the others to appropriate as much surplus value as possible and convert the bulk of it into capital. In this essential respect the guided market is identical to monopoly capitalism in the West. The central plan may modify the market mechanism, as indeed state intervention does in the West, but only within fairly narrow limits, especially when the enterprises compete in foreign and home markets. Since there is a disjunction between coordinated labour and control in this type of society,[8] there will be the two basic classes of collective worker and global capitalist.

This conclusion is rejected by Easern Marxists. Wesolowski writes:

The Marxist theory of class structure stipulates first of all the existence of two mutually antagonistic groups involved in the process of production. They are the so-called 'basic classes'. They differ from each other by their relations to the means of production. One of these classes owns them; the other is deprived of them although it operates them. The relation determines the character of the first as an exploiting and of the second as an exploited class.

This brief summary leads to what has become a commonplace that proletarian revolution abolishes the thus conceived class structure. Socialisation of the capitalist-owned means of production means the liquidation of one of the elements of the antagonistic capital–labour relations. And with this disappears the fundamental class relations typical of capitalist society.[9]

Wesolowski's argument rests entirely upon his *definition* of the capitalist class as the owners of the means of production and thus, tautologically, a society without private ownership of the means of production is non-capitalist. Rather than analyse the real relationships to the means of production, he focuses only on the juridical relation of ownership – but legal definitions may conceal rather than reveal class relationships. Marx was certainly right to consider that a necessary condition for the abolition of capitalism is the ending of private ownership of the means of production and it would be understandable, writing at the time that he did, if he suggested that it were a sufficient condition. However, in the changing conditions of contemporary capitalism, which we discussed at some length in Chapters Four, Five and Six, it is no longer possible to sustain this formalistic position. Would Weslowoski argue, for example, that the mixed economies of the West are only partly class stratified, as employees of state industry are not in an antagonistic class relationship *vis-à-vis* capital? As we have already noted, the neo-Weberian approach to class analysis also denies that Eastern societies have a capitalist class structure – this applies particularly to the directly planned system. This view is cogently expressed by Goldthorpe in a passage which it is worth quoting at length:

In Soviet society the economy operates within a 'monistic'

or totalitarian political order and is, in principle at least, totally planned, whereas in advanced Western societies political power is significantly less concentrated and the economy is planned in a far less centralized and detailed way. From this it results that in the West economic, and specifically market forces act as the crucial stratifying agency within society. They are, one could say, the major source of social inequality. And consequently, the *class* situation of individuals and groups, understood in terms of their economic power and resources, tends to be the most important single determinant of their general life-chances. That is why we can usefully speak of Western industrial society as being 'class' stratified. However in the case of Soviet society, market forces cannot be held to play a comparable role in the stratification process. These forces operate, of course, and differences in economic power and resources between individuals and groups have, as in the West, far-reaching social and human consequences. But, one would argue, to a significantly greater extent than in the West, stratification in Soviet society is subject to *political* regulation; market forces are not permitted to have the primacy or the degree of autonomy in this respect that they have even in a 'managed' capitalist society.[10]

Goldthorpe is of course correct in his assertion that the central authorities in Eastern Europe may impose substantial changes in the pattern of rewards: a striking example would be the increases in wage differentials and the implementation of regressive taxation in Russia from the 1930s until this policy was reversed in the early 1950s. More recent evidence has demonstrated that central authority has even the power to deliberately manipulate the occupational structure, by restricting the number of jobs in commerce, finance, and services and by other methods.[11] In the East, therefore, it is clear that market forces, even though they may contribute to the occupational structure and pattern of rewards, do not determine them.

Let us consider, however, the factors which do apparently structure the patterns of rewards in the East, in particular, 'political' decision making. In the extensive quote from

Goldthorpe we have just utilised, much emphasis is laid upon the concentration of political power in the East – a concentration of power which, it is implied, is such as to override economic factors. Giddens's theoretical discussion takes this point even further, indeed he argues that a major distinguishing feature of capitalist, as opposed to state socialist, society is the 'separation of the spheres of political and economic hegemony'.[12] Further support for this theoretical stance can apparently be drawn from contemporary capitalism, although we would stress that this interpretation has certainly not been received without criticism.[13] As we demonstrated in Chapter Six, the *relative* autonomy of the state in Western capitalism should not be taken to imply that political decisions can be made without regard to economic factors. The range of political debate and practice – for example, over the allocation of welfare benefits – can be extremely wide, but this should not obscure the fact that the total of values allocated to welfare will be constrained in the last instance by the need to maintain the rate of accumulation in the system as a whole. Similarly we would argue that in the East the decisions taken by the central authorities should not be treated as irreducible political phenomena. There are stringent limits on the range of choice, limits which need to be analysed concretely. Because the state, in a system of directive planning, both guards the social order and organises production, unlike private enterprise capitalism where the state does not perform the latter function,[14] every political decision is equally an economic decision, and vice versa; polity and economy are fused. However this does not imply, as Giddens would argue, that the societies of the Eastern bloc are not capitalist and therefore not class stratified.[15] Political manipulation of a stratification system does not mark it off from *class* stratification where it can be shown that political decision making is severely constrained by other social structures – in particular, and most significantly, the economic. We can illustrate our position through a review of some of the constraints upon the Russian leaders in the 1930s.

By any standards they presided over a very backward economy, unmechanised and inefficient agriculture and a tiny industrial sector, and were faced by hostile Western states. One conceivable strategy would have been to attempt to industrialise on the basis of imported machinery in return for surplus grain, supplies of which could be expected to expand if agricultural prices were allowed to rise and investment was concentrated in that sector; and seek to attract foreign loans and investment,[16] by allowing capital to move freely to the most potentially profitable areas, removing price control, bringing in low taxation, permissive foreign exchange controls and so on. Such a policy, if carried through systematically, would have enormously strengthened agrarian capital and made Russia permanently dependent on one or other grouping of Western states; in any case such a policy would probably have failed to develop industry significantly in the context of the continuing world depression. But as the military threat became more menacing the need for rapid industrialisation became ever more urgent; Russia could not be defended without modern arms, and modern arms need modern industry. Thus the Russian leaders were compelled to a desperate solution: forced industrialisation and the collectivisation of agriculture.[17] The only way to obtain food for the towns while keeping its price down was to take it by force and destroy private capital in the countryside, which would naturally resist such appropriation; collectivisation was designed to drive labour into the towns and squeeze the peasants' living standards in order to provide the resources for industrialisation. Such reorganisation of agriculture itself increased the need for industrialisation; electrification of the countryside, improvements in transport, and vast increases in supplies of oil, tractors and other agricultural machinery were essential for the new type of farming. Urban workers were also made to pay dearly for the industrialisation programme by the introduction of successively higher work norms and the wide-scale use of payment by results, in particular progressive piece-rate systems.[18] The plans decreed, and in practice it was more than achieved, that production should shift decisively away from consumer goods to producer goods; correspondingly, the price of consumer goods was particularly inflated by indirect taxation so that urban workers' living standards inevitably fell, and indeed there were permanent shortages. Resistance to such depradations had to be combated – by making the trade unions more thoroughly an arm of the state, controlled from above; establishing the party as a monolithic body, an agent for the leadership at the local level; creating a massive repressive apparatus of police, secret police, informers, prison camps. Rapid industrialisation opened up new channels for upward mobility: experts were needed in industry and agriculture, a hierarchical managerial structure was required in the enterprises to impose and supervise the new work norms, 'loyal' men were needed to staff a host of positions in the party and state apparatus. The widening of income differentials was an essential element in this refashioning of the class structure. In Deutscher's words,

> the highly paid and privileged managerial groups came to be the props of Stalin's regime. They had a vested interest in it. Stalin himself felt that his personal rule was the more secure the more solidly it rested on a rigid hierarchy of interest and influence.[19]

From this simplified account we can begin to see how the international environment, economic and military, limited the choices available to the Russian authorities and eventually determined the general character of the accumulation process and its associated class structure. As Stalin put it, 'We are fifty or a hundred years behind the advanced countries. We must make good this lag in ten years. Either we do it or they crush us.'[20] In part these pressures derived from international markets; in the depression years the prices of machinery, which Russia needed to import for the industrialisation programme, fell much less rapidly than that of food and other primary products, which therefore had to be exported in ever greater quantities – in spite of shortages at home – in order to get the same amount of machinery.[21] But the military threat was an even more potent constraint. Armaments were not produced in Russia for exchange but the effects of military competition were congruent with market competition; Russia was forced to manufacture arms comparable in quantity and technological sophistication to the Western states, which, given Russia's backward economy, required an extraordinarily high level of accumulation. The workers were forced to carry out surplus labour, thereby creating a surplus product which was appropriated by the authorities, but since armaments were not exchanged the surplus never took the form of surplus value. This fact does not in our view invalidate the identification of Russia as a capitalist society, with a division of labour on essentially the same principles as any capitalist enterprise.

Contemporary Russia does engage in overseas trade and even accepts foreign capital investments, world commodity and financial markets thus constraining state policy. It is certainly no new phenomenon for capitalist states to threaten or go to war, although such conflicts may be interpreted by the participants in non-economic terms such as 'struggles for freedom' and 'against dictatorship'. Whatever the conventional rationalisations, the arms race is not evidence as such of antagonism between Western capitalism and Eastern 'communism'. We accept that international rivalries may be partly explicable in the first instance by reference to relations of national political domination and dependence and by ideological notions of freedom, democracy, patriotism, racism and so on, but we would argue that there are generally underlying economic factors which tend to mould international political and ideological relationships – for example, security of raw material supplies, safe markets, colonial exploitation. Certainly Russian political and ideological domination of Eastern Europe is a condition for a continuing exploitative economic relationship.

Russian forces, then, have to cope with the threats of both the West and China, and attempt to maintain suzerainty over Eastern Europe.[22] After the Second World War the Russians were able to impose directive planning systems on the Eastern European states on somewhat similar lines to Russia. (Yugoslavia was exceptional in that the regime was established on the basis of an indigenous resistance movement rather than the Russian army, and although it first adopted a directive planning system it soon broke sharply with the Eastern bloc and established the guided market type.)

However, there has been considerable change, particularly since the mid-1950s, so the contemporary Eastern states present a picture of diverse forms intermediate between directive planning and guided market systems. [23]

Directive planning systems tend to suffer from characteristic economic irrationalities, particularly in the agricultural sphere and where there is sophisticated technology; these include autarky of enterprises and planning departments, prices which do not reflect costs of production, shortages of some goods and surpluses of others, low quality goods, overfulfilment of plans for producer goods and underfulfilment of plans for consumer goods – particularly agricultural products – labour hoarding, management avoidance of risk taking, and so on. There have been some attempts in the Eastern countries to ameliorate these problems by moving towards guided market systems, but such 'reforms' have often been modest and in some cases sharply reversed. Reforms generally threaten vested interests of important sections of the party and state bureaucracies, who are often able to block such measures, but when the conflict between 'reformers' and 'conservatives' becomes particularly bitter and public it may spill over into much wider political struggles. In any case, 'reforms' have not solved the tendencies to overinvestment in producer goods or enterprise autarky and have created new problems such as inflation, unemployment and large fluctuations in growth rates. Greater exposure to Western markets has meant that they have increasingly been affected by world booms and slumps.

We see no inevitable tendency for the Eastern societies to move progressively towards guided market systems. Neither do we envisage that the 'logic of industrialism' [24] will make the social structures and political systems of the East and West converge. All that we can say is that the Eastern countries, like the West, are capitalist, that there are many variations within this genus, and that there is no *general* theory about changes from one type to another.

Eastern social theorists analyse the social structures of their societies in conformity with the official ideology, a doctrine authoritatively pronounced under the imprimatur of the central leadership, supposedly based on a 'correct' interpretation and application of the theories of Marx and Lenin.[25] Wesolowski, as noted earlier, considers that the virtual elimination of privately owned capital leaves un-exploited classes remaining 'classes' only in a very weak sense. While it is true that privately owned smallholdings are a significant proportion of all agriculture in some Eastern countries, the farmers rarely, if ever, employ wage labour. Private non-agricultural capital seldom employs people outside the owner's family and is largely confined to creative, professional and service spheres. We agree with the official view that this vestigial class of private owners of the means of production appropriates an insignificant amount of surplus product, but deny that this disposes of the possibility that there is some other exploiting class.

The official social classifications are based on legally defined property relationships rather than actual control of the means of production. This approach allows the recogni-tion of two social classes, collectivised peasants and 'working class'; the former is related to the means of production as local jointly owned property 'socialised on a comparatively small scale',[26] while the latter is related to means of produc-tion which are 'socialised on a state scale and are therefore the property of the entire people.'[27] Whereas the income of the working class is based on national wage scales, the peasants' is a share of the difference between the collectives' sales and costs. It is true that peasants elect the collective's management and jointly decide details of the organisation of production but, in Russia at least, state planning authorities fix output quotas and planning policy.[28] State authorities take most, or all, of the collectively produced goods at a price they decide, thereby indirectly determining peasants' living standards. The low prices paid to the collec-tives for their product are no more evidence that the working class exploits the collective peasants than the high prices paid by the working class are proof that the reverse is the case; the difference between these two prices arises of course from taxation of agricultural goods. Any serious analysis of control of production and allocation must therefore examine the role of the state in this process, the uses to which state revenue is put and the constraints upon those uses.

The official theories accept that the working class is not homogeneous in income, education and social status but that such inequalities, while retaining an autonomous existence, will be increasingly 'removed from the determining influence of the relation to the means of production.'[29] They distinguish a number of strata within the working class, the principal division being between manual workers, the 'working class proper', and non-manual workers, the 'intelligentsia'; but they claim that the pattern of inequalities is rather complex with some manual workers higher on income and status than some non-manual workers. We accept that this may be so. We also readily agree that such inequalities are not in themselves proof of class differences.[30]

We have argued throughout this chapter that in the Eastern countries there is a class which controls the means of production as a whole but, to identify it, it is necessary to break down the category of 'intelligentsia', distinguishing senior state and party bureaucrats and enterprise managers (including collective farm chairmen).[31] It is evident that co-ordinated labour is separated from control in the East, but it is a rather futile exercise to fit each person into one box or another, just as with our analysis of the West we distinguish global capital from collective worker by their different functions in the accumulation of capital.

Lower officials, particularly party and trade union officials, may experience considerable strain in carrying out their roles as both agents of state capital among a particular group of workers and as the latter's representative to higher authorities. In periods of sharp class conflict these people are torn by conflicting loyalties.

As with capitalist classes in the West, there are more or less profound internal tensions and occasionally open conflict between sections of state capital. A recurrent source of controversy has been demands from national/regional factions for governmental decentralisation and reallocation of resources to the regions.

The enterprise manager is dependent upon both state and party officials for obtaining the resources necessary for achieving the targets, but needs to be free of their immediate supervision in order to make unorthodox innovations. This fact gives rise to a characteristic tension within the state capital, occasionally breaking out into factional conflicts between an alliance of managers and modernising officials against the 'old guard'.[32]

8

Class and Inequality

Inequalities of material reward are a recurring feature of all societies, except possibly the simplest hunting and gathering societies. In the case of Britain such inequalities have been increasingly well documented in recent years.[1] In the advanced capitalist societies of the West, of which Britain is but one example, the two most obvious sources of inequality are firstly inequalities of wealth (in particular inherited wealth), and secondly inequalities of earned income. Changes in the structure of both have occurred since the Second World War. For example, the proportion of large wealth holders has grown somewhat over the years – largely for reasons of tax avoidance[2] – and the earnings of lower-level white-collar workers have tended to overlap more and more with the earnings of better-paid manual workers.[3] Despite these modifications, however, the overall structure of inequalities of material condition in Britain has remained remarkably stable.

It is a sociological commonplace that inequality – whether in a positive or negative direction – is cumulative. Those with better-paid jobs are invariably likely to have longer holiday entitlements, better sick pay schemes, shorter hours of work, and other fringe benefits.[4] Additionally all of these advantages are often associated with inherently more interesting work tasks and better working conditions. It is self-evident that a better-than-average income enables the recipient to make better provision for himself and his family (if any) in respect of such things as housing, clothing, food, and entertainment, but even in areas of supposedly universal state provision such as health and education there are still considerable inequalities. For example, the most prestigious research and teaching hospitals are located in the 'middle-class' south-east, and (although of course there are exceptions) schools in working-class or slum areas are likely to be in old buildings, poorly equipped, with a subsequent difficulty in retaining the better teachers. Even more fundamentally, the less well paid die earlier, have a higher rate of infant mortality, and suffer more often from complaints such as stomach ulcers and heart disease, to say nothing of such occupational hazards as pneumonoconiosis and asbestosis, which are associated with *manual* work.[5] Nor are inequalities limited to those of material reward. Material advantages are causally connected with prestige, social esteem, or 'status', as Weber described it, access to power and the ability to influence decision making, and, crucially, the opportunity to do even better in the future.

We could document the kinds of inequalities referred to above in much more detail, but as we have already indicated this has already been done elsewhere, and is not a major focus of this book. The mapping of the differential distribution of material and non-material resources is an important empirical exercise, as is the development of the various taxonomies and classificatory schemes which lead to the effective description of these inequalities. However some sociologists have substituted, explicitly or implicitly, the documenting of such inequalities for class analysis itself.[6] Although such an approach is certainly less common nowadays, we would stress that the study of social class is not identical with the study of social inequality in general. Nevertheless any sound theory of social class should generate explanations of some of the facts of social inequality, although different theories will present different and possibly conflicting explanations. We would not claim that the class analysis we have been developing in this book is sufficient in itself to give a comprehensive explanation of the complex inequalities of distribution in all capitalist societies. However, we can utilise the general approach we have developed to give an explanation of the broad contours of inequality, and in so doing perhaps throw some light on the 'economic curiosities'[7] of the reward structure of contemporary capitalism.

Even in the capitalist societies of the West (where inheritance of capital is legally sanctioned, unlike the East) only a very small minority can expect to hold wealth sufficient to yield a return on investment which constitutes the whole, or a major part, of current income. For this reason, amongst others, our discussion of inequalities will focus on the vast majority of the population who either work for a living, are the dependants of employees, or exist on pensions which are themselves a reflection of income received during an active working life. This does not mean that we regard inequalities of wealth as unimportant. According to the most recent data, 1 per cent of the population owns 28 per cent, and 10 per cent of the population 67 per cent, of total private wealth.[8] If anything, these figures are an underestimate of the actual level of concentration of private wealth. They include, for example, housing. Although housing does in a sense constitute 'wealth', it is unlikely to be used as capital, as most housing in the wealth statistics is owner-occupied. Housing constituted 28 per cent of overall personal wealth in 1968, and 38 per cent by 1973, reflecting both an increase in the rate of owner-occupation and considerable inflation in house prices. However, for wealth holders in the £5000 bracket, housing constituted 59 per cent of their wealth, whereas at £200,000 housing only accounted for 8 per cent.[9] For this and other reasons the concentration of *productive* wealth in private hands is therefore certainly even greater than the figures indicate.

The reasons for the gross disparities in private wealth holding in the United Kingdom and other Western capitalist countries are not, in themselves, particularly difficult to explain. For these disparities depend, above all, on the institution of inheritance – the ability of wealth holders to pass on large amounts to their closest kin or other selected beneficiaries. Although examples of the 'self-made man' are widely publicised, they are in fact comparatively rare; the majority of major wealth holders began their careers backed by substantial inherited wealth.[10] Paradoxically, as has been pointed out:

inheritance has no logical place in that part of the
capitalist ethos which has paid lip service to the ideal
of the self-made man: to a right, and duty, of each
individual to make his own way in the world. Inheritance
is in flagrant breach of pretensions to equality of
opportunity.[11]

Given the continuing conflict between ideologies of equal
opportunity and the institution of inheritance, the problem
becomes one of explaining not why disparities of wealth
persist, but why such an obvious and built-in source of
advantage (and consequent disadvantage) as the institution
of inheritance should continue to be sanctioned. Such a
continuing sanction should certainly not be taken for granted.
Durkheim, for example, considered the institution of
inheritance 'abnormal', and argued that the problems
associated with the forced division of labour could not be
overcome without the abolition of inheritance.[12]

If we wish to explain the reasons for the persistence of
personal wealth in the West, despite the effects of various
forms of taxation such as (in Britain) death duties and capital
transfer tax, we must turn once again to our analysis of
the capitalist system of investment, production, realisation,
and accumulation. In the 'mixed economies' of the West,
as we demonstrated in Chapter Six, private capital exists side
by side with state capital. Private capital is found in a variety
of forms – agricultural estates, publicly quoted and private
companies, the great financial institutions such as banks,
insurance companies, pension funds and so on – all of which
amass wealth from small as well as large investors. Large
personal wealth holdings are characteristically distributed
through all of these forms of private capital, although of
course many great fortunes are also concentrated in a particular industrial firm, bank, or large estate. More often than
not the personal wealth holder acts as a *rentier*, and personal
capital is managed by industrial and commercial institutions.

In the West private wealth, itself a reflection of the rate
of accumulation, plays a vital role in maintaining the level
of investment and production. Any sustained attempt to break
up or take over private wealth (for example, by the state)

is likely to result in a flight of capital, usually abroad. Similarly, foreign capital would be extremely wary of placing investment in a country where it might be subject to excessive taxation, or even take-over. Investors will not continue to invest unless their capital is reasonably safe, and in addition yields a reasonable return on investment. For all of these reasons, therefore, large holdings are unlikely to be seriously eroded during the lifetime of the wealth holder (although they could be dissipated through overconsumption or bad investment), as such an attack would constitute an attack on capital itself. This would of course undermine the viability of the system as a whole. The structural dominance of capital, in addition, often ensures that capital is actually augmented during a lifetime, as well as providing a more than decent income for its possessor.

This relative 'safety' of personal wealth during the lifetime of the wealth holder to some extent explains the persistence of inheritance despite taxation. Most forms of wealth taxation to date have taken the biggest slice on the death of the wealth holder, therefore taxation has been avoided by transfers of wealth during his or her lifetime. The transfer of wealth *inter vivos* is to a large extent responsible for the redistribution of personal wealth from the top one or two per cent to the top ten per cent or so during the last fifty years. It is perhaps misleading to term this 'redistribution', as the desired effect, of course, is to retain this wealth within the family. More particularly, wealth holders, or their agents, have supremely privileged access to and participation in the dominant (capitalist) power structure, and are therefore in a unique position to protect their own interests and those of their dependants. The concentration of personal wealth, therefore, is likely to be a continuing feature of a mixed economy.

The argument summarised above is a major element in the central thesis advanced in a recent work on the British class structure: *Class in a Capitalist Society* by Westergaard and Resler. Although there is much in the book with which we would agree, we would fundamentally disagree with the theoretical approach to the class structure taken by the authors and consequently the central place of *private* property

ownership to their analysis. As defined by Westergaard and
Resler, class in itself is seen as a 'set of closely related inequalities of economic condition, power and opportunity.'[13]
These classes are identified as structured 'life-chances', much
as in Weberian class analysis. Westergaard and Resler then
provide a comprehensive and empirically detailed account
of the manner in which property ownership, labour market
pressures, and state activity combine so as to maintain a persisting structure of class inequality. A significant departure
from the neo-Weberian framework in their analysis, however,
is that property is not treated analytically as if it were a
particular kind of market capacity, but is given a central
place in the overall system of capitalist production and
accumulation. Thus *private* property is held to be *the* key
factor in the understanding of social class and the persistence
of class inequalities. 'Property and property relations play
the key part in forming the contours of inequality',[14] and
again, 'private capital is the central force behind . . .
inequalities of life circumstances'.[15] However, as we have
suggested, whereas we would concur with Westergaard and
Resler in their insistence that private property should be
analysed as *capital*, rather than simply as an enhancer of
'life-chances', it should be obvious by now that we would
not restrict the analysis of capital and its effect *vis-à-vis* the
class structure to private property; rather we would
emphasise the global function of capital. The global
function of capital, as we have seen, is by no means only
to be associated with the private ownership of capital.
It is true that:

> the concentration of high incomes in few hands arises in
> substantial part from a still sharper concentration of
> property in private ownership. Less directly but more
> significantly: because the principles which govern allo-
> cation and use of most resources reflect the dominance of
> private capital. The routine assumptions that set the
> principal parameters of life and policy are capitalist.[16]

However we would argue that it is not just *private* capital
whose dominance is reflected in the 'allocation and use of

most resources', and 'set the principal parameters of life
and policy', but the dominance of the global function of
capital.

Inequalities of wealth holding give rise, in large part,
to the concentration of incomes at the very top of the hierarchy
which has been documented by Westergaard and Resler. The
distribution of *earned* incomes, although it does not show
such great disparities as unearned incomes, still reveals considerable differences. In 1975, for example, whilst a sales
manager earned £85, and a higher civil servant £92, for
a 38-hour week, a goods driver earned £49 for a 48-hour
week, a dustman £47 for a 44-hour week, and, towards the
bottom of the income hierarchy, a farm worker £37 for a
45-hour week.[17] As with the wealth statistics, such figures
are probably an underestimate of existing inequalities. The
averaging technique will tend to obscure the really high
incomes – for example, in 1972 the director of a trading
stamp company was earning £260,000 a year. Neither do the
weekly incomes cited include any attempt to calculate the
value of fringe benefits – for example, it has recently (1976)
been calculated that the value of a company car to an
employee is about £808 a year.[18]

Although it would be a gross exaggeration to claim that
any sort of societal agreement existed concerning these
inequalities of earned income, it is nevertheless true that
they have persisted for many years, like the institution of
inheritance, without being seriously challenged. Indeed the
need to preserve differentials is built into the bargaining
strategy of many trade unions; there is no doubt that among
manual workers it is often considered right and proper that
a skilled man should receive more than an unskilled man.
All of this indicates that there are powerful forces at work
which apparently explain such inequalities.

Explanations – or legitimations – of inequalities of earned
income are many and various, and we cannot hope to review
all of them in detail here. For the sake of brevity, and
at the risk of some over simplification, we will consider
such explanations under three broad headings or categories.
Firstly, those explanations which assert that inequalities of
earned income are a measure of the market value or worth

of the employee. Secondly, those explanations which assert
that the pattern of income inequalities reflects the functional
importance (or lack of it) of various occupations to society,
and thirdly, those explanations which argue that the unequal
structure of rewards reflects some kind of 'social consensus'
as to the value of the work done.

The broad assumption that wage inequalities reflect the
price of labour in the market is the basis of traditional
economic theories of wage determination.[17] It is assumed that
the supply of labour and the demand for labour reach
an equilibrium point at which the wage rate will be
determined. The underlying assumptions of this model are
also rational and individualistic: labour will calculate its
maximum advantage, and thus offer itself where the highest
return can be obtained, and the employer will try to obtain
labour at the lowest rate possible. Wage rates, therefore,
are fixed by supply and demand, with each side trying to
maximise relative advantages. In real life, of course, nothing
approaching this hypothetical state of perfect competition is
ever found. For example, the model implicity assumes
mobility of labour, that labour will be able to make itself
available so as to maximise market opportunities. Many
factors however combine to inhibit the mobility of labour,
amongst the most important of which is housing. A man,
especially if he has a family, often cannot move in order
to gain a higher return for his labour, simply because he
has nowhere to live. Perhaps the employer might try to sur-
mount these difficulties by offering housing with the job,
but then a further imperfection will have to be accommo-
dated within the market model. For the provision of company
housing means that the worker is tied to employment by
other factors than the return for labour per se, thus labour
mobility is further hampered. Other features designed to
attract labour in the first place – for example, occupational
pension schemes – will also inhibit the mobility of labour.

Economists have to varying extents modified their theories
to take account of variations from the basic competitive
model. Perhaps foremost among the facts which demand
that the theory be modified is the emergence of the institutions of collective bargaining, institutions which funda-

mentally belie the rational individualism in which classical economic theories of wages are grounded. Economic theory in general has failed to reach any consensus as to whether trade union activity has had any permanent effect on the overall pattern of distribution between capital and labour, but it seems to be generally accepted that trade unions have had more or less significant effects on wage rates at less aggregate levels.[20] Conversely the employers, or more often the employers and the state in combination, can act so as to hold down wages below the level they would reach in a situation of free collective bargaining; this has been the effect of recent attempts at incomes policy. Different groups will be differentially affected according to the extent that they are 'caught' by legislation.

In the case of labour not all maximisation is rationally directed towards material rewards. Some workers may value certain features of the job – for example, congenial workmates, or inherently interesting work – to the extent of staying in that employment even if they could obtain better material rewards elsewhere.[21] Although such preferences *can* be built into a market model of wage determination, they are by their very nature unquantifiable, and as such difficult to accommodate within the framework of orthodox economics. A further complicating factor, once the notion of job preference has been introduced, is that many of the apparently more attractive areas of employment in the non-material sense, that is jobs offering creativity, interest, good working conditions, the ability to participate in the decision-making process, and so on, are in fact those which offer the highest levels of material reward as well.[22] If non-material factors are to be built into the economist's models, therefore, this would appear to be a major example of the theory being seriously at variance with the facts.

We have not outlined all of the difficulties encountered by a market-based model of wage inequalities, but the major thrust of our criticism has been to demonstrate that the structure of the market in the real world bears so little relation to the underlying competitive model that the general theory can be of only limited explanatory utility. If we want to explain the *actual* structure of differentials, substantial modifications must be built into any market-based model. In fact this is what has been achieved by much neo-Weberian class analysis. The major strength of neo-Weberian class analysis, as compared to economic theory, is that it has always perceived the market as a set of *social* relationships, embodying structures which go far beyond the simple sale and purchase of labour power as a commodity. Giddens' account of 'structuration', for example, focuses upon 'the modes in which "economic" relationships become translated into "non-economic" social structures'.[23] The three basic kinds of market capacity identified by Giddens, property ownership, educational or technical qualifications, and manual labour power, are embedded in and reinforced by a structure of work relationships, authority relationships and community relationships which are not, in the economist's sense, 'economic', but 'social'. Parkin's analysis of 'closure' has perhaps a closer affinity to economic theory in that it analyses attempts by different 'classes' to achieve a monopolistic or oligopolistic market situation.[24] Nevertheless his account of closure strategies takes full account of social as well as economic factors. As Parkin argues, claims of birth or race can be just as effective as apparently more rational elements such as 'qualifications' in laying claim to an enhanced share of material rewards.

Despite the criticisms we have made above, it must be accepted that market-based explanations do provide in part an explanation of income differentials from employment, especially when 'social' factors, such as those identified by neo-Weberian sociologists, are taken into account. If a skill – say medical skill – is absolutely vital to a society, and the skill is in short supply, then demand will exceed supply and the possessors of the skill will be able to obtain more for their services. However, we would still argue that much of the market-based explanation of differentials can only be partial. For ultimately in such explanations the only standard of value is price, therefore the definition or explanation of the value of skills, and thus differentials, is inherently circular. We can see how different groups vie for advantage in an imperfect market, but we have still not satisfactorily explained *why* particular attributes or skills are 'more valued' in the first place. In a minority of cases short-term differentials may realistically be explained by market factors – for example, the remuneration of computer programmers during the computer boom of the early sixties. In many more cases, however, such explanations are simply not sufficient. Historically the comparison of manual and non-manual labour is probably the best known example. Once universal literacy had been more or less achieved, the skills necessary for clerical work could hardly be said to be in short supply, yet the manual/non-manual differential is only now being slowly eroded.

An answer to the question as to why it is that some skills or attributes are more highly rewarded than others might initially appear to be supplied by the second broad category of explanations of inequality we have noted above – that of functional importance. That is, the rewards for particular skills or attributes are held to be not just an outcome of market forces, but also to reflect the functional importance of the skill or attribute to the society as a whole. The manager is worth more than the shop-floor employee because what the manager does is more important than what the shop-floor worker does. (Such explanations of societal worth overlap to a considerable extent with market-based explanations, especially as the supposed worth of functionally more necessary occupations is often further buttressed by pointing to the expensive and time-consuming training associated with such occupations.)[25] Thus, in the words of Davis and Moore, 'Social inequality is thus an unconsciously evolved device by which societies ensure that the most important positions are conscientiously filled by the most qualified persons'.[26] Criticisms of this explanation of inequality are legion, not least from within the broadly functionalist sociological perspective itself. Does functional importance have to be acknowledged by material rewards alone – what about the inner satisfactions deriving from functionally important work? What about the possible *dysfunctions* to which structures of inequality might give rise? For structures of inequality rarely, if ever, approach anything like a true meritocracy, and the existence of inheritance and cumulative advantage (to which we have already referred) might well result in 'the most important positions' being filled by *less* 'qualified persons', and conversely debar those with the relevant aptitudes from occupying the most important positions.[27] More fundamentally, how is 'functional importance' to be ascertained? If we claim that functional importance can be identified according to the degree of material reward, then the definition is circular, and in any case open to the kinds of objections noted above. If we attempt to define functional importance – say, according to the extent to which some occupational roles affect or control other work roles – we would find functional importance to be associated with power. But we would still not have broken out of the circularity of definition making – are roles functionally important because they are powerful or powerful because they are functionally important? – and we return yet again to the basic problem of providing a coherent explanation of exactly *why* particular attributes or work roles should be more highly rewarded.

In fact we often find that functional explanations of inequality are associated with the third broad category of explanation of inequality we have identified – that of the 'social consensus' as to occupational worth. We note this as an academic fact, although we would stress that 'functional importance' and 'social consensus' are logically independent explanations: logically functional importance could be demonstrated without there being any consensus as to the level of reward, and societal evaluation might not correctly identify functional importance. The consensus approach argues that the structure of income inequalities reflects some sort of moral consensus about what is 'most valuable' in society as a whole. For example, the medical practitioner cited above does not continue to receive a relatively high income because the medical profession controls the supply of entrants and is also monopolistically organised, but because his or her intrinsic worth as a healer is accepted by society as being more valuable than that of a primary school-teacher or a dustman. Empirically there is much that would seem to support such a view. With the possible exception of the very highest and the very lowest incomes, the structure of income differentials seems to be largely accepted as legitimate.[28] Data on occupational prestige – what Parkin has termed a 'moral referendum' – collected from random samples of the population has shown that those occupations ranked highest by the public at large are also likely to be those which generate the highest incomes; a finding which would seem to indicate some sort of consensus about the distribution of rewards.[29]

As with market-based explanations, we would not reject the social consensus explanation of differentials out of hand. There is no doubt that perceptions of 'customary standards' and 'traditional differentials' do play a large part in maintaining the structure of inequalities, and are viewed as acceptable by the population at large. However the fact that inequalities *are* viewed as acceptable has not been taken for granted by many social scientists. Briefly, it has been argued that, far from being an accurate reflection of a *common* value system (a basic assumption of the social consensus explanation), the acceptability of differentials in fact reflects the successful imposition of the *dominant* value system (or ideology) on the subordinate population. In Lockwood's words, 'a dominant class has never existed which did not seek to make its position legitimate by placing the highest value on those qualities and activities which come closest to its own.'[30] Indeed, when we examine the nature of the 'most valued' qualities and activities, as reflected in the income/occupation hierarchy, we find that they do tend to correspond to dominant class attributes. If we take, for example, the ubiquitous distinction between manual and non-manual labour, it requires little insight to perceive that the supposed superiority of non-manual work reflects the values of a dominant class for which work, if at all acceptable, should be as far removed from manual labour as possible. More specifically the increasing frequency of job-evaluation schemes enables us to identify which elements of work are in fact accorded the highest material rewards. As Hyman has pointed out, four features of the work task are conventionally identified in job evaluation schemes: 'responsibility', 'skill' (or educational qualifications), 'effort' (or manual labour) and 'working conditions', and 'the two former categories are normally assigned a weighting [i.e. entitlement to material reward] more than double that of the latter two.'[31] Why *should* greater material rewards be accorded to responsibility and educational qualifications? Hyman's answer is that both are associated with structures of power. Formal education 'is powerfully influenced by class origins, and . . . in turn provide[s] a crucial medium of career advancement to positions of high prestige and material reward.'[32] Responsibility 'in a hierarchical and undemocratic structure of industrial governance is primarily a euphemism for domination.'[33] In short the prevailing reward structure is nothing more than a reflection of the dominant power structure in Western industrial societies.

Hyman's conclusions have been echoed by many other social scientists. We would agree that the structure of income inequalities from employment is not a result of consensual evaluations of social worth, but to a large extent corresponds to established patterns of power and domination. However, as an explanation of income inequalities, it has analytical deficiencies which parallel those of the market forces explanation – it is inherently circular. 'Power and domination' has been substituted for 'price'; we still lack any explanation of *why* particular groups are powerful, or *why* particular attributes *are* associated with structures of power. It is here, we would suggest, that the framework of analysis we developed earlier in this book can be applied so as to give a coherent account of the structures which underlie patterns of power and domination. For distribution relations, we would argue, are in the broadest sense structured by capitalist relationships of production.

PRODUCTION AND DISTRIBUTION

In volume three of *Capital* Marx states that:

> The so-called distribution relations . . . correspond to and arise from historically determined specific social forms of the process of production and mutual relations entered into by men in the reproduction process of human life. The historical character of these distribution relations is the historical character of production relations, of which they express merely one aspect.[34]

This bald statement requires considerable expansion. As it stands, it is wide open to the kind of criticism pithily summarised by Giddens: 'it is not legitimate to claim that, because men must eat to live, their mode of life is necessarily determined by the manner in which they produce what they eat.[35] To take up such a position would be patently absurd. In particular we would emphasise that production relations in no sense determine the details of distribution; patterns of distribution in capitalist societies will show considerable variation depending on the history of the particular society, local labour market variations, the evolution of property ownership, the manner of capitalist development and so on. Although we are not therefore offering a universal explanation of *all* structures of distribution, we would claim that some features are common to the structure of earned incomes in all capitalist societies.

The development of the capitalist mode of production, as we argued earlier, results in a transformation of the labour process – indeed we may legitimately refer to the 'capitalist labour process'. To recognise the powerful constraining force of the economic system is not 'crude economic determinism'. It should be obvious, for example, that a capitalist entrepreneur simply could not survive competitively if the production techniques and scattered labour force of the precapitalist era were retained while his competitors were installing new machinery and establishing factories.[36] We would argue, therefore, that we can best begin to understand the unequal structure of incomes from employment if we examine the development of the capitalist labour process, and the associated emergence of the global function of capital on the one hand, and the collective worker on the other. Our starting point has been well summarised by Braverman: 'the technical features of the labor process are now dominated by the social features which the capitalist has introduced: that is to say, the new relations of production . . . *the labor process has become the responsibility of the capitalist* . . . it thus becomes essential for the capitalist that *control* over the labor process pass from the hands of the worker into his own.'[37] That is, the need to maintain and if possible increase the rate of capitalist accumulation means that the capitalist must assume control over the labour process, and as a result some elements of the labour process are now carried out by agents of the capitalist function – that is, management. The gradual development of control over the labour process, and the associated work-force, has been a long and painful business involving a variety of strategies which are now fused together in the 'managerial' role complex. Most obviously it may be attempted through the imposition of more or less rigorous work disciplines – what we have earlier referred to as the work of control. However, effective control is difficult to enforce and maintain if the organisation of the labour process itself is left to the discretion of the work-force. Thus, characteristically, this discretion – which we earlier referred to as coordination – is removed from the work-force and redefined as an element of the managerial role. Coordination within the capitalist labour process has been developed and carried out external to labour, on behalf of capital.[38] Although such coordination is analytically a part of the function of the collective worker, in practice it is almost invariably associated with strategies of control, and indeed.may be indistinguishable from control. Thus we find associated with the capitalist labour process hierarchical authority structures in which the coordination necessary to *any* complex labour process is fused with control. The supervisor does not simply supervise, but supervises as the agent of capital. We would suggest that authority relationships within the capitalist labour process (we refer to unproductive labour processes here as well as productive) are characteristically antagonistic not least because supervision is 'the personification of capital in the direct process of production'.[39] Differential rewards can be explained at least in part by the need to preserve and maintain a structure of authority, and ensure that it continues to be exercised on behalf of capital.[40] In some cases a particular work role may be only historically associated with authority, or, though lacking in any direct supervisory content, require the characteristics traditionally associated with authority (usually 'intellectual' as opposed to 'manual' skills; we would suggest that much white-collar work falls into these categories). In such cases a degree of material advantage is required if the integrity of the dominant structure of capitalist authority is to be preserved. In the establishing of different incomes from employment, there is no doubt that authority (or 'responsibility', or 'decision-making') is a key factor in justifying unequal rewards. For example, in a case known to one of the authors, skilled workers were hastily assigned completely fictitious 'supervisory' duties during the introduction of a job-evaluation scheme in order to ensure that more or less the existing pattern of differentials would be preserved after job evaluation.

In addition, those in positions of authority are in the unique position of being able to determine their own levels of income from employment, levels which are hardly likely to be low.

> Directors and senior managers cannot in real terms be seen as deriving their salaries and other rewards primarily from the sale of their labour in the market. They are able in large part to determine their own remuneration. . . . Their rewards, in considerable measure, are a claim on profit.[41]

However, although participation in or association with authority is probably the major factor influencing income differentials, it is clearly not the whole story. As we have seen in the examples cited above, both skills and technical expertise are in general widely regarded as deserving an enhanced level of material reward. Although market conditions and societal evaluation both play a part in determining the level of skilled incomes, we would argue, again, that the differentials accorded to skill can be seen as being at least in part a consequence of the development of the capitalist labour process.

In our preceding discussion we have described how co-ordination has been, as far as possible, isolated from the labourer and developed on behalf of the capitalist function. Although we can maintain the analytical distinction, in a very real sense, coordination is an aspect of *skill*, and the development of coordination by management incorporates, or is followed by, the 'deskilling' of the labour process. The deskilling of the labour process has been a continuing feature of the development of the capitalist labour process, and historically the work of Frederick Winslow Taylor (the father of scientific management) provides us with one of the clearest and best-documented examples. Taylor's own words make the strategy so clear that they require little commentary from us:

> to work according to scientific laws, the management must take over and perform much of the work which is now left to the men. . . . The managers assume . . . the burden of gathering together all of the traditional knowledge which in the past has been *possessed by the workmen* and then of classifying, tabulating, and reducing this knowledge to rules, laws and formulae. . . . It is only through *enforced* standardization of methods, *enforced* adoption of the best implements and working conditions, and *enforced* co-operation [sic!] that this faster work can be assured. And the duty of enforcing the adoption of standards and of enforcing this co-operation rests with the *management* alone. . . . All of those who, after proper teaching, either will not or cannot work in accordance with the new methods and at the higher speed must be discharged by the *management*.[42]

Taylor's prescription is obvious. The 'work' to be taken over by the management does not involve the managers in actually manning the lathes or loading the pig iron, rather, managerial 'work' is to systematically locate all of the elements of skill in the labour process, and from the best of these elements develop the 'one best way' of carrying out any task, then imposing this 'one best way' on the work-force. A consequence of course is that any skill or discretion possessed by the workman has been removed. The transfer of skill to the management (or global capitalist) function enhances both productivity and managerial control, and thus increases relative surplus value.

Work which has been successfully deskilled is characteristic of the 'low discretion' syndrome outlined by Fox.[43] Because discretion has been so effectively removed from the work task, the worker is subject to rigid supervision in order to ensure that work is carried out as prescribed. Communication is one-way from the manager to the managed, and little trust is experienced on either side. Inadequate performance by the worker is defined as 'insubordination', the worker feels no *personal* responsibility for maintaining the level of performance. Because of mutual distrust and associated factors, formal relationships between manager and managed take the form of conflict-ridden collective bargaining. Thus although the deskilling of the work task may enhance managerial control in one sense, it brings with it other control problems, to which we will shortly return. Also, although deskilling is a widespread feature of the development of the capitalist labour process, we would for obvious reasons never suggest that *all* paid employment has been similarly deskilled. In the first place, the administration of skills itself gives rise to work roles in which the use of discretion is a prescribed necessity. In the second place, by no means all work lends itself to the deskilling process.[44] Finally, there is considerable evidence that where possible the work-force will systematically resist attempts to remove discretion from the work process, and evolve methods of working which effectively feed back in control over the labour process.[45] Nevertheless these instances do not undermine our contention that on the whole the capitalist function will seek to remove and/or control the skill element from and in the labour process.

Thus although the majority of work roles in developed capitalist society are 'low discretion' there will always persist a substantial minority of 'high discretion' work roles, including such occupations as senior managers, functional specialists, research scientists, lawyers, small élite military units, top administrative groups, and so on.[46] In order that the process of capitalist production and accumulation may be maintained, it is essential that the commitment of such role occupants to the dominant social and political organisation (or mode of production) is assured. Because such work roles embody a high level of discretion these employees could be potentially dangerous, or at least a considerable nuisance, if they failed to make the decisions and judgements inherent in their work roles in the light of the interests and goals of their employers. The more discretion embodied in a work role the more real is such a danger. It is crucial therefore to ensure that as far as possible the occupants of high discretion work roles – 'experts' – have similar values, interests and goals to their superiors and employers. Experts can be and are assimilated socially, but, more importantly, they are usually offered a level of rewards and opportunities which make it clear that they are viewed as a part of the capitalist function.[47]

We would argue, therefore, that the expert is rewarded not only because of the enhanced market value of scarce skills, or because of proximity or association with a dominant class, but because the expert, given the development of the capitalist labour process, is an essential and integral adjunct of the global function of capital.

Our discussion so far has centred on the manner in which skills *initially* evolved *within* the labour process have been appropriated by, or brought under the control of, the capitalist function. Another aspect of 'expertise' to which we would draw attention is what we will term, for want of a better word, 'science'. Unlike 'skill', 'science' is initially developed outside of the labour process and subsequently applied to it. Much has been written on the relationship between science and production and we can only hope to give a crude summary here. Briefly, it would appear that the 'first industrial revolution' was carried out using the tools and techniques developed by previous modes of production. Scientific improvements were only applied as and when the increases in productivity engendered by the transformation of the *social* relations of production – the capitalist organisation of labour – made them necessary. For example, the use of chlorine and sulphuric acid in cloth finishing was introduced only when the amount of cloth produced was so great (as a result of factory organisation and technical improvements) that the supply of bleaching meadows and buttermilk simply was not sufficient to cope with the supply of cloth.[48] However, with the increasing dominance of the capitalist mode of production and the development of the capitalist labour process, science itself is transformed from a somewhat amateur preserve to be utilised as and when necessary, and is developed in association with the capitalist function. Science, as a social property, has become an adjunct of capital.[49] Massive resources are now diverted into research and development by industrial firms. In developed capitalist countries, the state bears much of the cost of scientific research, thus socialising the costs of production.[50] The tension between pure and applied scientific endeavour is of course still there. Even today pure scientists are gently berated for the lack of attention they pay, or low status they accord, to industry, but such is the effectiveness of the dominant ideology that this industry is represented as neutral, or even 'for the good of the whole', rather than for what it is – the capitalist mode of production and accumulation.[51] As with skill, science has been more or less successfully integrated with and is now developed by the capitalist function. The rewards accorded to the scientific expert must therefore be seen as at least in part as reflecting this integration of science.

In summary, differential incomes from employment *are* in part to be explained by the strategic manipulation of the market by particular occupational groups, and the over-all structure of differentials *is* buttressed by the dominant class and legitimated through the dominant ideology. Never-theless, as we have been attempting to illustrate in our dis-cussion above, if we wish to explain why particular features of employment have a high market value, or why they are closely associated with the dominant class, we would argue that the explanation is to be found in the development of capitalist relations of production, and the associated develop-ment of the capitalist labour process. For 'authority' and 'expertise' – and associated synonyms such as 'responsibility', 'decision making' and 'trouble shooting' on the one hand, together with 'scientific excellence', 'skill' or 'qualifications' on the other – are all attributes which have been developed and administered by the capitalist function and have had to be so developed in order to maintain the rate of accumula-tion of the capitalist production process.

In arguing our case we have certainly oversimplified a number of points, perhaps giving the impression that the explanation we have suggested is unproblematic. We would not wish to imply this as we feel that we have only sketched out the beginnings of an explanation of inequalities derived from Marxist class theory, rather than provided a comprehensive account. In particular, some problems associated with the analysis of skill and expertise can be indicated here. We have already indicated that although the deskilling of work enhances managerial control it also brings with it associated control problems. Firstly, as Fox has emphasised,[52] no work can be so completely deskilled as to remove all discretionary content, therefore all work, even if only to a very limited extent, depends upon the 'voluntary' cooperation of the work force. Such contractual participation is in fact a feature of the capitalist mode of production, work *could* be forced on a reluctant labour force through slavery or serfdom, but in such cases the analysis we have been developing through this book would not apply. There is ample evidence that the deskilling of work is covertly or overtly rejected and resented by the workforce, a resentment which may make even a minimal level of voluntary commitment difficult to obtain. For example, after Ford had developed the assembly line production of automobiles, 'so great was labor's distaste for the new machine system that toward the close of 1913 every time the company wanted to add 100 men to its factory personnel, it was necessary to hire 963'[53]. Such problems of recruitment will be particularly acute during periods of relatively full employment, when boring and unsatisfying work may be explicitly compensated by relatively high pay. But, as Westergaard has argued:

> if the . . . worker is tied to his work only by the size, security, and potential growth of his wage packet . . . his commitment is clearly a brittle one. He may be willing to accept the lack of other interests and satisfactions in the job, for the sake of the money. But should the amount and dependability of the money be threatened, his resigned toleration of the lack of discretion, control and 'meaning' attached to the job could no longer be guaranteed. The 'cash nexus' may snap just because it is *only* a cash nexus, because it is single-stranded; and if it does snap, there

is nothing else to bind the worker to acceptance of his situation.[54]

'Maintaining commitment' has thus become a *managerial* problem, along with the more usual managerial functions of control and decision making. This problem has been reflected in academic literature by the growth of the 'neo-human relations' school of management thinking, which, paradoxically, parallels Marx's analysis of the subjective effects of alienation in modern work with its emphasis on the need for 'self-actualisation', 'motivation', 'enrichment', etc.[55] Where such ideas have taken root we now find an initially confusing picture of the apparent reversal of the previous seventy years of managerial development, with conscious efforts being made by management to selectively feed back elements of discretion and variety into the work task, thus enhancing the level of participation and therefore commitment amongst the work force. Such attempts are not widespread, and are still at an early stage, but they apparently constitute such a radical departure from previous practices that we must at least raise the problem of their implications. Bosquet, for example, has argued that such attempts by management may boomerang against capital: the restoration of meaning to work itself may lead to the questioning of the structure of social relationships in which work is located.[56] At the moment such a radical requestioning seems unlikely. Management may be feeding in discretion, but it is very much a management-controlled process, and we should not suppose that managements are unaware of the potential dangers of unlimited discretion, even if we accept that many genuinely feel the need to modify dehumanising work. Indeed, as long as the feedback is controlled by management, the dictates of prudence are likely to ensure that, in the immortal words of one of Nichol's respondents:

> You move from one boring, dirty, monotonous job to another boring, dirty, monotonous job. And then to another boring, dirty, monotonous job. And somehow you're supposed to come out of it all 'enriched'. But I never feel enriched – I just feel knackered.[57]

Neither are such enrichment schemes likely to lend to any radical restructuring of differentials, apart from perhaps smoothing out even further the skill/semi-skilled distinctions *within* the manual sector. Such schemes are often associated with the implementation of productivity deals, and experience has shown that the initial income gains of a productivity deal are often subsequently eroded in the years following the deal.[58]

Another feature of capitalist industrial development which would initially appear to undermine the deskilling hypothesis are the changes in the nature of work and occupational structure brought about by the second industrial revolution. If the first industrial revolution utilised energy technology, the second industrial revolution is founded on information technology – in particular the introduction of electronic data processing and information provision. The kind of work generated by the second industrial revolution is said to be such that the worker no longer has to submit to the dictates and pace of a machine, but receives information, acts upon it, and in general *controls* the machine rather than being directly controlled by it.

> [The worker] is no longer embedded in the technology, contributing his energy to it or even his manipulative skill, but outside it, handling information from it and himself becoming a source of information critical for its management. This change of position and role makes him in fact a manager, different in degree but not in kind from those who traditionally have carried this title.[59]

If such a revolution in work is in fact occurring, the implications are profound. The demands of modern technology are held to be such that for practical purposes the dividing line between 'manager' and 'managed' is being broken down, thus a transformation in social relationships will eventually occur and a form of participatory democracy ensue. It is not suggested that income differentials would break down as well, but logically this should also be a consequence. This is what may be termed the 'orthodox' interpretation of the effect of such technological changes.[60] The more radical interpretation of such changes parallels Bosquet's comments on the effects of job enrichment. It has been argued that the central location of such workers in the production process, and their control and understanding of such processes, has the effect of placing these workers in the vanguard of the 'new working class'.[61] In short, their work experience will lead them to question the structure of production relationships, and such workers may well lead or radicalise the rest of the working class in revolutionary consciousness. In fact we are rather sceptical of both of the interpretations summarised above. It is by no means universally agreed that the second industrial revolution has invariably led to work of the nature described in the passage we have just quoted – Braverman, for example, argues that the main effect of information technology has been to further undermine craft work.[62] Whilst we feel it is incontestable that some information technology work is inherently satisfying, the technology has probably generated even more jobs which by any standards are routine, dull, and boring – automatic data card punching, for example. It has also been shown that although there may be cases where theoretically the technology could or should give rise to more interesting work, market demands and product changes have meant that this has not happened – it is not the technology *alone* which determines the nature of the work.[63] Finally, it is by no means clear that the technology of the second industrial revolution will or can be applied to all production. Even if we accept, therefore, that new technologies generate some more interesting, high discretion work, it would appear that for a variety of reasons only a very small minority of the occupations generated by the second industrial revolution fall into this category, so neither participatory democracy nor revolution should be realistically anticipated as a consequence. In any case, although work-place socialisation is crucial and important, not all such socialisation is mediated through work itself, and other, non-work factors are also important.[64]

We do not think, therefore, that the evidence so far has indicated that either neo-human relations, managerial administration or the effects of the second industrial revolution have had a fundamental effect on the capitalist labour process or the associated structure of income differentials. Our basic argument – that the enhanced rewards accorded to authority and expertise reflect their incorporation and association with the capitalist function – therefore still holds good. What this discussion has demonstrated, however, is the ongoing nature of the development of the capitalist mode of production and the capitalist labour process, and the consequent need to maintain a flexible approach to both theory and its interpretation, rather than doggedly trying to force facts into a stationary theoretical mould.

In this chapter we have tried to provide a coherent theoretical explanation of the structure and persistence of material inequalities – in particular inequalities of earned income – in developed capitalist society. In developing our explanation (derived from capitalist production relationships) we have tried at all times to emphasise that it is not comprehensive: it cannot explain the detail of and variations in material inequality across the whole range of developed capitalist societies. We have, however, tried to establish some general principles. Firstly, in mixed capitalist economies (generally speaking, those of the West) concentrations of wealth outside state control are unlikely to be eroded for as long as they continue to maintain the rate of accumulation. Secondly, the broad structure of income inequalities from employment can to a large extent be explained by the development of the global function of capital in monopoly capitalism and the capitalist labour process. These kinds of inequalities are to be found in state capitalist countries of the East, as well as in the West – authority and expertise are universally rewarded. The fact that we have identified authority as a major determinant of income inequality does not in any sense imply that we consider authority to be an independent dimension in relation to the class structure; we would stress that authority assumes a *particular* (and antagonistic) form given capitalist production relationships. Dahrendorf, for example, has argued that authority *is* such an independent dimension. [65] We would argue that he persists in this mistaken assumption because he has failed, in his rejection of Marx's analytical framework, to systematically consider production relationships, concentrating instead on the role of *private* property in Marx's analysis. Dahrendorf thus assumes that authority relationships are invariably antagonistic and subsequently give rise to conflicts and tensions. We, on the other hand, have argued that the antagonistic form assumed by authoritative coordination in modern society can be seen as a manifestation of the antagonistic *social* relations engendered by the capitalist mode of production, and it is not inconceivable that, given an alternative mode of production, coordination could be achieved without giving rise to tensions and antagonsims.

9

The Political Economy
of Class

In this chapter we bring together arguments developed earlier in the book in order to draw a preliminary 'map' of the capitalist class structure. This map will be constructed directly from the elements we have identified in our analysis of the capitalist economy in Chapters Five and Six – that is, the generation, realisation and allocation of value in complex capitalist societies.

We define class situations by locations in the flows of surplus product, the primary axis of differentiation being control versus coordinated labour, other axes being capital versus non-capital, and state versus private ownership. More explicitly, class situations are initially defined by three elements: (1) whether the position entails control, coordinated labour or both; (2) whether the enterprise in which the position is located is a capital, non-capital, or both (i.e. quasi-capital); (3) whether the capital, non-capital or quasi-capital is state owned or privately owned. (In practice state ownership will be confined to quasi-capitals and non-capitals.)

All three of the elements defined above derive directly from our account of the structure of the capitalist mode of production in contemporary capitalism. The distinction between capital and labour embodied in the first element is a universal feature of *any* capitalist mode of production at *any* stage of development. This distinction, and the irreconcilable conflict of interests implied by this distinction is therefore, we would argue, the primary axis of class differentiation in any capitalist society. Although the second and third elements, like the first element, have been derived from an economic analysis of contemporary capitalism, they are to a large extent a consequence of the *development* of the capitalist mode of production. Much of our argument and discussion so far has been concerned to demonstrate that despite modifications the underlying functions of control and coordination, global capitalist and collective worker, still persist in capitalist societies. Therefore, although we insist that the distinction between control and coordinated labour is the primary axis of class differentiation in capitalist societies, its presence and significance cannot be grasped unless we simultaneously locate both functions within the complex sectional structure of modern capitalism. For this reason we develop our initial class map in terms of all three elements, although the capital/non-capital and state/ private distinctions are, we argue, not primary axes of class differentiation. Indeed, as our discussion will illustrate, these axes may often effectively obscure underlying class relationships along the primary axis – that is, control/coordinated labour and in particular global capitalist/collective worker.

In capitalist societies there are many tendencies towards identification and action as primary classes. There are also factors working against this, creating individual and sectional competitiveness. Specific socio-historical studies are required for any given society to assess the weight and likely changes of these conflicting forces. We make no prediction that primary class consciousness and behaviour will inevitably grow, that people increasingly become aware of their broadest class interests as they lose their 'selfishness' and 'parochialism'. Nonetheless this is a possibility, a potential for class polarisation which would present an acute threat to capitalism as such. The functional dichotomy between control and coordinated labour *must* be given institutional form in capitalism; any challenge to their separation is also a challenge to the capitalist order.

There is a large amount of evidence as to the wide-ranging effects of primary class stratification.[1] Opportunities or disadvantages in acquiring employment, wealth, skills and knowledge are associated with primary class, being passed on inter-generationally. Status and power in the community are also correlated with control and coordinated labour. Whatever the function or ownership of the enterprise they work in, people tend to socialise exclusively with others in the same primary class, people who have similar backgrounds, education, status and power. There is a significant degree of job mobility between enterprises of different function and ownership but within primary classes. While admitting that there are numerous exceptions to these generalisations, the overall patterns cannot be seriously challenged.[2]

The primary class of controllers is fairly firmly wedded to the capitalist social order in attitudes and action, their class consciousness often being expressed in terms of 'order' rather than 'power over', emphasising nationality, law and the 'naturalness' of capitalist market and production relations – challenges to which are seen as leading to anarchy.

Class identifications among the primary class of coordinated labourers are more mixed, fragmented and tenuous, a complex amalgam in varying proportions of acceptance of the above-mentioned dominant values, adaptation to them and rejection of them. There have been a number of insightful attempts to typify forms and causes of working-class consciousness in the sociological literature and we select four of these for brief discussion: deferential, traditional, affluent and radical ideal types.[3]

Deference involves recognition and respect for social superiors and acceptance of one's role, however humble it may be, in a society conceived of as an organic unity. Such an attitude is characteristically associated with face-to-face relations with employers in small firms or local dignitaries in small towns or villages. Broader strains towards deference derive from churches, monarchy and conservative political parties. Traditional working-class perspectives recognise the fact of their subordination, a subordination which may rankle but is nonetheless seen as inevitable. The 'authorities' are conceived of rather diffusely, while 'we' are identified in a highly localised fashion. The long-settled solidly working-class community is the major source of such traditional consciousness. The so-called affluent worker's prime goal is home-centred consumption, combination with other workers only being valued in so far as it serves that end. The existing social order is accepted pragmatically, at least as long as there are good prospects of rising living standards. This sort of outlook is characteristic of large-scale modern production and 'anonymous' housing estates. Finally, the radical consciousness values collective sentiment and action, on as class-wide a basis as possible, this being seen as the means for overturning present exploitative class relationships. According to Parkin radical values are generated, if at all, by radical mass political parties.

Undoubtedly this typology captures something of the rich variety of workers' attitudes and actions, but it needs to be complemented by a dynamic analysis exploring the factors which lead to the growth, collapse or transformation of particular congeries of ideas and dispositions. Deferential attitudes are difficult to sustain in large urban settings and where modern industry destroys the viability of employers' paternalism. Disappointment that one's 'betters' fail to do the 'right thing' may lead to sharp breaks from deference. Both traditional and affluent worker perspectives contain seeds of radicalism since they recognise cleavage in society and adapt to the fact of their subordination rather than embrace it; whether those seeds germinate or not is an open question. Certainly modernisation or decline of old industries like dock-work, shipbuilding and mining have combined with urban redevelopment programmes to strain the traditional working-class perspective, but it is uncertain whether the outcome will be the crystallisation of a broader class consciousness or a relapse into intensified parochialism. The affluent workers' fixation on consumption leads to a shattering of this type of consciousness with increasing job insecurity and stagnant living standards; if the system does not 'deliver the goods', affluent workers may swing violently between radicalism and sectionalism based on locality, craft or race. If economic crisis does lead to any significant crumbling of deferential, traditional and affluent worker perspectives, large new audiences for radical and sectional values may be created.

The fragmentation and fragility of working-class consciousness derives in large part from the central dichotomy of control versus coordinated labour, the alternative logical responses to subordination being acceptance, adaptation and rejection, but it is also patterned by other features of class structure.

A major complication to primary class division comes with the recognition that some roles involve *both* control and coordinated labour, a situation we refer to as 'structural ambiguity'. We prefer this rather elaborate term to Carchedi's 'middle class'[4] since the latter incorrectly implies coherent class interests, whereas these positions are characterised by internally inconsistent interests derived from opposed objectives. Under capitalism, the functional distinction between control and coordinated labour tends to be realised concretely in disjunct role complexes, but this separation is not now complete nor is ever likely to be. Those who carry out both control and coordinated labour are in an objectively ambiguous position, whether they are conscious of it or not. Later in this chapter we shall discuss more fully the forces strengthening and weakening the effects of primary structural ambiguity.

Those carrying out both capital and labour functions are faced with contradictory ways of understanding their situation. On the one hand they could identify with the goals of the global capital, viewing labour only as a means to those ends and so seeking to increase surplus labour appropriated by the capital. In this perspective their income is seen as a share of profit, from which low productivity of labour detracts. Alternatively people in this ambiguous position could identify with the collective labourer, regarding the control functions they carry out as purely technical. Income is then seen as wages, with profits being created out of the surplus labour performed by them and others.

In reality those who carry out both functions often adopt an inconsistent and vacillating combination of these two perspectives or synthesise them by regarding their income as a share of total profit which they have contributed to creating.

The primary axis of class differentiation therefore gives rise immediately to three distinct groupings; control, coordinated labour and structurally ambiguous class situations which contain elements of both. As we stated in our introduction to this chapter, the location of the groupings generated by this primary axis can only be grasped if we simultaneously consider sectoral differentiation within the total system of the generation and allocation of surplus product.

The first distinction we build on to our basic model is that between capitals and non-capitals. In practice the great majority of non-capitals will be state controlled – the health service, national and local government administration, education, etc. Private non-capitals include activities such as churches, charities, and voluntary organisations.

In general we find that coordinated labour, whether employed by a capital or non-capital, is paid at the current rate for the job, supervised with respect to speed and quality of work and subjected to such alterations in methods of work as are devised by the controllers in the light of their calculations as to relative costs and benefits. The controllers also evaluate pricing and investment policies. As discussed in Chapter Five, in capitals both control of labour and investment decisions are evaluated with respect to their contribution to capital accumulation.[5] Although the pursuit of capital accumulation does not constitute a goal for non-capitals, we still find there are compulsive pressures to pay market wages, supervise work strictly and evaluate costs systematically by a distinct 'control' role complex.

This is because state non-capitals are financed from taxation and are therefore a drain on all incomes and profits. It is easy to see that there will be inbuilt pressures for cost-effectiveness; there are needs which some or all sections of society want to be met socially, but all sections apparently have a stake in their being met cheaply. Indeed a very large part of the activity and effort of parliaments and local councils is devoted to an examination of costs incurred to see whether they are all 'necessary' or whether the money of the taxpayer and ratepayer could be saved by reducing 'waste.' What expenditures are 'necessary' or 'wasteful' changes with shifts in political and economic forces, a notorious example in Britain being free medical prescriptions, which have twice changed from 'necessary' to 'unnecessary' since the war! Disputes on such issues may appear as conflicts between political parties, but they are more deeply rooted in economic interests as is evidenced by shifts in party policy – in practice, if not in theory – as a result of economic changes. At the time of writing, for example, a Labour Government has turned its back on the party's traditional defence of the Welfare State and is imposing severe cuts as a result of the current economic crisis. In any case, whether state expenditure is rising or falling, governments adopt elaborate accounting procedures in order to monitor and control it. Public scrutiny and the direct concern of powerful economic interests for costs and benefits ensure that, whatever niches of bureaucratic wastefulness there may be, there are strong and continuous pressures for cost reduction. These pressures ensure a separation between control and co-ordinated labour with the latter in similar work and market situations to their counterparts working for capitals. Although, as we have just demonstrated, there are powerful pressures reproducing the functional role complexes of control and coordinated labour within non-capitals, the fact that such sectors *are* non-capitals has important consequences for those engaged in both control and coordinated labour functions within them. One problem lies in the definition of the goals of the organisation. Non-capital objectives – market regulation, legitimation, socialisation of constant and variable capital, and external functions – lack the precision and measurability of capital goals, namely capital accumulation. The diffuseness of goals does not necessarily detract from powerful drives toward cost-effectiveness, although it does mean that there is likely to be constant dispute about what counts as effectiveness. For example, effectiveness of care for the elderly may be measured by net weekly cost per resident in old people's homes, level of old-age pension, net hourly cost of domestic help provided for old people, and so on – but there is con-siderable scope for disagreement about the relative importance of different sorts of provision, whether and how the indices should include subjective factors such as dignity and happiness, and how the indices should weight numbers helped as compared with the extent to which they are helped.

In the armed forces the goal of 'national defence' has an open-ended nature, thus seeming to be threatened by any attempts to cut costs, a circumstance which necessitates a system of indices: costs of army rations, probable megadeaths for a missile of given cost, training costs, and so on; these indices are used to measure efficiency and provide a framework within which 'rational' decisions can be made.

Similar remarks would apply to all other non-capital functions undertaken by the state; there is a relative shortage of resources as compared with the diffuseness and open-endedness of goals. Therefore, although the class situation of coordinated labour in capitals and non-capitals is similar, this similarity is qualified by the fact that the diffuseness of goals within non-capitals makes it very difficult, indeed contentious, to systematically evaluate 'productivity' for such workers. Furthermore the capital/non-capital distinction may obscure the common class interests of coordinated labour in so far as collective workers come to regard coordinated labour in non-capital sectors, (i.e., the majority of state employees) as supported out of the taxes they pay. Indeed where governments wish to generate popular support for cuts in state expenditure they often argue that non-capitals are an expensive luxury.

The situation of the controllers in state non-capitals is considerably more complex than in capitals, for one aspect of control is characteristically removed from the enterprise itself and located in government. Olin Wright, following Poulantzas, distinguishes two elements of control – possession and economic ownership.[6] Possession refers to control over plant and equipment together with corresponding supervisory powers over labour, whereas economic ownership refers to the capacity to make long-term strategic decisions, especially over investment and the allocation of resources. In the case of capitals, both elements of control are located within the enterprise itself, typically with economic ownership concentrated in the top echelons. This fact may be responsible for tensions between differentiated functions and levels in a bureaucratic hierarchy, tensions which may also enhance or obscure the primary structural ambiguity of roles involving both global capital and collective worker functions. But in state non-capitals economic ownership is to a substantial degree located outside the enterprise in the government; for it is government which decides the basic shape and size of the health service, the army, the social security system and so on, with the boards concerned only exercising possession.[7] This division of control creates both a characteristic tension between government and internal controllers and, in significant conflicts between control and coordinated labour, the appearance of the internal controllers as 'intermediaries'. On the one hand the fact that those at the top of the managerial hierarchy evidently do not have economic ownership may lead labour in such enterprises to a resigned acceptance that it is pointless bargaining with an 'authority' which cannot deliver, or on the other hand the relative impotence of the internal controllers may give labour's discontents an immediate political flavour.

In discussing non-capitals so far, we have considered only those that are state owned, for we do not regard private non-capitals as part of the capitalist mode of production. Some enterprises appear to be marginal cases, for example, workers' cooperatives and mutual companies (such as insurance companies where ownership is formally vested in the policy-holders). These are clearly *economic* enterprises and the evidence demonstrates that they develop managerial hierarchies, separating control from coordinated labour. Thus as they operate in the market they come to be capitals rather than non-capitals, even though their controllers may be elected or the members subscribe to a cooperative ideology. The most democratic firm can only maintain its viability in the market if the bulk of its members accept no more than market wages and work at no lower productivity levels than comparable enterprises; cooperatives cannot opt out of capitalism.[8]

So far we have related the basic elements of class situation – control/global capital and coordinated labour/collective worker and associated structural ambiguities – to the capital/non-capital distinction. This has inevitably involved building in the state/private dichotomy, as the significant non-capitals are invariably state owned. Any consideration of quasi-capitals must also simultaneously incorporate the state/non-state dichotomy, since state quasi-capitals may have very different properties from private quasi-capitals.

As discussed in Chapter Five, most state-owned enterprises trading in the market must be regarded as quasi-capitals since their pricing and investment policies are strongly influenced, or determined, by the government. Possession is vested in the top management but economic ownership is shared with the government. In addition to the diffuseness and open-endedness of the non-capital functions it performs, a futher source of uncertainty lies in the problem of appropriately balancing capital against non-capital functions. This is often expressed as a conflict between 'social service' and 'commercial' orientations, a confusion of goals which is apparently deeply frustrating to top managers in state firms. For labour the collective worker/global capitalist dichotomy is overlaid by a consciousness of the 'subsidy' element inherent in non-capital functions, a dependence on the government's goodwill.' This phenomenon is very evident in cases where the state nationalises a bankrupt company, 'rescuing' it and 'generously' saving jobs. Such potential for harmonious labour relations in state quasi-capitals may be enhanced if the government ensures that it is a model employer. On the other hand, as with state non-capitals, discontent can take a strongly political form since the government evidently stands close behind the internal controllers. In Britain, this was particularly evident in recent strikes in coalmining and the Post Office. Perhaps the potential for conflicts is greater than in non-capitals since profits are actually being made in some quasi-capitals, providing some indication of surplus product appropriated by labour.

Privately owned quasi-capitals may operate regulated prices either through contracting with the government or by cartel and monopoly – or both. The former situation is characteristic of armaments and some high technology industries, effectively locating part of economic ownership in government. The significance of such cases for class relationships is very similar to that of state quasi-capitals.

But where privately organised cartels or monopolies provide a degree of market regulation, thus making the firms quasi-capitals, the principal complicating factor in class situations is not their relation to the state but their involvement in market manipulation as such. If a firm is able to fix prices at a higher level than market competition would allow, it effectively appropriates additional surplus value from its customers. Where those customers are other firms, their employees may be susceptible to the view that they are making sacrifices to benefit coordinated labour as well as control in quasi-capitals. O'Connor argues that American capitalism has developed two distinct private sectors – a monopoly and a competitive sector. The former rewards its workers in proportion to increasing productivity but, since wage increases are passed on as price increases in that sector, competitive sector workers suffer. 'On the one hand, their wages are relatively low; on the other, they have to buy at relatively high monopolistic prices.'[9] Even if competitive and monopolistic sectors are not as distinct as O'Connor claims, the mechanism of monopolistic exploitation in the market he describes is undoubtedly valid. Private quasi-capital creates two alternative perspectives: a basis for loyalty to one's own firm against the threats of others, or a hostility to monopoly control of the economy as such. This latter perspective is capable of developing into a radical critique of monopoly *capital* or a reactionary defence of the 'little man'.

As discussed in Chapter Five, there will be competition between different sorts of capital despite their common interest in maximising total surplus product. For example, high interest rates favour finance capital at the expense of other types of capital and high trading profits favour commercial capital at the expense of industrial capital. The different types of capital – industry, services, commerce, finance and property – may effectively form factions, each one pursuing its distinctive interests in conflict with the others and, in particular, pressing its claims upon the state. The state is clearly very important in securing relative advantages between these factions through its fiscal and monetary policies. Interest rates are largely tied to those fixed by the state central bank. Taxation may favour one faction against others, an example being selective employment tax in the late sixties in Britain, which was a discriminatory burden for all non-industrial capitals. Between these different types of capital there are characteristic but shifting alliances, perhaps the most secure of which is that between finance and property. The most generally significant division among types of capital is that between those in productive and unproductive spheres, for, from the point of view of the former, the latter, however necessary they may be, are a drain on surplus product.

This conflict of interests between *capitals* over shares of the total surplus product is often presented as a conflict between productive and unproductive *activities* so that, to the extent that this perspective is accepted, productive workers may come to regard unproductive workers as living at their expense. Conversely, unproductive workers may insist that their work is necessary for production to take place, a claim which is of course true in capitalist society. The potential for tensions among different types of collective worker can be seen most graphically where a firm engaged in both sectors is experiencing low profits and reductions in business turnover; for example, sales staff and manufacturing workers may dispute *which* group should make most sacrifices in wages, conditions and jobs rather than combine to minimise total losses.[10] Tension between types of collective worker is not the result of capitals' conscious decision to 'divide and rule', although any such policy will naturally exacerbate divisiveness, but because the different capital functions require separate hierarchies of authority, conditions of work and systems of payment. The conflicts of interests between factions of capital thus reproduce in more or less attenuated form splits among the primary class of coordinated labour, splits which are institutionalised to some degree in trade union structure in the United Kingdom.

As already mentioned, non-capitals are, like capitals in unproductive spheres, a drain on surplus product so they and their workers are liable to be castigated as an unnecessary luxury. Since the most economically important non-capitals are within the state sector, attacks on 'unproductive activities' often slide into general attacks on state expenditure, including state investment in quasi-capitals. Such criticisms in fact often relate to the potential threat of immensely powerful state competition with private capitals, even though such investment is customarily described as an excessive expenditure of *national* resources.

While such polemics may serve the interests of private capital and divide public sector workers from private sector workers, the supposed association of the state with unproductive activities is fallacious;[11] there are clearly both large unproductive private sectors and productive state sectors. It is of course true that enterprises in the state sector are inevitably pressed into non-capital functions so that there are no pure state capitals, but only state quasi-capitals. This does mean that state enterprises which are predominantly in the productive sphere do, to a greater or lesser extent, absorb as well as generate surplus product. The substantial loss-making nationalised industries like British Railways are a clear case in point. However, this is a rather fine point, for in spite of all the free enterprise rhetoric large corporations are increasingly interdependent with the state.

Whatever the validity of the supposed conflict of interests between private and state activities, it remains true that these arguments to some extent divide coordinated labour. This is again evident in trade union structure.

We have seen how the primary class divisions based on control versus coordinated labour are complicated when taken in conjunction with the other two defining elements of class situation, capital versus non-capital and state versus private ownership. These bases of classification were derived from our general model of flows of value, but the class situations to which they give rise are further complicated by other secondary structural factors. We term these factors 'secondary' because, although they may be extremely important – in particular, in contributing to the *actor's* perception of the class structure – they are not directly derived from the basic framework we have developed above. Furthermore it is a feature of these secondary structural factors that the conflicts between the interest groupings they generate may be resolved without a radical change in the underlying capitalist mode of production, thus they cannot be considered to be *determinants* of social class.

We begin by discussing two secondary structural factors – differentiation within sectors and bureaucracy – which broadly speaking have developed as a consequence of the pressures to increase the rate of accumulation through raising the mass of relative surplus value. Both the division of labour within the enterprise and the development of universalistic, predictable, chains of command are techniques developed to increase efficiency by making the best possible use of available resources. In the case of capitalist production these techniques have been developed in order to achieve maximum production for the *market*. Of course methods have to be developed in order to administer *any* complex structure, and neither bureaucracy nor the division of labour are peculiar to capitalist production. However the development of both in capitalist society has been dominated by the requirements of the capitalist mode of production, therefore – to give an example – differentiation within the capitalist function has reflected the different aspects of capital, and bureaucratic structures have reflected the dominance of global capital over collective worker.

DIFFERENTIATION AND SPECIALISATION WITHIN SECTORS

Within the functionally specialised sectors we have identified above, we typically find in developed capitalist society that the many tasks necessary to the creation, acquisition and distribution of surplus value are carried out by specially trained groups possessing the skills relevant to a particular task. We have already described in Chapter Five how under capitalism the labour process has been developed to the extent that it is now carried out by the collective worker and, as we shall shortly demonstrate, this differentiation may well lead to conflicts of interest between workers carrying out different functions, even though their underlying *class* interests are the same. Similarly the many and varied aspects of the capitalist function are now commonly carried out by specialised managers, who may not necessarily own (in a legal sense) the means of production. (The emergence of the managerial stratum has been discussed in Chapters Four and Five.) Although the capitalist function *is* largely carried out by 'management' because, as we have argued, management also carries out a part of the function of the collective worker, the category of 'management' is not synonymous with that of global capital. Some of the strains and conflicts which can be empirically observed within the differentiated managerial stratum are therefore attributable to the structurally ambiguous class situation of many managers. At the same time conflicts may be generated between different parts of the managerial stratum in the absence of structural ambiguity. Parallel conflicts may also develop within the collective worker/coordinated labour function.

A. *Global Capital/Control*

Management theory has identified four basic activities associated with a manufacturing organisation – financing the enterprise, developing the product, supervising production, and marketing.[12] These four basic activities may be simply adapted to apply to non-manufacturing activities such as finance or commerce. The simplest form of specialisation involves the creation of separate departments to deal with each of these aspects. It is not difficult to see that conflicts may easily arise between managers so identified – for example, marketing departments may complain that production departments fail to reach the desired volume or quality, production or research departments that they are starved of financial resources and so on. Also familiar in the literature are the conflicts between 'line' and 'staff' management – that is, between managers directly responsible for and integrated into an authority structure which carries out any of the basic activities listed above, and the 'expert', not necessarily part of the hierarchy of authority, but there to advise on particular problems.[13] The extent of differentiation of function within the managerial stratum will vary widely, as will the relative power of the groupings so identified. These variations will not necessarily be arbitrary; it has been argued that both tend to vary with the kind of technology employed.[14] Neither are such variations without consequences for individual managers or groups of managers: relative power within an organisation, for example, will be an important factor in deciding remuneration. The point, however, we wish to make in identifying these differentiated managerial functions is that it is more than likely that essentially short-term conflicts of interest between these groupings may tend to obscure their common interest as agents of global capital.

So far we have been considering the effects of what we would describe as *task* specialisation within management, although it is worth noting that such task specialisation – in particular in respect of the four basic activities identified above – corresponds broadly to different aspects of the function of global capital. A recent discussion of the class situation of management has similarly related their class position to the extent to which managers carry out the function of capital.[15] Wright identifies three processes underlying the social relations of capitalist production: (1) economic or *de facto ownership*, the control of investments and resources, and two aspects of *possession*; (2) the control of the physical means of production; and (3) the control of labour power. Full control in respect of all three of these processes locates an agent unambiguously in the bourgeoisie, total lack of control, in the proletariat. Those managers, therefore, who have more or less full control in respect of economic ownership and the two aspects of possession are to be considered as part of the bourgeoisie, attenuated control in respect of any of these three processes, or control in respect of only one or two of them leads, according to Wright, to a contradictory class location. We will deal with the question of *degrees* of control in our discussion of bureaucracy – the next secondary structural factor we identify. In this section we will evaluate Wright's claim that control in respect of only one or two of the three processes underlying capitalist relations of production places the agent in a 'contradictory class location'.

We would argue, contrary to Wright, that the fact that an agent carries out only a part of the function of global capital – be it economic ownership, control over physical resources, or control over labour power – does not automatically place the agent in a structurally ambiguous (or contradictory) class location in a *fundamental* sense. The carrying out of only a part of the capitalist function by an agent does not make it any the less capitalist, neither does it automatically imply that the agent carries out any part of the function of the collective worker. (We have reserved the term 'structural ambiguity' only for those class positions which embody *both* global capitalist *and* collective worker functions.) For example, a *rentier* capitalist, living entirely from investment income and taking no part in management, is not any less a capitalist because he/she does not control the labour power of others or the physical means of production. Taken to its logical conclusion Wright's analysis would place such *rentier* capitalists in a 'contradictory class location' – which would be odd, to say the least.

We also find it difficult to maintain a rigid analytical distinction between the two aspects of possession identified by Wright – the control of the physical means of production, and control over labour power. Empirically they will invariably be associated, and furthermore the aspect of possession which involves the control over the physical means of production seems to us to be particularly ill-defined. In Wright's discussion such control ranges from full discretion over material resources to individual control over tools and/or control over one's individual labour process – by craft workers, for example. Wright argues that such 'semi-autonomous employees', because of their minimal control over the physical means of production, are therefore in a contradictory class location, marginal between the proletariat and petty bourgeoisie. In our opinion this is not the case. If we adopt Wright's own strategy of arguing from a perspective of interests, it is difficult to see how relative autonomy in respect of tools, or a part of the labour process, would lead to any identification with the petty bourgeoisie, or any other aspect of capital; such autonomy does not make a worker any less a worker. If it did, then semi-skilled workers in technologically advanced industries – for example, chemicals – would have to be located as marginal to the petty bourgeoisie as technological developments have certainly increased their control over the physical means of production (as discussed in Chapter Eight). We would argue that typically control over the physical means of production in respect of the immediate labour process is an aspect of *work* which has been systematically appropriated by management in order to maximise control over the other aspect of possession identified by Wright – the labour power of others.

Therefore, although we would agree with Wright that the fact that many managers are only responsible for an aspect of the capitalist function may well lead to strains, tensions and conflicts of interest, we would not agree that such functional splits constitute a *basic* or fundamental axis of class differentiation, such as to place managers who do not carry out all of the capitalist functions in a 'contradictory class location'. While we are highly critical of some aspects of Wright's work, the value of his analysis lies in the fact that he has systematically related the differentiation of the managerial function to the development of the capitalist mode of production, and the social processes underlying this mode of production. He has thus contributed to the better understanding of developments within the managerial stratum – an understanding which can be easily fitted within the framework of class analysis which we have been developing.

B. *Collective Worker/Coordinated Labour*

The collective worker, as we have already described, is the expression of the differentiation of the labour process in developed capitalism. As such differentiation has to date *only* occurred within capitalist production relationships, we cannot assert with any confidence whether or not all of the kinds of division of labour we observe empirically are only associated with the capitalist mode of production. We can however be reasonably confident that some aspects of this differentiation *are* peculiar to capitalism – for example, the carrying out of coordination and unity by management rather than labour, and similarly the appropriation of skill within the managerial function so forcefully prescribed by Taylor. However, if we turn to those aspects of the function of the collective worker which are carried out by labour, there is much empirical evidence available of the potential for conflict between workers carrying out the different parts of the complex labour process. Brown and Brannen's study of shipbuilding workers provides a particularly good example.[16] Shipbuilding is an industry which gives rise to work and community situations which have been termed 'traditional proletarian'; workers in such industries (shipbuilding, coal, steel) tend to be relatively isolated geographically, living in 'one-class' (i.e. working-class) local communities, which reinforce the friendships and loyalties developed within the work situation. Such features, it is argued, give rise to considerable group solidarity, the 'us' of the community and work-place being ranged against 'them' – employers, managers, etc. This is the so-called traditional working-class perspective referred to earlier in this chapter. However Brown and Brannen's empirical findings revealed that only a minority of shipbuilding workers actually held such a two-class 'oppositional' model of the social order, most perceived the social order as a more or less complex hierarchy of conflicting interest groups. Brown and Brannen argue that the source of this perception of society was to be found in the work situation of shipbuilding workers. Shipbuilding, as a craft industry, presents a picture of a wide variety of different crafts all engaged on different parts of the same product – a ship. In the United Kingdom, at any rate, each craft grouping is organised by a separate union, and the different crafts or their representatives are involved in constant short-term conflicts of interest over both relative wage rates, and the 'right' area of work for a particular craft – that is, demarcation disputes. Although their common identity as shipbuilding workers might at times override their sectional differences, the continuing short-term conflicts of interest experienced by different groups of shipbuilding workers has had a significant effect on their 'world-views' and thus, we may infer, on any potential development of class consciousness.

The kind of evidence summarised above clearly demonstrates how functional differentiation within the labour process can lead to antagonism between different groupings of the collective worker. As with conflicts between different sections of management, therefore, this may effectively obscure more basic elements in their class situation – their common interest as workers.

BUREAUCRACY

As initially developed by Weber, 'bureaucracy' is an ideal-typical construct which describes the characteristic mode of administration of rational-legal authority. Bureaucratic administration is characterised by the marking off of specialised areas of competence which are bounded by rules and hierarchically organised. Recruitment to bureaucratic positions is on the basis of appointment rather than election, nepotism, or other personal ties; technical competence is the major basis for selection. Each sphere of operation is insulated from other spheres, and the roles constitute a chain of command extending progressively down the hierarchy of the bureaucratic structure. As described by Weber, bureaucratic structures represent a supremely efficient mode of administration although, as we have seen in Chapter Four, he also thought such structures contained the seeds of paradox which could become an 'iron-hard cage'. As our brief sketch of Weber's formulation indicates, the differentiation of function resulting in the specialised areas of competence we have discussed above could well be subsumed under Weber's identification of bureaucracy. For our purposes, however, we shall use the term to refer to the system of administration through essentially impersonal rules and regulations.[17]

Leaving aside the tendency for bureaucratic organisations to subvert democracy, which was Weber's major preoccupation, many modern writers in this field of what has become known as 'organisation theory' have drawn attention to the *dysfunctions* of this supposedly efficient form of administration. As several authors have pointed out, bureaucracy tends to generate antagonisms between layers and sections of the organisation.

To further the present discussion such malfunctions may be identified under two broad categories. Firstly, the development of bureaucratic structures effectively curtails control and stunts initiative, especially for those lower down the bureaucratic hierarchy, who only carry out orders formulated above, even though the carrying out of such orders may well involve control over the labour power of others. Additionally the fact that rules and regulations *are* impersonal makes no allowance for any personal weakness or failing, leaving the individual insecure and unprotected. Secondly (a more general observation), those subject to bureaucratic authority may simply not accept the legitimacy of this authority, or of the rules through which this authority is administered. (As bureaucracy was described by Weber as the mode of administration of rational-legal authority, legitimation did not, technically, present a problem for Weber.)

Responses to the first kind of malfunction we have identified are varied. Officials can retire behind the protection of bureaucratic rules, slavishly carrying out instructions (however inappropriate) and thus avoiding censure. Alternatively bureaucratically identified departments may seek to protect themselves, or increase their importance by selectively withholding information and otherwise jealously guarding whatever limited autonomy they possess.[18] In either case efficiency will be impaired, and conflict engendered between different groups both horizontally and vertically. When legitimacy is denied by those ultimately subject to authority – that is, those on the receiving end of the bureaucratic structure – the denial may in extreme cases take the form of a refusal to carry out orders, or at the very least an attempt to subvert the orders given falling short of actual refusal.

As a secondary structural factor, we would argue that the development of bureaucratic structures has two opposing effects. Within the hierarchy of managerial authority the imposition of rules and limitations on discretion brought about by bureaucratic developments will tend to increase conflict between different levels, thus obscuring common class interests. On the other hand the successful imposition of bureaucratic rules will sharpen the distinction between those who administer the rules and orders, in however a routine and attenuated a fashion, and those who simply carry them out. In short it will emphasise the distinction between global capital and collective worker and more generally, control and coordinated labour.

Gouldner's empirical study, *Patterns of Industrial Bureaucracy*, can be used to illustrate our point.[19] A gypsum mine and wallboard factory had long been managed, in a rather lackadaisical fashion, by a plant manager who had allowed a considerable degree of latitude in respect of timekeeping, job allocation, and general leniency described by Gouldner as the 'indulgency pattern'. On the demise of the lenient manager the controlling company, who were facing economic difficulties, installed a new plant manager with instructions to tighten things up. The new manager set about his task in a typically bureaucratic fashion, enforcing rules which already existed, developing new rules to cover 'grey areas' of administration and creating new departments to administer the rules. Not surprisingly these developments were bitterly resented by the work-force, and management–worker relations declined to the point of the first serious strike for many years.[20] This study of a changing situation therefore shows clearly how the imposition of bureaucratic authority may heighten the distinction between global capitalist and collective worker – after all, these two antagonistic functions existed during the time of the 'indulgency pattern' but did not manifest themselves in overt conflict.

At the same time it must be remembered that the new plant manager was to a large extent carrying out orders formulated above in bringing the plant into line with other units of the parent company.[21] The carrying out of these orders was by no means a pleasant task, and there can be little doubt that the new manager resented the superiors who had put him in this position. Similarly those responsible for imposing his commands were not universally content with the changed situation, especially those who had been supervisors under the old regime. They tended to identify more with the 'old' work-force than with the 'new' management, presenting the new manager with a problem which he attempted to solve by bringing in his own lieutenants, thereby replacing the old guard. As we can see from this example, bureaucratic structures may well lead to conflict between different levels of the command hierarchy.

The development of bureaucratic hierarchies has certainly had a significant effect in both obscuring and clarifying class relationships. On the one hand the difference between global capital and collective worker is emphasised by a systematisation of authority which separates those who command from those who obey. On the other hand the fact that the different functions and levels within the command hierarchy are themselves constrained by bureaucratic rules and varying degrees of authority is likely to lead to tensions *within* the hierarchy. Although these effects are undoubtedly important, we regard the development of bureaucracy as a secondary structural factor in our analysis of the class structure, rather than an absolutely basic element in its patterning. Particular functions are not transformed by changes in their administration, and if anything the functions of global capital and collective worker are made even clearer by the development of bureaucracy. Even though conflicts may well develop between bureaucratically identified groups, such conflicts are susceptible to resolution in the absence of any fundamental changes in the underlying mode of production, and may be analysed as intra- rather than inter-class conflicts, adding further to the complexity of the class structure of contemporary capitalist societies.

In our identification of bureaucracy as a secondary, rather than a primary, factor in the structuring of class relationships, our analysis again diverges significantly from that of Wright. His approach may be briefly summarised: The carrying out of the different aspects of the capitalist function – the control of investments and resources, control over the physical means of production, and control over labour power – is typically administered through a complex bureaucratic hierarchy. Thus control at different levels ranges from almost full control through partial to minimal. Therefore the *degree* of control – reflected in the position in the bureaucratic hierarchy – possessed by an agent is a crucial factor in *determining* 'contradictory class locations'. Taken together with the number of functions carried out, the degree of control determines class location.[22] For example, if an agent has full control in respect of the physical means of production and labour power, then the class location, although contradictory, will lie very near that of the bourgeoisie. Alternatively an agent with control over labour power, and only minimal control at that, will be located very near the boundary of the proletariat. From this and previous summaries of Wright's approach we can see that Wright identifies two factors which actually *structure* class relations – the differentiation of the functions of capital and the development of complex hierarchies.[23] We have argued that these factors are secondary, rather than primary. Both contribute essentially to intra- rather than inter-class conflicts, and the kinds of conflicts engendered by these factors are technically possible to overcome without radically changing or transcending the capitalist mode of production. We can further develop our criticism by looking at Wright's discussion of foremen, who have 'moved further from workers by becoming less involved in direct production, and (they have moved) closer to workers by gradually having their personal power bureaucratised'.[24] Whilst we would agree that the fact that foremen participate less in the labour process will move them further from workers, we would not agree that the bureaucratisation of personal power moves them any closer. Even if the foreman only supervises labour in accordance with rules laid down from above, this does not make his control over labour power – or the carrying out of the capitalist function – any less real. A function is not transformed by the *manner* in which it is carried out. Attenuation of control therefore does not change the essential nature of a class situation, although it may further complicate a class situation which is already ambiguous. (For example, a foreman may resent management and *feel* that he is closer to the work-force because he is 'pushed around' in a similar fashion, but he is unlikely to be accepted by the work-force as long as his major task is the administration of delegated authority.)

Although we have been critical of much of Wright's approach, we would stress that in many respects his work represents a significant improvement on many existing strategies of class analysis. Firstly, he locates class relationships firmly in *production*, rather than the market, status groupings, or whatever. Secondly, Wright has identified the differentiation of the capitalist function and the development of bureaucratic hierarchies through a historical analysis of capitalist developments. Logically they are not, therefore, 'the inevitable developments of advanced industrialism', but the *particular* accompaniments of monopoly capitalism.[25]

Although we have recognised that neither the division of labour nor bureaucracy is a phenomenon unique to capitalism, we have stressed that in a capitalist society they cannot be analysed without reference to the underlying mode of production and its development. Although both will show variations between sectors and nation states, we would claim that to a large extent the analysis we have developed above will be generalisable across the whole range of sectors and nation states. This is not necessarily the case, however, with the second set of secondary structural factors we identify – social market and status factors. Both of these factors are pre-eminently historical – that is, the form they take will depend above all on the particular manner of capitalist development in a particular society, the characteristics of dominant groups, the presence or absence of subordinate ethnic groups and so on.

SOCIAL MARKET FACTORS

In Chapter Eight we discussed at some length the importance of the market in the determination of income differentials. We argued there that the market must be seen as *socially* structured. That is, the structure of the market is not simply determined by supply and demand, but is heavily influenced by the relative *power* of different groups in society, which will include the power to define which capacities or aptitudes are 'worth' more than others. (This point overlaps considerably with the consideration of status factors, which we discuss in the next section.) Indeed the complex structure of differential rewards in contemporary capitalist societies is influenced to varying degrees by all of the factors we are building into our approach to the analysis of the class structure.

In this section we will briefly examine the effect of the market – manifest in the overt structure of unequal material rewards – on the underlying structure of class relationships and consequent patterning of interests. Indeed this patterning of interests, and associated conflicts between different groupings in the market, will often assume such importance as to appear *the* basis of class stratification, in particular for the actors involved. Thus any group which does particularly well in the market – which receives a relatively high level of material reward – may justifiably consider they have an interest in maintaining the *status quo*. This may effectively obscure underlying class relationships if the groups concerned *de facto* carry out the function of the collective worker. Similarly, because material differences so obviously reflect and are translated into conflicts of interest, it is a simple matter to understand how such conflicts may well occur *within* classes At the same time, because historically labour has had to fight for improvements in wages and conditions, most usually through trade union organisation, the market is in a very real sense the arena in which overt conflicts between global capital and collective worker are manifest. Thus the operation of the market mediated through trade union activity can sharpen the differences between capital and labour, marshalling wageworkers as a whole against the employers as a whole.

Nevertheless, even if *all* wage labour were systematically organised in respect of *all* units of capital (and such unity is, in any case, highly unlikely), it would not be correct to describe this as conflict between global capital and collective worker in the capitalist societies of today. For many agents who carry out the capitalist function will technically be wageworkers. Thus, with the contemporary spread of unionism into the managerial hierarchy, trade union activity encompasses conflicts between different sections of global capital over the allocation of surplus value, as well as between capital and labour.

In fact trade unions in capitalist societies are complex and often contradictory phenomena, the nature of which we can only briefly touch on here. The crux of the difficulties we encounter in the analysis of unionism can be illustrated by a quotation from Gramsci:

> Trade unionism is evidently nothing but a reflection of capitalist society, not a potential means of transcending capitalist society. It organises workers, not as producers but as wage-earners, that is as creations of the capitalist system of private property, as sellers of their labour power.

Unionism unites workers according to the tools of their trade or the nature of their product, that is according to the contours imposed on them by capitalist society. [26]

This moulding of unionism according to the 'contours of capitalism' has two major consequences. Firstly, groups of workers identified by skills or product may develop as interest groups in conflict with one another (as in the example of the shipbuilding workers cited above). Secondly, the organisation of workers *as wage-earners* tacitly accepts the basic structuring of capitalist society (by labour and capital). The major problem for unionism is thus to maintain the level and continuing payment of the *wage*; therefore, para-doxically, unionism develops an interest in the *successful* per-petuation of the capitalist system, and we may find trade unionists more or less willingly making short-term sacrifices in order to meet capitalist crises (for example, the current Social Contract in the United Kingdom). Many writers – Giddens (whose work we have drawn on heavily in this book) is one example – have argued that trade union commitment to 'economism' means that such trade unions can *never* be the basis for the development of ideologies or systems of belief that radically challenge the existing social order. If this is so, then market conflicts mediated through trade unionism will always, to varying degrees, effectively obscure class interests. Whilst we must accept the validity of much of this kind of argument, the fact that trade unionism also expresses, as Hyman has agreed, a fundamental resistance to attempts at control, means that trade unionism can also serve to focus underlying class differences. [27]

The particular form taken by trade union activity, and thus to some extent the degree to which union action serves to obscure or make more relevant underlying class differ-ences, will vary considerably from society to society, de-pending upon the rate and kind of capitalist development within a particular nation state. [28] Of course the social market is only partly mediated through trade unionism in *any* society. In general market advantages may be secured in a number of ways. The classic case occurs when the possessors of a particular skill – for example, doctors, or some craft groupings such as printers – act to restrict entry into training for their speciality. Thus a shortage of qualified personnel results, and those who are qualified may 'justifiably' lay claim to greater rewards. Alternatively there may be no real lack of trained personnel but a limited number of better-rewarded positions, in which case there will be intense competition for these positions. Such positions may be better rewarded, despite the ready availability of personnel, either because they are 'key workers' within the organisation – for example, crane drivers in the docks, who are able to demand a high level of reward because of their potential for disruption – or alternatively a position may be well rewarded because of a complex set of factors including status and association with global capital (as discussed in Chapter Eight) – for example, management or higher civil servants. (We omit genuine cases of short-term market shortage, for example, the computer programmers already cited, as such demands are not *socially* structured.) As we argued in Chapter Eight, neo-Weberian class theory has developed a valuable set of analytical tools for the analysis of the social market. Giddens, for example, after identifying 'classes' according to their particular kind of market capacity (or 'mediate' structuration), then identifies three 'proximate' sources of structuration which parallel our identification of secondary structural factors, i.e., the division of labour within the enterprise (differentiation of function), authority relationships (bureaucratisation), and 'distributive groupings' (status factors).

To repeat and summarise our position: in capitalist societies, especially where more or less free wage bargaining is the rule, conflicts in the market will lead to the formation of interest groups which can either obscure or sharpen underlying class divisions. We have stressed that the market is *socially* structured, both by the underlying relations of production as discussed in our previous chapter, and the secondary structural factors we discuss here.

STATUS

Social status refers to subjective states; claims to enhanced status will only be valid if they are accepted as such by other members of the society. There will therefore be considerable variations in this respect between societies; in some societies aristocratic birth and breeding will be considered important, in others ritual status, and elsewhere education, or the ability to amass considerable personal wealth. Although there will be local and national variations, in general enhanced status does tend to be associated with wealth, power and dominance. Status factors play an important part in determining the nature of the social market: for example, it is often easier to enter the better-rewarded positions in short supply if individuals are from the 'right' background – what is popularly known as the 'old boy' network. Very often groups rising in power attempt to legitimate their dominance by taking over the status characteristics of the earlier dominant groups. In Britain and Europe, for example, the rising bourgeoisie aped the manners and practices of the waning aristocracy. Such pretensions, described by Weber as 'status usurpation', have long been satirised in literature, from Moliere's *Bourgeois Gentilhomme* to Jane Austen's Mrs. Elton. Even today there is no doubt that a large part of the explanation of the generally higher status of mental as opposed to manual labour derives from the prejudices of an age when only those who could afford it did not perform manual work. It is because so many of the attributes contributing to enhanced social status have their roots in the past that we argue that no universal framework can be developed for the analysis of the status systems. Instead the particular features of individual societies have to be taken into account in any such analyses.

As with other secondary structural factors, status factors may operate in two opposing ways. In general, because (to re-quote Lockwood) 'a dominant class has never existed which did not seek to make its position legitimate by placing the highest value on those qualities and activities which come closest to it own', status differences will reflect the split between control and coordinated labour, between global capitalist and collective worker. On the other hand status factors may effectively obscure class differences. Such opacity may come about through open, not to say cynical, manipulation: for example, the 'buying off' of lower management and technicians (or even some groups of workers) through the bestowal of 'staff status', with its associated paraphernalia of separate lavatories, canteens, relative desk sizes, and so on. (We would not suggest that all of the elements of staff status are an illusion; of course many contribute to significantly better terms and conditions of employment.) More significantly a preoccupation with social status may effectively limit class action. There is little doubt, for example, that the antipathy of white-collar workers (until recently) to trade unions stemmed to a large extent from the association of union activity with 'lower' (i.e., manual) class behaviour and action.[29]

Differentiation of function, bureaucracy, the social market and status factors are, then, the most important secondary structural factors we would identify as relevant to the analysis of the class structure of advanced capitalist society. As we have noted in our commentary, many writers have argued that the factors we identify as 'secondary' are in fact the major axes of class differentiation in capitalist society. We recognise these factors as important – indeed to the actors involved they may well appear to be *the* most important – but we would argue that, far from determining the class structure of contemporary capitalist societies, they may often have the opposite effect of covering up more fundamental class antagonisms. They must therefore be systematically taken into account in the detailed empirical analysis of the class structure of any particular society.

STRUCTURALLY AMBIGUOUS CLASS SITUATIONS

In our initial definition of the class structure of modern capitalism we defined as structurally ambiguous those roles and positions which contain elements of both global capitalist and collective worker, control and coordinated labour. The extent of structural ambiguity will vary: in the case of top managers it will be minimal (or absent) and present no real problems of class identification for the agent or the social scientist, whereas the technician not only presents difficulties for theoretical analysis, but also may be acutely aware of his or her marginal position. It has often been noted that the so-called middle strata – which include empirically many of the class positions we have defined as structurally ambiguous – are politically unstable and volatile in their loyalties. As Wright Mills vividly expressed it, 'the new middle classes are up for sale',[30] and political parties of every shade assiduously court the 'middle ground' – their permanent support would give the lucky winners perpetual tenure of office. We would suggest that in the last analysis the wide and often changing spectrum of opinion and action within this heterogeneous grouping is a reflection of their structurally ambiguous class situation. Lacking a clearly defined class base, they may, without doing violence to their interests ally themselves at times with global capital, at times with the collective worker.

Life is not all violent swings of opinion, however, and we would expect extreme partisanship only to manifest itself in times of crisis. (In the United Kingdom during the General Strike, for example, the majority of the middle strata were firmly on the side of the bourgeoisie, whereas in France in 1968 many supported the workers and students). In general, structural ambiguity is resolved in gentler, more pedestrian ways. Ultimately, of course, structural ambiguity can only be resolved by a change in the nature of the position itself – by its transformation wholly or in major part into either collective worker or global capital. However it would be flying in the face of reality not to recognise that to a large extent structural ambiguity is apparently resolved for the *agent* in the absence of either of these two processes. In many, if not the majority of cases, structural ambiguity is apparently resolved for the agent through the operation of the secondary structural factors we have identified above. In our discussion of differentiation within the enterprise, we have noted that the differentiation of the capitalist function has given rise to managerial specialisation, corresponding very broadly to the different aspects of the capitalist function. We have already made the point that although management typically acts as the agent for all aspects of global capital, management as a whole is not synonymous with global capital as it also carries out a part of the function of the collective worker. In fact the incorporation of some elements of the labour process – in particular coordination and unity and the development and nurturing of 'expertise' – into the managerial function is an instance of differentiation consequent upon the development of the capitalist mode of production and associated relations of production. It is in this differentiation that the structural ambiguity of many class situations originates. On the other hand the definition of these aspects of the function of the collective worker as 'management', and their subsequent close association with the capitalist function, has the effect of apparently resolving structural ambiguity for the agent. For many managers the issue will simply never be salient. Thus, when the function of the collective worker embodied in a structurally ambiguous class situation is carried out as a part of management, we would expect the agent unambiguously to identify with the bourgeoisie. The emergence of bureaucratic hierarchies also plays an important part in apparently resolving structurally ambiguous class situations. As we have already noted, in our discussion in Chapter Five, empirically, coordination and unity are invariably associated with control and surveillance, indeed coordination has become an aspect of control. Thus, when the aspect of the collective worker function within a structurally ambiguous class situation has been incorporated as part of a hierarchical structure of authority, it is most unlikely that the agent will feel any sense of ambiguity.

By no means all structurally ambiguous class situations are apparently resolved for the agent by role definition as 'management', incorporation into a bureaucratic hierarchy, or both. The *fact* of structural ambiguity will be much more overt in some cases – for example, the technician, or 'staff' as opposed to 'line' management. Many technicians, as highly skilled *workers*, are overtly engaged in a part of the process of production *per se*, although their work may involve the giving of orders, and may also be used to police the work of other workers (as with quality control). However, because their work can clearly be seen to be part of the production process, the extent to which they perform the function of the collective worker is seen as such and not easily defined as a part of management. Similarly, staff management is not easily incorporated into a hierarchical structure. On organisation charts, staff functions are often represented in mid-air (or mid-page!), related horizontally to the hierarchical structure of line organisation. This horizontal 'slotting in' does not usually carry with it any authority over the levels 'below' the staff function in the line hierarchy. Indeed the precise level at which staff management is horizontally related often seems to be rather arbitrary, and corresponds to some sort of approximation of the placing which the skills and capacities the staff function would merit if they *were* part of the line hierarchy. There may of course be hierarchies of authority *within* staff functions, but in general the fact that such structurally ambiguous class situations may lack a clear placement within the bureaucratic hierarchy implies that structural ambiguity cannot be resolved for the agent by these means.

Better material rewards and enhanced prestige (social market and status factors) must be accepted as very important factors in the apparent resolution of class ambiguity. In Chapter Eight we suggested that enhanced material rewards are associated with the carrying out of the capitalist function, even if such agents are nominally 'employees'. Similarly loyalty is easier to ensure if rewards are good, and the dependability of those in structurally ambiguous class situations often crucial to the success of the enterprise. In addition differential reward structures are probably the most important factor in the creation of interest groupings. It is obvious that if those in structurally ambiguous class situations can be persuaded, through better material rewards, that their interests 'really' lie with the capitalist function, much potential conflict will be avoided. (Of course in the short-term it is perfectly rational for those in structurally ambiguous class situations to maximise their level of reward.) Status factors are similarly influential. Indeed it would appear that so important is the need for self-esteem that many in structurally ambiguous class situations associate themselves with the capitalist function in the absence of significantly higher levels of material reward; enhanced status through association would appear to be sufficient.

The success of both better material rewards and relatively

high status in apparently resolving structural ambiguity
depends of course on their continuing presence. (Similar processes may occur in respect of structurally unambiguous class
situations, for example, the 'affluent worker' referred to
earlier.) If, due to the economic and/or organisational
changes, the level of either material or status rewards
declines, the way is open for those in structurally
ambiguous class situations to transfer their allegiances; and
there is some evidence that they do. The recent rise in white-
collar unionism in the United Kingdom, for example, has
been associated with a decline in both status and rewards
amongst many groups of workers. Empirical evidence of this
decline, and the subsequent increase in the level of trade
union activity, is provided by a recent study of technicians
by Roberts, Loveridge, and Gennard.[31] Basic information and
attitudinal data was collected from a sample of over a
thousand technicians, working in a variety of industries –
petroleum products, metal manufacture, electrical engineering and vehicles.[32] The study showed that technicians have
always been in a somewhat marginal position within the
organisation (a reflection in many cases of their structurally
ambiguous class situation), but historically had tended to
identify themselves with management and the employers.
Their cooperation and loyalty had been rewarded with 'staff'
(i.e., enhanced) status and relatively high rates of pay.
However increasing technological sophistication, combined
with economic and trade union pressures in the sixties, has
led to a relative decline in both status and pay. The technician
is under pressure from above from the increasing number
of college-trained technologists who are usurping the
technicians' position because of their formal, and better,
qualifications. At the same time the technician is under pressure from below, as productivity deals often allocated to
the skilled work-force the more complex aspects of the
labour process which had once been the province of the
technician. Thus the relative status of the technician within
the organisation is in decline. Together with this decline
in status has occurred a worsening of the market situation,
both absolutely and relatively: 'The increasing number of
technical staff in employment has meant an increase in the

wage costs of technicians and a rising concern with the need to economise this factor.'[33] Mergers and rationalisations during the sixties resulted in many technicians being made redundant; previously, their 'staff' status had afforded them protection. Productivity deals considerably increased (in the short term) the pay of skilled manual workers, whose pay sometimes overlapped with, or was greater than, that of the technicians as a result of these deals. Because of their past tradition of cooperation with management, technicians had no restrictive practices to sell and thus did not benefit from the 'productivity wage explosion' at all.

The decline in the status and market situation of the technician has led, understandably, to considerable questioning of their past strategy of cooperation with management (or the capitalist function). New strategies of behaviour are being tested, and increasing trade unionism is one major response within the technician grouping. Notwithstanding the qualifications about the role of trade union organisation we expressed earlier in this chapter, there is no doubt that for many technicians trade union activity represents a significant break with tradition and a realignment of traditional loyalties. A.S.T.M.S., a union busily recruiting in the technician field, touched the nerve of this shift of loyalties in its full-page recruiting advertisement in *The Times* headed 'Management has decided it does not like the colour of your eyes.'

Largely because of the lack of suitable empirical material, we have made no attempt to estimate the overall size of the many and various groupings that we would argue are in a structurally ambiguous class situation. Many such class situations are encompassed in the rather loose amalgam that has come to be known as the 'middle class' – new or otherwise. In this category we can include such occupations as middle to lower-level management in all sectors, including foremen, many technicians and other 'experts', much of state and local government administration and others in state non-capitals such as health, education, etc. We would stress however that our analysis would associate many occupations which have historically been termed 'middle class' in sociological and popular literature firmly with the collective worker function (or proletariat). We can mention here the great mass of retail and sales workers, routine clerical or white-collar occupations, low-level civil servants and local government employees, and workers employed in state non-capitals. That many such occupations *have* been associated with the middle class is due above all to the operation of secondary structural factors – in particular social market and status factors.

Even though our approach would exclude many who have formerly been termed 'middle class', the total number of those in occupations we would claim to be structurally ambiguous is still considerable. Wright has recently attempted to estimate the size of the 'contradictory class location[s]' in the United States. As our discussion has indicated, we would not define as 'structurally ambiguous' some of the occupations Wright has argued are in a con-tradictory class location – craftsmen, for example – and our theoretical reasons for arguing that a class situation *is* structurally ambiguous are rather different from those which Wright employs to ascertain contradictory class locations. Nevertheless, adapting Wright's empirical material, we would give a rough estimate of 30 per cent as the size of the structurally ambiguous class locations in the United States; the figure is probably very similar for Britain.[34]

Although we have recognised the association of struc-turally ambiguous class situations with the middle class, this does not mean that we would regard the heterogeneous complex of structurally ambiguous class situations as con-stituting a class in any sense. In a Marxist sense, such class situations lack a firmly defined class base. As they contain elements of both global capital and collective worker, control and coordinated labour, they may potentially associate with either function, although the net effect of secondary structural factors has historically tended to orient them towards global capital rather than collective worker.

Even if we employ non-Marxist strategies of class analysis, it is difficult to fit this heterogeneous grouping into a single class. In particular the range of market differences and status differentials will commonly be so wide so as to preclude firm identification on the basis of interests.

For ourselves, we see no analytical difficulties in locating such structurally ambiguous elements within the class structure of capitalist society, yet at the same time arguing that they do not constitute a social class in themselves. They are significantly different from the 'old' middle classes, for example, the peasantry and the petty bourgeoisie. The 'old' middle classes were located externally to capitalist relationships of production, as independent artisans, small landholders, or small family-based, productive units. They were dominated by capitalist production relationships without being integrated into the capitalist class structure. However the so-called 'new' middle class – or structurally ambiguous class situations – draw their ambiguous character directly from the structure of capitalist relations of production.

Although in developed capitalist societies the class situation of the majority of the members of the society will be determined in the last analysis by capitalist relationships of production, it does not follow that the class situation of all societal members is so determined. In particular there may be significant numbers of people lying outside the scope of capitalist production relations. To conclude our discussion of the class structure of capitalist societies we will therefore briefly draw attention to two groupings external to the capitalist mode – the petty bourgeoisie and lumpenproletariat. The relative importance of these groupings will show considerable variation as between different capitalist nation states, and of course both will be greatly influenced by capitalist dominance.

As petty bourgeoisie we identify those who contract their services on an individual basis as independent artisans – say, the jobbing builder – and small-scale family businesses which rarely, if ever, employ wage labour. In this latter category are found small shopkeepers and productive enterprises, as well as the great mass of the landowning peasantry. Individual or small-scale family production was a feature of society before the advent of the capitalist mode of production, and it has persisted with the development of monopoly capitalism; even in the Eastern bloc countries, the small producer is widely tolerated, even if not officially sanctioned.

However, although individual and family enterprise is a continuing feature of capitalist society, and operates in similar spheres of activity to capitalist enterprises, the class situation of those engaged in such enterprises is not determined by capitalist relationships of production. As they do not employ wage labour they do not extract or acquire surplus value in the manner of the capitalist. As they do not hire out their labour power to the capitalist function they are not exploited through the appropriation of surplus labour power. Therefore, although we may for analytical purposes term the petty bourgeoisie a 'class', we must be constantly aware that this class situation is not determined by capitalist relationships of production, and their class position is located outside these relations.

The second grouping we discuss here, the lumpenproletariat, is similarly located outside the dominant structure of capitalist production relationships, indeed it is a feature of the lumpenproletariat that they are more or less chronically unemployed. As examples we can cite immigrants from rural areas who exist on the fringes of metropolitan districts – as in the *bidonvilles* of Paris or the shanty towns of Latin America – refugee populations, poor immigrants from ex-colonial territories who fail to become integrated into the 'host' society, and so on. Employment, if any, tends to be sporadic and of a casual and unskilled nature, and life is often only barely maintained through national and international poor relief, supplemented by a myriad of activities such as street selling and other odd jobs. Analytically, the lumpenproletariat corresponds to the 'underclass' identified by Giddens, in that they are more or less excluded from the prevailing structure of market opportunities and have to scratch a living where and when they can.

Because the class interest of neither grouping is determined by the structure of capitalist production relationships, we would suggest that market factors are extremely important in determining the interests and ideology of both the petty bourgeoisie and the lumpenproletariat. The petty bourgeois operate in markets dominated by large-scale capital and the state; as such, their class interests are located closest to small-scale capital. Because of their economic position, both petty bourgeois and small-scale capital will be firmly wedded to the values of individualism, free enterprise and free markets, values which are a part of the official ideology of conservatism. Yet paradoxically the increasing interdependence of the state and larger corporations in monopoly capitalism makes it highly unlikely that conservative parties will ever do very much for some of their firmest supporters. Feelings of betrayal may lead to attempts at independent political organisation – Poujadism in France, for example – but the political critique so engendered will be of monopoly or 'state-dominated' capitalism, rather than of capitalism as such. In other words, although at times the petty bourgeoisie and small employers may be very vocal in their criticisms of the *prevailing* structure of capitalism (which may lead to short-term alliances with the proletariat), it is unlikely that they will ever unambiguously ally themselves with the proletariat in any long-term struggle for the overthrow of capitalism as such.

At first sight it might appear that the class interests of the lumpenproletariat lie closest to the proletariat. Historically, however, this has by no means been the case; we would argue that this is largely because of the virtual exclusion of this poorest section of the 'industrial' community from access to the market and the prevailing structure of production relationships. Acute material deprivation makes them relatively easy game for the highest bidder: having little to lose and relatively much to gain they may be and are used by the capitalist function as strike breakers, *agents provocateurs*, or persuaded to work on terms and conditions of employment unacceptable to organised labour. In these circumstances there may well be considerable conflict between them and the proletariat. On the other hand there is also evidence that the lumpenproletariat may identify with left-wing political organisation – as in Allende's Chile. Unlike the petty bourgeoisie, therefore, the lumpenproletariat may manifest shifting class identifications, although material want and degradation will make apolitical apathy the most common 'response'.

Throughout this book we have tried to emphasise that, although much of our analysis is at a very abstract level and can be applied to any capitalist society, we fully recognise that particular capitalist nation states will show considerable variations in occupational structures, dominance of particular factions, class alliances, and so on. These variations are in part due to the operation of the secondary structural factors we have discussed in this chapter, but more particularly due to the unique historical development of the many and various societies which go to make up the international structure of capitalism. The importance of historical factors is nowhere more relevant than in the determination of the size and relative importance of these two groups which we have located outside of the structure of capitalist production relationships. The size of the petty bourgeoisie will depend on patterns of inheritance and land tenure, the rate and timing of capitalist development, population density, etc. (In capitalist societies with a scattered population there is likely to be a continuing demand for small-scale services which are characteristically provided by the petty bourgeoisie.) The size of the lumpenproletariat will depend on specific historical factors such as the manner and the rate of decolonisation, the presence or absence of subordinate ethnic groups, and so on. In the majority of advanced societies with a hundred or more years of capitalist development behind them it is likely that the lumpenproletariat will be a residual grouping (unless the economic situation gives rise to widespread, chronic, unemployment as in the depression of the thirties), almost completely unimportant for any social or political analysis. However, in the so-called developing nations, especially where there has been a rapid transition to capitalist production in the monopoly stage, the lumpenproletariat will be correspondingly large. In such cases capitalist production relationships have released a pool of potential wage labour on to the market much larger than actually required by non-labour-intensive production techniques. The presence or absence of a significant stratum of petty bourgeoisie or lumpenproletariat may have significant political consequences for particular societies, which should be taken into account in any class analysis of these societies.

As with many other points discussed in this book, therefore, our brief review of the location of the petty bourgeoisie and lumpenproletariat in the class structure has raised issues which can only be explicated through more or less detailed analyses of particular situations. We have attempted, through an investigation of the economic structure of contemporary capitalism, to demonstrate that Marx's approach to class analysis is still relevant to contemporary capitalism. We would suggest that the framework we have developed from Marx's work can be applied whilst still retaining many of the insights and theories developed by more conventional 'sociological' class theorists. In the final instance, however, the class structure of any particular society can only properly be understood by the systematic empirical and historical investigation of that society – informed, we hope, by the theoretical approach we have attempted to develop.

Appendix

A NOTE ON THE LABOUR THEORY OF VALUE

Capitalist production, as analysed by Marx, is production of commodities, that is, of goods which are exchanged in the market. Shifts in supply and demand may result in *fluctuations* in price but, since such features of the market themselves need to be explained, supply and demand cannot account for the *general level* of prices.

Marx argues that two commodities can exchange freely because they are equal in a certain respect, namely in the one thing that they necessarily have in common – that they are products of human labour. The value of a commodity in exchange is dependent on the amount of labour expended in creating it.

> A commodity has a *value* because it is a *crystallization of social labour*. The *greatness* of its value, of its relative value, depends upon the greater or less amount of that social substance contained in it; that is to say, on the relative mass of labour necessary for its production.[1]

The value of a commodity is thus measured as

> the *quantity of labour necessary* for its production in a given state of society, under certain social average conditions of production, with a given social average intensity and average skill of the labour employed.[2]

It is crucial to Marx's argument that values are defined relative to a particular society, specifying current technology and work organisation and current work norms and levels of skill. Although there are severe practical and conceptual difficulties in precisely quantifying socially necessary labour time, we do not consider that this refutes the theoretical validity of the notion of value.

Neither are values directly observable as exchange ratios in the market, in the first place because of market fluctuations. It could be argued that in the early stages of a competitive market economy average prices of commodities are approximately proportional to average labour time expended in making them, but with the development of capital this cannot be so. On the basis of Marx's theory, the fact of variations in the organic composition of capital, together with the tendency to profitability equalisation in different branches of industry, implies that prices depart from proportionality to values.[3] Marx and later authors have suggested ingenious solutions to 'the transformation problem', showing, on the basis of the labour theory of value, how prices might systematically differ from values by redistribution of surplus value between capitals of different organic composition.

Whatever the validity of these solutions might be, our argument in this book does not assume that the labour theory of value provides a sufficient basis for an adequate price theory. Whilst the economy of labour times powerfully constrains the price system, the mechanisms involved are undoubtedly very complex and varied. The very fact of monopoly and state planning certainly prejudices prospects of constructing a valid theory deriving prices from values.

In Marx's theory the value of any commodity depends on the amount of labour embodied in it. Labour is an activity rather than a commodity so it is clearly nonsense to refer to the value of labour. However, the capacity to labour, labour power, is bought and sold on the market and thus like all other commodities has a value – a value depending on the amount of labour embodied in it. More explicitly, the value of labour power is equal to the value of the necessaries required to reproduce and maintain the labourer. Marx insists that what is necessary may extend far beyond physical needs to include established standards of living. These standards may alter over time, occasionally quite rapidly, rising, for example, with the development of new technology and work organisation or where capitals seek to induce greater commitment by their employees, or falling as wage cuts are imposed in times of 'national crisis'. The level of unemployment is clearly a major factor in determining wage levels and indeed the circumstance of full employment and increasing prosperity since the war (until recently) has been widely taken as refuting Marx's wage theory. On this point we believe that such a judgement is premature, although we do doubt that necessaries *independently* determine wage levels. It is not a tautology but a fact of the way capitalist societies operate that actual living standards become necessaries; aspirations and expectations for standards of living are generated socially by reference to socially justified differentials and the promises, predictions and inducements of capital's spokesmen (as sellers, employers and ideologists). Nevertheless we are sceptical of the notion that the labour theory of values enables wage rates to be predicted with any accuracy.

In our view Marx's value theory exposes the logic of relations between capital, labour and commodities – a logic which enables us to start to understand the aggregate flows of value in the total capitalist system.

As we have argued in the text, the 'flow of value' picture does require modification in the light of the growth of quasi capital, but it still provides a basis for understanding class relations. Whether or not the product is realised in the market, Marx's analysis shows that the 'equal' exchange involved in hiring wage labour masks exploitative social relationships.

Notes and References

CHAPTER 2

1. The two references are: 'Class, Status, and Party', in H. Gerth and C. W. Mills, eds., and the concluding section of M. Weber, ed. T. Parsons (1966).
2. M. Weber (1966) p. 424.
3. H. Gerth and C. W. Mills, pp. 181–2.
4. Ibid. p. 183.
5. Ibid. p. 185.
6. A. Giddens (1973) p. 47.
7. 'The development of rational economic action from its origins in the instinctively reactive search for food or in traditional acceptance of inherited techniques and customary social relationships has been to a large extent determined by non-economic events and actions.' M. Weber (1966) p. 166.
8. See, for example, K. Marx (1970b).
9. H. Gerth and C. W. Mills, p. 193–4.
10. M. Weber (1966) p. 424.
11. Ibid. p. 429.
12. Engels quoted in M. Nicolaus (1972).
13. K. Marx and F. Engels (1968a).
14. M. Nicolaus (1972).
15. K. Marx (1968c).
16. Ibid. pp. 64–5.
17. Ibid. p. 69.
18. K. Marx (1974b) p. 242.
19. B. Malinowski.
20. K. Polanyi.
21. K. Marx (1974b) p. 274.
22. Ibid. p. 324.
23. F. Engels, Introduction to K. Marx (1968d).
24. A. Giddens (1971) p. 46. See also Chapter Four below.

25. T. Bottomore (1965) p. 21.
26. J. Goldthorpe (1964).

CHAPTER 3

1. A. Giddens (1973) chaps. 1, 2 and 3.
2. D. Lockwood (1958) pp. 15–16.
3. R. Crompton (1976).
4. See above, p. 9.
5. F. Parkin (1972a).
6. Ibid. p. 18.
7. Ibid. p. 26.
8. Ibid. p. 24.
9. Ibid. pp. 25–6.
10. See, for example, B. Roberts *et al.*
11. G. S. Bain and R. Price.
12. J. Mitchell.
13. F. Parkin (1974).
14. Ibid. p. 14. In fact Parkin is here unnecessarily restricted by his own assertions as to what is logically possible. For example, an important part of the scheme of class analysis we develop is that some groups – often located in these 'middle strata – perform the functions of capital *and* labour. This is both logically and empirically possible.
15. Ibid. p. 3.
16. Ibid. p. 5.
17. Ibid. p. 15 (our emphasis).
18. F. Parkin (1972a) p. 26.
19. Ibid. p. 145.
20. Ibid. p. 144.
21. Ibid. p. 147.
22. Given the subsequent development of his analysis (F. Parkin, 1974), perhaps he would now argue that the higher echelons of the party constitute 'classes of nomination'.
23. F. Parkin (1972b).
24. D. Lane (1977). Lane argues that the overlap between the party and intelligentsia is in fact sufficient to characterise the Soviet élite as 'unitary'.
25. D. Lane (1970) p. 333.
26. Ibid. chap. 10.
27. C. Crouch.
28. A. Giddens (1973) p. 95.
29. Ibid. p. 127 (our emphasis).

30. Ibid. pp. 96–7.
31. R. Rowthorn.
32. A. Giddens (1973) p. 96.
33. Ibid. p. 130.
34. See Chapter Two above, p. 8.
35. A. Giddens (1973) p. 107.
36. Ibid. pp. 134–5.
37. Ibid. pp. 112–13.
38. Ibid. p. 205.
39. Ibid. p. 214.
40. Ibid. p. 291.
41. Ibid. p. 292.
42. Ibid. p. 112.
43. Ibid. p. 249.
44. Ibid. p. 250.
45. Ibid. p. 251.
46. Ibid. p. 269.

CHAPTER 4

1. D. McClellan.
2. S. Pollard.
3. C. M. Cipolla, ed., p. 468.
4. Ibid. p. 370.
5. B. Supple, pp. 308–9.
6. Ibid. pp. 326 ff.
7. See above, p. 32f.
8. T. Bottomore and M. Rubel, eds. (1973) p. 198.
9. K. Marx, *Theories of Surplus Value*, vol. 1, quoted in M. Nicolaus (1970).
10. K. Marx (1974*a*) p. 299.
11. Ibid. p. 292.
12. M. Nicolaus (1970).
13. A. Giddens (1973) p. 177.
14. K. Marx (1974*a*) p. 436.
15. Ibid. p. 438.
16. Ibid. p. 439.
17. Ibid. p. 440.
18. P. A. Baran and P. M. Sweezy, chap. 2.
19. That is, Marx failed to anticipate the 'Keynesian revolution'. Perhaps this criticism is unduly severe!
20. See in particular R. Miliband, and N. Poulantzas.
21. K. Marx (1970*a*) p. 751.

23.   K. Marx (1968*e*) p. 211.
23.   Given the continuing debate about the autonomy (or other-wise) of the state (see in particular N. Poulantzas), it is interes-ting to note that Marx's discussions of state autonomy largely concern a society in the 'early' stages of capitalist development in the nineteenth century – i.e., France. See, for example, K. Marx (1974*c*) pp. 246–9.
24.   T. H. Marshall.
25.   C. Kerr *et al.*, J. K. Galbraith (1961, 1969), T. H. Marshall, R. Dahrendorf, C. Kaysen.
26.   K. Marx and F. Engels (1968*a*) pp. 34–5.
27.   See, for example, R. Dahrendorf, T. Parsons, A. Giddens (1973), K. Davis (1958).
28.   M. Weber (1969) p. 103.
29.   D. Beetham.
30.   Ibid. pp. 242–3.
31.   M. Weber in H. Gerth and C. W. Mills, eds, chap. 8, sects 6, 9 and 10.
32.   D. Beetham, chap. 3.
34.   M. Weber (1966) p. 339.
34.   D. Beetham, p. 83.
35.   See, in particular, M. Weber (1965).
36.   E. Durkheim (1966) p. 35.
37.   S. Lukes.
38.   T. Parsons, and the discussion by D. Lockwood (1967).
39.   A. Giddens (1971).
40.   E. Durkheim (1968) p. 384.
41.   Ibid. p. 377.
42.   Durkheim developed further his prescriptions for the for-mation of such 'secondary groupings' – see E. Durkheim (1957, 1958).
43.   A. Giddens (1971) pp. 203–4.
44.   See, for example, the discussion in A. Gamble and P. Walton, chaps 2, 6.

CHAPTER 5

1.   Large numbers of independent shops have to face competition from the multiples and so are often forced into specialised trade or into retreating from 'high street' to 'corner'. Furthermore many shops have to purchase the goods they sell from large corporations. In agriculture, big firms dominate the many small farmers as buyers of their products and, even

in this sphere, corporations have in recent years been taking over more and more farms.

2. According to M. Barratt Brown, 30 per cent of the 120 top quoted British companies in 1966 were controlled by tycoons or members of the founding family.

3. The separation of ownership and control has been widely discussed over many years. Recent contributions to the continuing debate include M. Barratt Brown (1968), G. Domhoff (1967), R. V. Clements (1958), C. Crosland (1962), J. K. Galbraith (1969), C. Kerr *et al.* (1973), C. W. Mills (1959), T. Nichols (1969), P. Baran and P. Sweezy (1968).

4. R. Dahrendorf, p. 43.

5. See, for example, C. W. Mills (1959), G. Domhoff, T. Nichols (1969), J. Westergaard and H. Resler (1975), C. Yanaga.

6. See, for example, C. A. R. Crosland, C. Kaysen, J. K. Galbraith (1969).

7. For a valuable discussion of this point see P. Baran and P. Sweezy, chap. 2.

8. Precisely because a large number of small shareholders are typically unorganised, a few major shareholders may be sure of winning support from a sufficient number of small shareholders to obtain a majority at shareholders' meetings.

9. While we certainly do not wish to present a picture of finance capital dominating industrial capital, it is undoubtedly true that share portfolios held by the great financial institutions give them a capacity to intervene in company policy even to the extent of coordinating a number of industrial capitals. Interlocking directorships, particularly between financial and other companies, are perhaps some indication of such coordination.

10. R. Dahrendorf, p. 43.

11. K. Marx (1970a).

12. That Marx refers to material objects being created is incidental to the logic of his argument here; the emphasis is on the worker's submission to capital's authority.

13. See G. Bannock, C. Tugenhadt, R. Likert, J. Woodward.

14. It should not be assumed that ascending the hierarchy of the formal management chart is equivalent to identifying roles which are more and more 'capital' rather than 'labour'; in some cases the lowest rung of the managerial ladder, the foreman, is almost entirely a control role.

15. H. Braverman, chap. 3.

16. Ibid. p. 58.

17. E. P. Thompson.
18. K. Marx (1970a) parts 3, 4, 5.
19. We are referring here to the detailed (or technical) division of labour *inside* the work-place, not to the social division of labour between occupations in branches of production and circulation. Braverman (p. 73) draws the contrast as follows: 'In capitalism, the social division of labour is enforced chaotically and anarchically by the market, while the work-shop division of labour is imposed by planning and control.'
20. See H. Braverman, chap. 3.
21. See Chapter Nine.
22. The above discussion owes much to G. Carchedi.
23. The following discussion draws from I. Gough, although our conclusions differ significantly from his.
24. In the early stages of capitalist development 'initial' capital was obtained to a large degree not as surplus value but as direct expropriation of peasants' products, trade backed by force with pre-capitalist societies and commercial exploitation of artisan labour.
25. Finance capitalists may make loans to capitalists in non-productive spheres also, such as commerce, but then they acquire in interest a share of the surplus value that capitalist obtained from an industrial or service capitalist.
26. We are concerned with property here as a means of production or consumption hired out on the market, not traditional dues by which a tenant is tied personally to his 'lord' politically and ideologically as well as economically.
27. Land is given by nature rather than a human product, but in capitalist societies it is treated as if it were a commodity. Note also that some things which are technically indispensable for production are not bought but socially provided, for example roads. This socialisation of costs will be discussed extensively in Chapter Six. Marx's terminology distinguishes variable capital (labour) from constant capital (raw materials and 'fixed' capital such as plant, machinery, vehicles, etc.). The amount of value created in a production process with given technology and organisation of production is in principle proportional to the total labour time expended – thence the term 'variable capital'. In the production process the value 'congealed' in the constant capital is transferred to the product, using up the raw materials and wearing out the fixed capital.
28. Surplus value, reckoned as labour time, is the difference

NOTES AND REFERENCES

average energy and using the current technology and methods
of production, and the amount necessary to produce the
equivalent of goods and services to maintain the worker and
his family at the customary standard (according to physically
and socially generated needs).

29. See above, p. 71.
30. See G. Carchedi.
31. E. O. Wright.
32. These usually include, with significance for our discussion of
    the relation between owners and managers, options to
    purchase shares on favourable terms.
33. There are also debentures, which bear a fixed rate of interest
    but which differ from loans in that they entitle the holder to a
    share of the assets in the case of the company winding up.
    Debenture income seems to be a mixture of loan interest and
    share of profits but we are not concerned by the problem of
    which is the most apt way of classifying it; the important point
    for our analysis is that it is a portion of surplus value.
34. That is, the service does not contribute to the accumulation of
    capital but is personally consumed (for example, hairdresser,
    waiter, house decorator, where such labourers are employed
    by a capitalist who gets them to serve clients).
35. K. Marx (1970a) p. 509. As we shall argue later, a teaching
    factory owned by the state puts the schoolmaster in a similar
    class situation to the worker in the state-owned sausage factory,
    provided costs are covered by school fees. Where education is
    'free' the teacher's class situation is somewhat altered even
    though they remain wage labourers.
36. For example, hotels and property capital in so far as rent is
    charged, industrial capital in so far as food is prepared, service
    capital in so far as rooms are cleaned and food is served,
    and so on.
37. Marx (1967), p. 301, makes this point very cogently:

    The commercial worker produces no surplus value directly.
    But the price of his labour is determined by the value of his
    labour power, hence its cost of production, while the applica-
    tion of this labour power, its exertion, expenditure of
    energy, and wear and tear, is as in the case of every other
    wage labourer by no means limited to its value. His wage,
    therefore, is not necessarily proportionate to the mass of
    profit which he helps the capitalist to realise. What he costs
    the capitalist and what he brings in for him, are two different

things. He creates no surplus value, but adds to the capitalist's income by helping him to reduce the cost of realising surplus value, in as much as he performs partly unpaid labour.

38. This could be an extremely long time, particularly if the product is exported.

39. For completeness, it should be noted that one commercial capital often trades with another. This arises in two main ways – wholesaler to retailer and between commercial capitals in different countries.

40. Mandel neatly expresses the function and role of finance capital in capitalist society:

> The function of credit institutions under capitalism is to fulfil the . . . role of intermediary between those who hold unproductive sums of money and those who are looking for opportunities to increase their own capital with the aid of borrowed capital. . . . He (the finance capitalist) is useful to the capitalist mode of production only to the extent that he can overcome the fragmentation of social capital into a multitude of individual properties. It is this function of *mobiliser and centraliser of social capital* that his whole importance to society consists. This function goes beyond the class limits of the bourgeoisie in the strict sense and embraces the centralisation of the funds saved by landowners, rich and middle peasants, craftsmen, civil servants, technicians, and even skilled workers in prosperous periods (p. 221, Mandel's italics.)

41. Note that in many countries finance capital has played a major part in the lives of those engaged in petty production and circulation, particularly peasants, who spend their whole lives (or at least the periods between harvests) in debt to financiers.

42. The diagram is easily modified to show the case where some of the outlay is provided by the industrial capital and our argument about the function of credit for industry is not altered significantly.

43. Thus the ideological justification of profit as a reward for saving is invalidated, in its own terms.

44. This is likely to be particularly important in international trade.

45. This can be represented diagrammatically as in Figure 9.

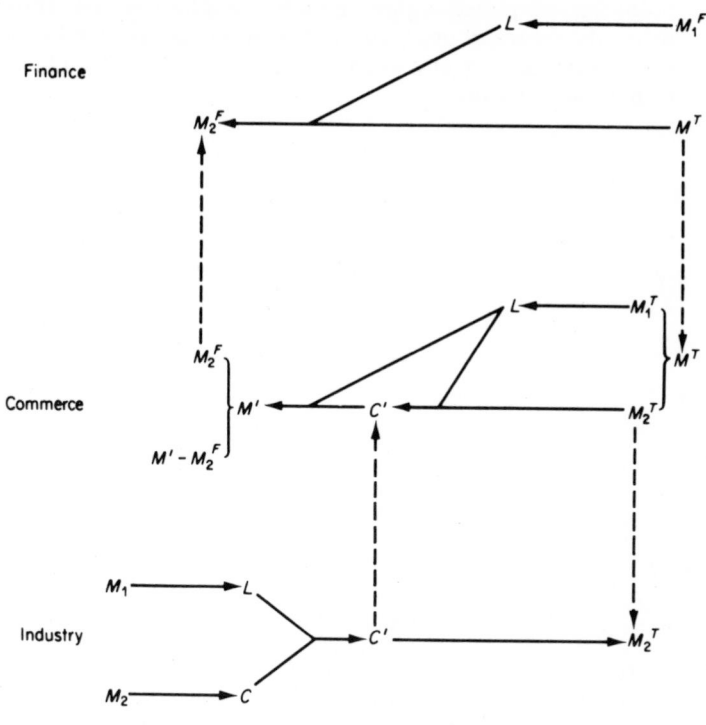

Figure 9

Of the total surplus value $M' - (M_1 + M_2)$ commerce *initially* obtains $M' - M_2{}^T$ but $M_1{}^T$ of this has to be paid in wages to the commercial worker and $M_2{}^F - M^T$ in interest, leaving the commercial capital with $M' - M_2{}^F$. Of the interest the finance capital gets $M_2{}^F - (M_1{}^F + M^T)$ and the finance worker $M_1{}^F$. All these sums are shares of surplus value.

46. See pp. 69–71.
47. It is not necessary for the purposes of our argument to provide an explanation of rent – we simply take if for granted that the use of some types of property allow the owner to extract a rental from the users. For an explanation of the phenomenon see K. Marx (1974a), E. Mandel, or M. Howard and J. King (1975) chaps 4, 5.
48. The portion of payments which cover depreciation of the property is not so much rent as purchase of goods. The

following simplified figure ignores depreciation. We show below the means of production C^P, which is not altered by the production process, and which is presumed to have been hired to an industrial capital.

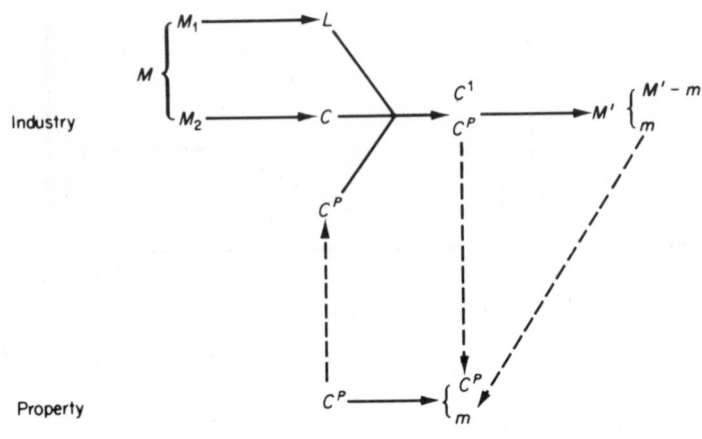

Figure 10

Of the total surplus value $M' - M$ the industrial capital has to pay the rent of m. Out of this the property capital has to pay the wages of the property workers (not shown on the figure).

49. For example, the class situation of the rent collector will be affected by the class situation of the tenant. This will affect his interests and consequently his likely consciousness, possible enemies and possible allies.

50. According to P. A. Baran and P. M. Sweezy, the situation has increasingly developed where 'the sales and production efforts interpenetrate to such an extent as to become virtually indistinguishable' (p. 135). They expand on the theoretical significance of this point:

No one doubts that a large part of the actual labour which goes into producing an automobile – how much we shall examine presently – has the purpose not of making a more serviceable product but of making a more saleable product. But the automobile, once designed, is a unit which is turned out by the combined efforts of all the workers in the shop and on the assembly line. How can the productive workers be distinguished from the unproductive? How can selling costs and production costs be separated? (p. 137)

While we do not share these authors' implicit assumption that to make a product serviceable, as distinct from saleable, is equivalent to being engaged in production, we recognise that they are posing important questions which demand a theory about the generation of social needs under capitalism.

51. It is true that such assets could be incorporated in the means of production C in Figure 2 for the case of industry. Also the figures showing finance and commerce could be modified to show fixed capital required for buying and selling, and making credit available. Whereas such procedures are in no way objectionable there may be advantages in analysing property capital explicity in such cases, as argued in the text.

52. For example, I.T.T. is engaged in a wide range of electronics manufacturing, hotels, care hire and insurance. See A. Sampson.

53. Indeed in Germany and Japan industrialisation was launched on the basis of state-protected markets and monopoly.

54. The tensions inherent in the foreman's work role have been reasonably well-documented, although not within the framework utilised here. See Wedderburn and Crompton (1972) on the conflict between 'authority' (or global capital) and 'expertise' (or collective worker) in respect of expectations of foremen.

55. E. O. Wright, p. 28.

CHAPTER 6

1.   *Employment in the United Kingdom in '000s in 1973*

Central Government	
H.M. Forces and Women's Services	361
Civilians	1,608
Local Authorities	2,714
Public Corporations	1,858
Total employed population	23,238

SOURCE: *British Labour Statistics Yearbook* 1973, pp. 196 and 122.

2. Even where nationalised enterprises do make a profit, none of this goes to enrich individuals in the form of dividends or capital gains.

3. Capitals can and do combine in cartels, thereby foregoing competition in certain respects. However, if a capital in a cartel is able to secure greater cost reductions than others or obtain priveleged access to factor or product markets, it has an interest in quitting; this very possibility makes cartel members compete with one another in cost reduction, vertical integration and sales promotion. On the other hand, really effective control over mutual competition would mark a transformation from cartel to conglomerate capital.

    Capitals also regulate their relations with labour, for example by setting up agencies to promote their point of view publicly or pressure the government, mutual assistance in the case of labour disputes and blacklisting of militant workers.

4. R. Miliband, pp. 78–9.

5. Several distinct circumstances give rise to quasi-capitals including state-owned enterprises, enterprises entering into planning agreements with the government, firms dependent on the state for raw materials, markets or technology, and constituent members of a cartel.

6. N. Harris, pp. 204–5. We have altered the tense in this quotation. See also J. Winkler, M. Kidron, J. Leruez. Whereas Winkler argues that massive state regulation of the economy signifies a new type of society – neither capitalist nor socialist – our view is that these changes can best be explained as the form taken by the capitalist state in circumstances of international oligopolistic competition.

7. See P. Bachrach and M. Baratz. More explicitly, the 'bias' in capitalist societies is that nothing should be done that hinders overall capital accumulation.

8. At any one time one or more sections of the capitalist class may be dominant, in Poulantzas's terminology, constitute a 'hegemonic fraction'. See N. Poulantzas.

9. At the time of writing, the Confederation of British Industries and the Conservative Party are pressing strongly for reduced taxation on firms and higher level incomes and demanding major cuts in state expenditure, with the notable exceptions of defence and grants to businesses. They argue that there should be cuts in what they call 'non-productive' areas of state expenditure such as health services, administration, social services, and subsidies on rents, food and school meals. Such

policies are not put forward, at least in public, as claims for sectional privilege but as being necessary for economic growth and the ultimate benefit of everybody.

10. *Pace* Weber, the modern state cannot be a perfectly integrated administrative machine; its various branches and hierarchies will reflect class antagonisms and indeed provide an important focus for them. Each part of the state apparatus may recruit personnel from particular social origins – the bourgeoisie, the aristocracy, the 'old' or 'new' middle class or even the lumpenproletariat. Patterns of élite recruitment may correspond to types of capitalist regime such as fascism, Bonapartism, military dictatorship, parliamentary democracy, autocracy etc. See Poulantzas.

11. Effective demand means the total of goods and services that capitals and workers want to buy and have the means to do so.

12. High interest rates cut workers living standards directly in increasing payments on hire purchases and mortgages, and indirectly because the burden of interest on the government, property capitals and capitals generally is passed on in taxation, rents and other prices.

13. Too low a level of working-class consumption prejudices commitment to work efficiency and even threatens reproduction of the labour force with appropriate skills. Socialisation of costs, such as state provision for training labour and building roads, benefits all capitals. Necessary through these expenses are for long-term capital accumulation, they are most vulnerable to attack when the economy is under pressure.

14. As Kincaid points out, in recent years, there has been a marked tendency for the taxation threshold as a proportion of average wages to decline; because of means tests, there is a punitive marginal rate of taxation on low incomes; furthermore, while direct taxation is progressive, rates, national insurance and taxation on expenditure are all sharply regressive.

15. A. Gamble and P. Walton, pp. 171–2.

16. In Britain a ministry department is responsible to a minister and thence, in theory, to Parliament. The employees are civil servants and it is financed out of the exchequer. The Post Office used to operate as a ministerial department but is now a public corporation, and there are few remaining 'trading' sections of departments. The most substantial manufacturing element under ministerial control is the Ministry of Defence –

141,660 industrial civil servants employed in 1971 in dock-yards, ordnance factories and maintenance departments. As we make clear on p. 102, these enterprises should properly be regarded as quasi-capitals rather than capitals.

A public corporation is a wholly state-owned enterprise directed by a government-appointed board but not subject to day-to-day ministerial control. It is financed by issues of bonds and government loans, which it has to pay at a given rate of interest. Examples of public corporations in Britain are British Railways, British Steel, Electricity Council, Gas Council, National Enterprise Board, National Bus Company, National Coal Board, British Airways, Post Office. While these public corporations should undoubtedly be regarded as capitals (or quasi-capitals) some others cannot be so readily classified. For example, the water authorities act as a capital in selling water to industry by quantity but sell to consumers at a rate proportional to the local taxation (rates), while they also have statutory duties with regard to upkeep of rivers, pollution control and effluent disposal. Again, it is not at all clear whether the Bank of England should be regarded more as a finance capital or an arm of government. We incline to the latter view.

The State also partly or totally owns the shares in a number of companies, which are subject to normal company law. The government may appoint some of the directors but does not normally interfere with details of company affairs. Examples of firms with major state shareholdings in Britain are Rolls-Royce (1971) Ltd, British Petroleum, British Sugar Corporation.

17.   The British Broadcasting Corporation receives some or all of the licence fees people have to pay annually to be allowed to use a television, but the Corporation's income depends on the number of televisions in use rather than the amount they are used in total. It is true that the Corporation seeks to obtain high ratings, in audience measurement surveys, but this is not so much selling their 'product' as trying to prove to the Government that, since their 'product' is popular, the licence fees represent good value for money. However, it is clear from this account, that although the Corporation is bound to be concerned about obtaining adequate income, its central goal is not capital accumulation. Even less can the Ministry of Transport section responsible for collecting vehicle licence fees be regarded as a capital. The fact that

the National Health Service does make some charges does not really affect its predominant character, not as a capital, but as an agent of social consumption and legitimation. We refer to all these enterprises as 'non-capitals'. See Chapter Nine.

18. There have been a number of attempts to define the principles by which nationalised industries should operate, although practice has often departed sharply from theory. A fairly consistent emphasis has been placed upon the duty of the corporation to act purely commercially except as specifically instructed to depart from this by statutory provision or explicit ministerial instruction. See A. H. Hansen and M. Walles (1975), pp. 174–89 for a brief summary. Other useful references are M. Rees, A. H. Hansen (1963) and R. Pryke.

19. R. Pryke, p. 460.

20. Ibid., p. 461.

21. The argument of this paragraph applies with equal force to cartels of privately owned corporations. If we wished to be pedantic, the partners in a cartel should be referred to as quasi-capitals rather than capitals but, as we have repeatedly argued, there is no practical difference for the relations between control and coordinated labour, that is, global capital and collective worker.

22. The discussion of this paragraph applies with equal force to the cases where there are similarly close relations between the government and privately owned corporations.

23. Any long-term contract between a state coal firm and a state electricity generating firm would become vulnerable to changes in prices of other fuels; if oil-generated electricity were cheaper than coal-generated electricity, the government would be under strong pressure to instruct the generating firm to increase the proportion of oil purchased. Such pressure might be resisted for a number of possible reasons such as military/strategic advantages of self-sufficiency in fuels, opposition by coal-miners to a decline in their industry and desire not to worsen balance of payments problems by importing oil. But reluctance to take decisions on the basis of price relativities exacts a substantial penalty in high electricity prices or exchequer subsidies – in either case costs to home capitals will be increased relative to other countries thus threatening their international competitiveness.

24. 'it is quite probable that no leader of a government in this country has been more hated, and even more feared, by business élites than was Roosevelt in the early (and even later)

stages of the New Deal. . . . Yet no one believes that Roosevelt
sought to (or did) weaken American Capitalism' (R. Miliband,
p. 102).

At the time of writing there is a debate within the Labour
Party as to whether a decline or an increase in state involvement in production is the most effective way to 'regenerate
British industry', i.e., promote capital accumulation. The
Labour Government, like the other major parties, seems to
have come down in favour of limiting state intervention and
emphasising 'encouragement' to private manufacturing
industry.

25. J. O'Connor, p. 6. See also chapters 4 and 5, on which we have
    drawn for some of the discussion in the rest of this section.
    We prefer to use the term 'social variable capital' rather than
    O'Connor's term 'social consumption' since we wish to
    emphasise its aspect as a subsidy to an input for capital rather
    than an unnecessary expense from capitals' point of view to
    workers' advantage.

26. J. O'Connor, p. 6. We prefer the term 'social constant capital'
    as being more explicit than O'Connor's 'social investment'.

27. See S. Melman, and M. Kidron.

28. R. Miliband, p. 178.

29. See M. Barratt Brown, chap. 3. Also see J. Kincaid.

30. See M. Kidron.

31. See C. Tugenhadt, and the useful collection of essays edited
    by H. Radice.

32. R. Bacon and W. Eltis. The apologetic use of the term 'pro-
    ductive' to identify it with profit-making, making it as
    applicable to employers as employees, needs no comment.

CHAPTER 7

1. We will refer to the Eastern countries as a convenient short-
   hand for the USSR, Poland, Hungary, Yugoslavia, Romania,
   Czechoslovakia, Bulgaria and the German Democratic
   Republic. We believe that the basic arguments of this chapter
   apply also to China, North Korea, Albania and Cuba
   although there are very great differences in the levels of
   industrial development. We do not use the term 'state socialist'
   to refer to these societies since that begs the question whether
   they are socialist or not. This chapter presents a similar
   analysis to T. Cliff (1970a).

2.   Nove describes the functions of Russian trade unions in the
     following terms:

> The structure of the unions is nominally democratic, with
> elections of officials and the all-union central council
> (AUCCTU) elected at national conferences. However, the
> Communist Party is in full control at all levels, and
> indeed there was only one national conference to elect the
> AUCCTU between 1932 and 1954. This central body must
> be regarded as a quasi-governmental labour agency, which
> is charged with administering the social fund, and with
> taking such action as will mobilise the workers in the
> struggle to fulfil output plans and other policies of the
> party and government. At the local level, trade union
> officials are supposed to reconcile these essentially official
> functions with the task of protecting workers from abuses on
> the part of management. . . . Subject to the overriding
> general aim of increasing production and fulfilling the
> plan, union officials on the spot are concerned with
> planned piece-rate and thereby have a hand in deciding
> how much is in fact earned by the workers, even though
> they have no power to negotiate about basic rates. (1965,
> p. 132.)

3.   Introducing these ideal types is an analytical device designed
     to identify the essential dynamic of the Eastern societies.
     Contemporary Yugoslavia approximates to the guided market
     type and Russia between 1930 and 1955 approximates to the
     directive planning type. We argue that both types are capitalist,
     so that logically all combinations of them are capitalist.
     We do not assume that the Eastern countries can be ranged on
     a single continuum between these two types.
4.   See an account of the planning process in A. Nove (1965).
5.   Profit in a directive planning system is one of a number of
     accounting devices used by the authorities to measure and
     control the performance of enterprises. By the way they fix
     prices and wages the planners can set corresponding profit
     targets, which may be high, low or even negative. We agree
     with Mandel's comment about enterprise profits: 'Profit is
     neither the purpose nor chief driving force of production. It is
     merely an accessory instrument in the hands of the state in
     order to facilitate the fulfilment of the plan and checking on
     how it is being carried out by each enterprise' (E. Mandel,
     p. 561).

6.   This is because goods are subject to very different rates of subsidy, taxation and profit target in their manufacture.

7.   Naturally the prime measure of competence is the success in obtaining premiums and bonuses.

8.   Control is separated from coordinated labour, in spite of 'workers' control' in the enterprise, because the economic and political environment – which the workers do not control – forces them to accept labour discipline and work norms applied by the management.

9.   W. Wesolowski (1967) pp. 22–3.

10.   J. Goldthorpe (1964) p. 10.

11.   E. Garnsey.

12.   A. Giddens (1973).

13.   See N. Poulantzas, and B. Fine and L. Harris.

14.   Although recent crises have resulted in increasing participation of the state in the organisation of production in the West, due to the need to restructure capital. See Fine and Harris.

15.   A. Giddens (1973) p. 239.

16.   In fact the Western states organised a financial boycott of Russia which deprived her of virtually any credit and made trade relations extraordinarily difficult.

17.   The strategy eventually adopted was only arrived at as the outcome of bitter internal political conflict – the defeat both of those who urged slow industrialisation on the basis of concessions to the peasants, and those who denied the premise that revolutions in the West were unlikely to occur and that encouraging such developments should be the keystone of policy.

18.   Payment by results encourages workers to solve their own economic problems by increasing their work rate rather than combining with fellow workers to demand a rise in wage levels. This individualistic effect is particularly marked in progressive piece-rate systems where the bonus is increased successively with each higher level of overfulfilment of the norms. 'Rate-busters' were held up as heroes whom other workers should emulate.

19.   I. Deutscher, p. 339.

20.   Quoted in I. Deutscher, p. 328.

21.   A. Nove (1972) p. 194.

22.   The potential threat of Russian forces is often sufficient to deter the leaders of Eastern European states from implementing policies of which the Russian leaders disapprove. At times, as in Hungary in 1956 and Czechoslovakia in 1968, the threat is translated into reality.

23. Perhaps Russia and East Germany provide the nearest approximation to the directive planning type and Hungary and Czechoslovakia the nearest to the guided market type.

24. The phrase is due to C. Kerr *et al.*

25. Marxism in the East is an ideology, a system of concepts and propositions legitimising a ruling class; in our view, it is a complete distortion of Marx's own theories.

26. R. Kosolapov, p. 60.

27. Ibid.

28. D. Lane (1970) pp. 282–3. According to Lane, the authorities may dismiss elected chairmen of collectives.

29. W. Wesolowski (1969).

30. We have argued this point extensively in Chapters Two and Three.

31. There is considerable ambiguity in Eastern theorists on who should be counted as 'intelligentsia'. The term is sometimes used generally to refer to all non-manual employees, but often restricted to specialists possessing higher educational qualifications, the rest being referred to as 'employees'. This narrow use of the term does not correspond to our conception of controllers of the means of production since it excludes control functions of lower supervisory staff and we would not necessarily include technical, scientific, educational and cultural personnel.

32. The reform movement in Czechoslovakia in 1968 was initially fuelled by Slovak nationalism.

CHAPTER 8

1. There are, however, still considerable gaps in our empirical knowledge – for example, in the areas of fringe benefits, tax avoidance and tax evasion. General discussions of the range and nature of inequality in Britain can be found in P. Townsend and N. Bosanquet, J. Kincaid, D. Wedderburn, ed. (1974), and J. Westergaard and H. Resler (1975).

2. J. Westergaard and H. Resler, p. 113.

3. Ibid. pp. 73–6.

4. D. Wedderburn and C. Craig, 'Inequality at Work', in D. Wedderburn, ed. (1974).

5. See R. Kinnersley.

6. A most explicit theoretical elaboration of this approach is to be found in W. G. Runciman. 'Economic class' is defined as 'wealth' and individual class positions 'mapped' in a three-dimensional space according to class, status, and power. A

cogent critique of Runciman is developed in G. K. Ingham (1970a). A similar approach to that of Runciman has been more implicitly assumed by some American sociologists, especially in the 1950s. Communities are divided into 'lower lower', 'lower middle', 'upper middle', etc., 'classes' on the basis of material possessions and reputational analysis. See, for example, W. Lloyd Warner.

7.   B. Wootton.
8.   Report of the Royal Commission on the Distribution of Income and Wealth, July 1975, table 29 (Cmnd 6171).
9.   Ibid. tables 30, 48.
10.   J. Westergaard and H. Resler (1975) p. 114.
11.   Ibid. p. 116.
12.   See the discussion in Chapter Four above.
13.   J. Westergaard and H. Resler (1975) p. 27.
14.   Ibid. p. 27.
15.   Ibid. p. 344.
16.   Ibid.
17.   Data adapted from the *New Earnings Survey 1975*, table 8.
18.   *The Times*, 7 Aug 1976.
19.   For a critical review of such theories see R. Hyman (1974), R. Hyman and I. Brough (1975), and B. Wootton, chap. 1.
20.   See E. H. Phelps-Brown. A. Glyn and B. Sutcliffe argue that union militancy *has* had an effect on overall patterns of distribution.
21.   See the discussion in G. K. Ingham (1970b).
22.   B. Wootton, chap. 2.
23.   A. Giddens (1973) p. 105. See also the discussion in Chapter Three above.
24.   See Chapter Three above.
25.   K. Davis and W. Moore (1966), T. Parsons.
26.   K. Davis and W. Moore (1966) p. 415.
27.   M. Tumin. For a general critique of functionalist explanations, see R. Hyman and I. Brough (1975).
28.   R. Hyman and I. Brough (1975). Hyman and Brough further argue that the acceptability of income differentials is being increasingly challenged.
29.   F. Parkin (1972a) p. 40.
30.   D. Lockwood (1958) p. 209.
31.   R. Hyman (1974) p. 184, R. Hyman and I. Brough (1975). These are two of the most recent discussions of the ideological underpinnings of the occupational structure: this topic is also discussed in F. Parkin (1972a), J. Rex, and A. Giddens (1973).

32. R. Hyman (1974) p. 185.
33. Ibid.
34. K. Marx (1974a) p. 883.
35. A. Giddens (1973) p. 87.
36. Of course, if labour is sufficiently cheap 'outworking' is still profitable, especially if it is already skilled and requires little or no training – for example, married 'homeworkers' in the shoe industry. The example cited holds as long as the cost of labour is broadly the same to every capitalist. The actual details of the capitalist labour process can assume a variety of forms.
37. H. Braverman, p. 87 (our emphasis).
38. We feel that this *external* development of coordination, and its *practical* fusion with control, is a point insufficiently stressed by G. Carchedi, although at other points we draw quite heavily on his analysis.
39. K. Marx (1974a) p. 881.
40. Marx clearly recognised this particular nature of capitalist authority, although his discussion is not very extensive:

    > The authority assumed by the capitalist as the personification of capital in the direct process of production, the social function performed by him in his capacity as manager and ruler of production, is essentially different from the authority exercised on the basis of production by means of slaves, serfs, etc.

    An interesting parallel can be drawn here with Weber's analysis of types of authority relationships: traditional, charismatic and rational-legal. Weber associates different kinds of authority with different epochs, but not different modes of production. Rational-legal authority, associated with bureaucratic authority structures, we may infer is the 'characteristic' mode of authority associated with capitalist production. Rational-legal authority, is not, in Weber's analysis, in itself problematic, and conflicts and tensions analysed by Weber derive from the nature of the structure of authority itself – bureaucracy – rather than its association with exploitation (see above, Chapter Four). This is entirely congruent with Weber's analysis as a whole, which, as we have argued, implicitly denies that the capitalist mode of production is inherently antagonistic.
41. J. Westergaard and H. Resler (1975) p. 53. See also their discussion on p. 107 ff. Also R. Hyman (1974) p. 185.

42. F. W. Taylor, pp. 27, 29. First set of italics ours, others in the original. Taylor's work is extensively discussed in H. Braverman, chap. 4.
43. A. Fox.
44. See E. Trist. Trist argues that whereas work in the 'mechanised' phase of industrial development leads itself to 'scientific management' techniques and thus deskilling, this is not the case for work in the 'automated' phase of industrial development.
45. Direct resistance to deskilling is probably most common (for obvious reasons) amongst skilled craftsmen, but semi-skilled workers have also evolved highly complex control strategies. See, for example, D. Roy, and T. Lupton.
46. A. Fox, p.36.
47. Ibid. pp. 57–8.
48. See S. Lilley, 'Technological Progress and the Industrial Revolution 1700–1914', in C. M. Cipolla, ed.
49. H. Braverman, p. 156.
50. See above, Chapter Six.
51. See, for example, Sir J. Baker's inaugural address to the British Association for the Advancement of Science. Reported in *The Times*, 2 Sep 1976.
52. A. Fox, p. 16 ff.
53. Quoted in H. Braverman, p. 149. For other empirical discussions of the resentment engendered by assembly-line work see C. R. Walker and R. H. Guest, H. Beynon, R. Blauner, and J. Goldthorpe *et al.* (1968).
54. J. Westergaard (1970) p. 120.
55. The field is a wide one, but see, for example, F. Herzberg, D. McGregor, and R. Likert.
56. M. Bosquet.
57. T. Nichols (1975) p. 253.
58. For example, in the case of the archetypical British productivity deal, Fawley workers' pay had reached the average of that of the surrounding area some four to five years after the deal. See T. Cliff (1970b).
59. E. Trist.
60. Ibid.; also R. Blauner.
61. See S. Mallet, and various works by A. Touraine. Touraine's approach has been summarised in English in M. Mann, and C. Posner (editor's introduction).
62. H. Braverman, chap. 9.
63. D. Wedderburn and R. Crompton (1972).

64. Ibid.; also R. Brown (1973).
65. R. Dahrendorf. This also applies (to a lesser extent) to Giddens, where work relationships and authority relationships are identified as important 'proximate sources of structuration' Giddens, however, takes authority relationships for granted, rather than explaining them.

CHAPTER 9

1. Inequalities in income, status, power and opportunity have been recently documented for Britain by J. Westergaard and H. Resler (1976).
2. See J. Goldthorpe *et al.* (1969), D. Lockwood (1966), F. Parkin (1972*a*).
3. Perhaps 'sectionalism' might usefully be added to typologies of working-class consciousness.
4. G. Carchedi.
5. See Chapter Five, pp. 69–71.
6. E. O. Wright.
7. There are undoubtedly cases where the possessors profoundly contrain government decision making *in spite of* the government's formal legal powers. This is notoriously true of the armed forces and the administrative apparatus in some countries.
8. The concept of the capitalist mode of production involves a considerable abstraction from actual capitalist societies; we limit the concept to the general relations between control and coordinated labour in quasi-capitals, private capitals and state non-capitals. In reality there are social groups outside the categories of the capitalist mode of production such as aristocrats, lumpenproletariat, children, retired people and the sick, and domestic labourers (in particular, housewives). All these elements, together with such institutions as churches, social clubs, political parties and families, clearly play important parts in the functioning of any social order. For an examination of the way in which the capitalist mode of production is integrated into a total society we require more specific and historical studies than this book attempts.
9. J. O'Connor, p. 22.
10. For an interesting study of divisions among shop-floor workers see T. Nichols and P. Armstrong (1976).
11. We differ here fundamentally from R. Bacon and W. Eltis.
12. J. Woodward, p. 17.

13. See M. Dalton, and J. Woodward, chap. 7.
14. J. Woodward, and T. Burns and M. Stalker.
15. E. O. Wright.
16. R. Brown and P. Brannen (1970).
17. D. Lockwood (1958) p. 209.
18. See M. Crozier, and P. Blau.
19. A. Gouldner (1964).
20. A. Gouldner (1965).
21. Ibid. p. 95.
22. E. O. Wright, p. 33.
23. Ibid. pp. 29–33.
24. Ibid. p. 33.
25. For an exposition of the former approach see C. Kerr *et al.*
26. Quoted in R. Hyman (1971) p. 12.
27. R. Hyman (1971).
28. See M. Mann, G. Ingham (1974), and R. Dore.
29. C. W. Mills (1956).
30. Ibid. p. 354.
31. B. C. Roberts *et al.*
32. Ibid. p. 25.
33. Ibid. p. 322.
34. This figure is arrived at by retaining Wright's estimates of the proportion of top managers, middle managers, technocrats, foremen and supervisors and adding professionals etc., included as 'semi-autonomous employees'. Craftsmen have been placed in the proletariat. We reserve judgement on whether or not small employers are in a structurally ambiguous class position. See E. O. Wright, p. 37.

APPENDIX

1. K. Marx (1968*e*) p. 202.
2. K. Marx (1968*e*) p. 204.
3. For a brief introduction to this topic and a guide to further sources see M. Howard and J. King (1975) chap. 5.

Bibliography

P. Bachrach and M. Baratz (1962), 'Two Faces of Power', *American Political Science Review*, **56**, 4.

R. Bacon and W. Eltis (1976), *Britain's Economic Problem: Too Few Producers* (London: Macmillan).

G. S. Bain and R. Price (1972), 'Who Is a White-collar Employee?', *British Journal of Industrial Relations*, **10**, 3.

G. J. Bannock (1971), *The Juggernauts: The Age of the Big Corporation* (London: Weidenfield & Nicholson).

P. A. Baran and P. M. Sweezy (1968), *Monopoly Capital* (Harmondsworth, Middx: Penguin).

D. Beetham (1974), *Max Weber and the Theory of Modern Politics* (London: Allen & Unwin).

H. Beynon (1973), *Working for Ford* (Harmondsworth, Middx: Allen Lane/Penguin Education).

P. Blau (1966), *The Dynamics of Bureaucracy* (Chicago and London: University of Chicago Press).

R. Blauner (1964), *Alienation and Freedom* (Chicago and London: The University of Chicago Press).

M. Bosquet (1972), 'The Prison Factory', *New Left Review*, 73, (May/June).

T. Bottomore (1965), *Classes in Modern Society* (London: Allen & Unwin).

— and M. Rubel, eds. (1963), *Karl Marx: Selected Writings* (Harmondsworth, Middx: Penguin).

H. Braverman (1974), *Labour and Monopoly Capital* (New York: Monthly Review Press).

S. Brittain (1971), *Steering the Economy* (Harmondsworth, Middx: Penguin).

M. Barratt Brown (1968), 'The Controllers of British Industry', in *Can the Workers Run Industry?*, ed. K. Coates (London: Sphere Books).

— (1972), *From Labourism to Socialism* (Nottingham: Spokesman Books).

R. Brown (1973), 'Sources of Objectives in Work and Employment', in *Man and Organisation*, ed. J. Child (London: Allen & Unwin).

— and P. Brannen (1970), 'Shipbuilders' (parts 1 and 2), *Sociology*, **4**, 1 and 2.

T. Burns and M. Stalker (1961), *The Management of Innovation* (London: Tavistock).

G. Carchedi (1975), 'On the Economic Identification of the New Middle Class', *Economy and Society*, **4**, 1.

C. M. Cipolla, ed. (1973), *The Fontana Economic History of Europe*, **3**, *The Industrial Revolution* (London: Collins/Fontana).

R. V. Clements (1968), *Managers: A Study of Their Careers in Industry* (London: Allen & Unwin).

T. Cliff (1970a), *Russia: A Marxist Analysis* (London: International Socialism).

— (1970b), *The Employers' Offensive: Productivity Deals and How to Fight Them* (London: Pluto).

R. Crompton (1976), 'Approaches to the Study of White Collar Unionism', *Sociology* (September).

C. A. R. Crosland (1962), *The Conservative Enemy* (London: Jonathan Cape).

C. Crouch (1974), 'The Ideology of a Managerial Elite' in I. Crewe (ed.), *Political Sociology Yearbook*, 1.

M. Crozier (1964), *The Bureaucratic Phenomenon* (London: Tavistock).

R. Dahrendorf (1967), *Class and Class Conflict in an Industrial Society* (London: Routledge & Kegan Paul).

M. Dalton (1966), *Men Who Manage* (Wiley: New York).

K. Davis (1958), *Human Society* (New York: Macmillan).

— and W. Moore (1966), 'Some Principles of Stratification' in *Sociological Theory*, eds. L. Coser, and B. Rosenberg (New York: Collier/Macmillan).

I. Deutscher (1961), *Stalin: A Political Biography* (London: Oxford University Press).

G. Domhoff (1967), *Who Rules America?* (Englewood Cliffs, N. J.: Prentice-Hall).

R. Dore (1973), *British Factory, Japanese Factory* (London: Allen & Unwin).

E. Durkheim (1957), *Professional Ethics and Civic Morals* (London: Routledge & Kegan Paul).

— (1958), *Socialism and Saint Simon* (London: Routledge & Kegan Paul).

— (1966), *Suicide* (London: Routledge & Kegan Paul).

— (1968), *The Division of Labour in Society* (New York: The Free Press).

B. Fine and L. Harris (1976), 'The Debate on State Expenditure', *New Left Review*, 98 (July/August).

A. Fox (1974), *Beyond Contract: Work, Power and Trust Relations*, (London: Faber).

J. K. Galbraith (1961), *American Capitalism* (London: Hamish Hamilton).

— (1969), *The New Industrial State* (Harmondsworth, Middx: Penguin).

A. Gamble and P. Walton (1976), *Capitalism in Crisis* (London: Macmillan).

E. Garnsey (1975), 'Occupational Structure in Industrialised Societies', *Sociology*, **9**, 3.

H. Gerth and C. W. Mills, eds. (1964), *From Max Weber* (London: Routledge & Kegan Paul).

A. Giddens (1971), *Capitalism and Modern Social Theory* (Cambridge: Cambridge University Press).

— (1973), *The Class Structure of the Advanced Societies* (London: Hutchinson).

A. Glyn and B. Sutcliffe (1972), *British Capitalism, Workers and the Profits Squeeze* (Harmondsworth, Middx: Penguin).

J. Goldthorpe (1964), 'Social Stratification in Industrial Society', in *The Development of Industrial Societies*, ed. P. Halmos, *Sociological Review* Monograph, 8, University of Keele (Oct.).

—, D. Lockwood, F. Bechhofer and J. Platt (1968), *The Affluent Worker, Industrial Attitudes and Behaviour* (Cambridge: Cambridge University Press).

—, D. Lockwood, F. Bechhofer and J. Platt (1969), *The Affluent Worker in the Class Structure* (Cambridge: Cambridge University Press).

I. Gough (1972), 'Marx's Theory of Productive and Unproductive Labour', *New Left Review*, 76.

A. Gouldner (1964), *Patterns of Industrial Bureaucracy* (New York: The Free Press).

— (1965), *Wildcat Strike* (New York: Harper & Row).

A. H. Hansen (1963), *Nationalization* (London: Allen & Unwin).

— and M. Walles (1975), *Governing Britain* (London: Fontana).

N. Harris (1972), *Competition and the Corporate Society* (London: Methuen).

F. Herzberg (1968), *Work and the Nature of Man* (London: Staples).

M. C. Howard and J. E. King (1975), *The Political Economy of Marx* (Harlow, Essex: Longman).

—, eds. (1976), *The Economics of Marx*, (Harmondsworth, Middx: Penguin).

R. Hyman (1971), *Marxism and the Sociology of Trade Unions* (London: Pluto Press).
— (1974), 'Inequality, Ideology and Industrial Relations', *British Journal of Industrial Relations*, **12**.
— and I. Brough (1975), *Social Values and Industrial Relations* (Oxford: Basil Blackwell).
G. K. Ingham (1970a), 'Social Stratification: Individual Attributes and Social Relationships', *Sociology*, **4**, 1 (Jan).
— (1970b), *Size of Industrial Organisation and Worker Behaviour* (Cambridge: Cambridge University Press).
— (1974), *Strikes and Industrial Conflict* (London: Macmillan).
C. Kaysen (1966), 'The Modern Corporation: How Much Power? What Scope?' in *Class, Status and Power*, ed. S. M. Lipset and R. Bendix (London: Routledge).
C. Kerr, J. Dunlop, F. Harbinson and C. Myers (1973), *Industrialism and Industrial Man* (Harmondsworth, Middx: Penguin).
M. Kidron (1970), *Western Capitalism Since the War* (Harmondsworth, Middx: Penguin).
J. Kincaid (1975), *Poverty and Equality in Britain*, (Harmondsworth, Middx: Penguin).
R. Kinnersley (1975), *The Hazards of Work* (London: Pluto).
R. Kosolapov (1972), 'On the Way to a Classless Society', *Social Sciences*, 1.
D. Lane (1970), *Politics and Society in the USSR* (London: Weidenfeld & Nicolson).
D. Lane (1977), 'Marxist Class Conflict Analyses of State Socialist Society' in R. Scase (ed.) *Industrial Society: Class, Cleavage and Control* (London: Allen & Unwin).
J. Leruez (1975), *Economic Planning and Politics in Britain* (London: Martin Robertson).
R. Likert (1961), *New Patterns of Management* (New York: McGraw-Hill).
D. Lockwood (1958), *The Blackcoated Worker* (London: Allen & Unwin).
— (1966, 'Sources of Variation in Working Class Images of Society', *Sociological Review*, **14**.
— (1967), 'Some Remarks on "The Social System"', in *System, Change and Conflict*, ed. N. Demerath and R. Peterson (New York: The Free Press).
S. Lukes (1975), *Emile Durkheim: His Life and Work* (Harmondsworth, Middx: Penguin Books).
T. Lupton (1963), *On the Shop Floor* (Oxford: Pergamon).
B. Malinowski (1960), *Argonauts of the Western Pacific* (New York: Dutton).

S. Mallet (1975), *The New Working Class* (Nottingham: Bertand Russell Peace Foundation for Spokesman Books).

E. Mandel (1971), *Marxist Economic Theory* (London: Merlin Press).

M. Mann (1973), *Consciousness and Action amongst the Western Working Class* (London: Macmillan).

T. H. Marshall, *Sociology at the Crossroads* (London: Heinemann).

D. McClellan (1975), *Marx* (London: Fontana/Collins).

D. McGregor (1960), *The Human Side of Enterprise* (New York: McGraw-Hill).

K. Marx (1967), *Capital*, vol. 2 (Moscow: Foreign Languages Publishing House).

— (1970a), *Capital,* vol. 1 (Moscow: Foreign Languages Publishing House).

— (1970b), *The German Ideology* (London: Lawrence & Wishart).

— (1974a), *Capital*, vol. 3 (Moscow: Foreign Languages Publishing House).

— (1974b), *Grundrisse* (Harmondsworth, Middx: Penguin).

— (1974c), 'The Civil War in France' (draft), in *The First International and After*, ed. D. Fernbach, Pelican Marx Library vol. 3 (Harmondsworth, Middx: Penguin).

— and F. Engels (1968), *Marx and Engels: Selected Works* (London: Lawrence & Wishart): (a) 'Manifesto of the Communist Party'; (b) 'The Class Struggles in France'; (c) 'Wage Labour and Capital'; (d) 'The 18th Brumaire of Louis Bonaparte'; (e) 'Wages, Prices and Profit'.

S. Melman (1970), *Pentagon Capitalism* (New York: McGraw-Hill).

R. Miliband (1969), *The State in Capitalist Society* (London: Weidenfeld & Nicholson).

C. W. Mills (1956), *White Collar* (New York: Oxford University Press).

— (1959), *The Power Elite* (New York: Oxford University Press).

J. Mitchell (1972), *The National Board for Prices and Incomes* (London: Secker & Warburg).

T. Nichols (1969), *Ownership, Control and Ideology* (London: Allen & Unwin).

— (1975), 'The Socialism of Management: Some Comments on the New "Human Relations" ', *Sociological Review*, **23**, 2.

— and P. Armstrong (1976), *Workers Divided* (London: Fontana/Collins).

M. Nicolaus (1970), 'Proletariat and Middle Class in Marx', in *For a New America*, ed. D. Weinstein and J. Eakins (New York: Random House).

M. Nicolaus (1972), 'The Unknown Marx', in *Ideology in Social Science*, ed. R. Blackburn (London: Fontana/Collins).

A. Nove (1965), *The Soviet Economy* (London: Allen & Unwin).

— (1972, *An Economic History of the USSR* (Harmondsworth, Middx: Allen Lane, The Penguin Press).

J. O'Connor (1973), *The Fiscal Crisis of the State* (New York: St. Martin's Press).

F. Parkin (1972*a*), *Class Inequality and Political Order* (London: Paladin).

— (1972*b*), 'System Contradiction and Political Transformation', *Archives Européennes de Sociologie*, 13, 1.

— (1974), 'Strategies of Social Closure in Class Formation' in *The Social Analysis of Class Structure*, ed. F. Parkin (London: Tavistock).

T. Parsons (1964), 'Social Classes and Class Conflict in the Light of Recent Sociological Theory', in T. Parsons, *Essays in Sociological Theory* (New York: The Free Press).

E. H. Phelps-Brown (1972), 'The Influence of Trade Unions and Collective Bargaining on Pay Levels and Pay Structure', in *Trade Unions*, ed. W. E. J. McCarthy (Harmondsworth, Middx: Penguin).

K. Polanyi (1957), *The Great Transformation* (Boston: Beacon Press).

S. Pollard (1968), *The Genesis of Modern Management* (Harmondsworth, Middx: Penguin).

C. Posner, ed. (1970), *Reflections on the Revolution in France* (Harmondsworth, Middx: Penguin).

N. Poulantzas (1973), *Political Power and Social Class* (London: New Text Books).

R. Pryke (1971), *Public Enterprise in Practice* (London: MacGibbon & Kee).

H. Radice, ed. (1976), *International Firms and Modern Imperialism* (Harmondsworth, Middx: Penguin).

M. Rees (1973), *The Public Sector in the Mixed Economy* (London: Batsford).

J. Rex (1968), *Key Problems of Sociological Theory* (London: Routledge & Kegan Paul).

B. Roberts, R. Loveridge and J. Gennard (1972), *Reluctant Militants* (London: Heinemann).

R. Rowthorn (1974), 'Neo-Ricardianism or Marxism?', *New Left Review*, 86 (July/August).

D. Roy (1969), 'Efficiency and the Fix', in *Industrial Man*, ed. T. Burns (Harmondsworth, Middx: Penguin).

W. G. Runciman (1968), 'Class, Status and Party?' in *Social Stratification*, ed. J. A. Jackson, Sociological Studies 1 (Cambridge: Cambridge University Press).

A. Sampson (1973), *The Sovereign State* (London: Hodder & Stoughton).

B. Supple (1973), 'The State and the Industrial Revolution 1700–1914', in *The Fontana Economic History of Europe*, ed. C. M. Cipolla vol. 3 (London: Fontana/Collins).

F. W. Taylor (1972), 'The Principles of Scientific Management' in *Design of Jobs*, ed. E. Davis and J. C. Taylor (Harmondsworth, Middx: Penguin).

E. P. Thompson (1967), 'Time, Work Discipline and Industrial Capitalism', *Past and Present*, December.

P. Townsend and N. Bosanquet (1972), *Labour and Inequality* (London: Fabian Society).

E. Trist (1973), 'A Socio-technical Critique of Scientific Management', in *Meaning and Control*, ed. D. O. Edge and J. N. Wolfe (London: Tavistock).

C. Tugenhadt (1971), *The Multinationals* (London: Eyre & Spottiswoode).

M. Tumin (1966), 'Some Principles of Stratification: A Critical Analysis', in *Sociological Theory*, ed. L. Coser and B. Rosenberg (New York: Collier/Macmillan).

C. R. Walker and R. H. Guest (1952), *The Man on the Assembly Line* (Cambridge, Mass.: Harvard University Press).

W. Lloyd Warner (1960), *Social Class in America* (New York: Harper & Row).

M. Weber (1965), *The Protestant Ethic and the Spirit of Capitalism* (London: Allen & Unwin).

— (1966), *The Theory of Social and Economic Organisation*, ed T. Parsons (New York: The Free Press).

— (1969), *The Methodology of the Social Sciences* (New York: The Free Press).

D. Wedderburn and R. Crompton (1972), *Workers' Attitudes and Technology* (Cambridge: Cambridge University Press).

D. Wedderburn, (1974), *Poverty, Inequality and the Class Structure* (Cambridge: Cambridge University Press).

W. Wesolowski (1967), 'Social Stratification in Socialist Society', *Polish Sociological Bulletin*, 1.

— (1969), 'Strata and Strata Interests in Socialist Society', in *Structured Social Inequality*, ed. C. S. Heller (New York: Macmillan).

J. Westergaard (1970), 'The Rediscovery of the Cash Nexus', in *The Socialist Register*, ed. R. Miliband and J. Saville (London: Merlin).

— and H. Resler (1975), *Class in a Capitalist Society* (London: Heinemann).

J. Winkler (1976) 'Corporatism', *Archives Européennes de Sociologie*, **17**.

J. Woodward (1965), *Industrial Organisation: Theory and Practice* (London: Oxford University Press).

B. Wootton (1955), *The Social Foundations of Wages Policy* (London: Allen & Unwin).

E. O. Wright (1976), 'Class Boundaries in Advanced Capitalist Societies', *New Left Review*, 98.

C. Yanaga (1968), *Big Business in Japanese Politics* (New Haven, Conn.: Yale University Press).

Index

feudalism 11, 15, 30
finance 50–1, 68, 87–9, 92, 105,
  215, 216, 218
in early stage of capitalism 52
fixed capital 75, 78, 91, 216
foreman 95, 190. *See also* structural ambiguity
Fox, A. 157, 161

Gamble, A., and Walton, P. 100,
  106
Giddens, A. 132, 149, 154, 193,
  194
  class analysis 34–7
  class structure in the East 37–9
  labour theory of value 30–2
global capital, *see* capital
Goldthorpe, J. 130–1
Gough, I. 216
Gouldner, A. 187
Gramsci, A. 192

Harris, N. 102
Health Services 112, 116–17, 122,
  140
Housing 112, 117, 147
Hyman, R. 152–3, 193

ideology 204–5
  dominant value system 152–3
  ideological functions of the state
    114–18
  ideology in the East 27, 136–7
industry 78–81
  types of industry 81
inequalities
  class and inequality 125, 141
  cumulative inequality 140–1,
    150, 168–9
  differential rewards as a source
    of 'loyalty' 134, 155–6,
    192, 199
  income inequalities 140, 145–6
  inequalities of wealth 142–4
  inequalities politically deter-
    mined 26–7, 131–2
inequality, causes of
  functional explanation 151–2
  market value explanation
    147–50
  power explanation 150–1, 153
  social consensus explanation
    152–3

inflation 106–7
inheritance 27, 37–8, 60–1, 142,
  144. *See also* private property
interest 81, 105, 177. *See also*
  finance
investment 78, 79, 86, 105. *See also*
  capital accumulation

job evaluation 152–3, 155–6, 164.
  See also productivity
joint-stock company 50–1
  goals 66–8
  legal basis 45, 50

Keynes, J. M. 104, 106

labour (collective worker) 94–5,
  154–5, 180–1, 184–5, 197
  functional definition 3, 71–3
  See also class, coordination
labour power 10–11, 78–9
  labour power as a commodity
    12–13, 209
  relationship between wage
    labour and capital 68–70
labour theory of value 10–13,
    30–1, 69, 208–10
  socially necessary labour time
    72
  socially necessary wage 112,
    116, 209–10, 216–17
Lane, D. 28
legal system 118
  company law 45, 50
  ownership as a legal rather thn
    an economic category
    68–70, 128, 130
life chances 5–6, 34, 145
  affected by non-economic factors
    7–8.
  See also Weberian class theory
Lockwood, D. 152, 195
  class analysis 20–3
lumpenproletariat 204–5

management 70, 72, 79–80, 154–8,
  180–1, 198
  class situation of managers 73,
    180
  goals of management 66–7
  human relations and manage-
    ment 54, 148, 161–3

248 INDEX

relative surplus value 72–3, 157

taxation 14, 81, 105–6, 112, 123, 131, 133, 137, 143–4, 172, 177, 223
Taylor, F. W. 157. *See also* scientific management
technicians 44, 49, 198, 200–1
trade unions 35, 121, 147–8, 179, 192–3
trade unions and the state 103, 107
trade unions in the East 29, 127, 129, 227
white-collar unionism 23, 192, 196, 200–1
traditional worker consciousness 169, 185. *See also* class consciousness
transport 81
state support of transport 46, 112, 117

underclass 37. *See also* lumpen-proletariat
unemployment 55, 104, 106, 116, 204, 206, 209
unproductive labour, *see* productive and unproductive labour
use value 11, 30
use value equivalences in the military effort 114, 119
See also labour theory of value

variable capital 216

Weber, M. 2, 55–8, 195
bureaucracy 17, 57–8, 186–91, 231
ideal types 55
Weber's class theory 5–9, 16–19
Weberian class theory 5–9, 18–19, 125, 130, 149, 194
contrast with Marxist theory 2–3, 10, 16–17, 39–40
critique 3
demarcation problem 23–4, 34
A. Giddens 34–9
D. Lockwood 20–3
F. Parkin 23–7
See also property class, acquisition class, social class
welfare 55, 112, 116, 140, 172–3. *See also* state expenditure
Wesolowski, W. 129–30, 137
Westergaard, J. 161
Westergaard, J., and Resler, H. 144–5
work situation 20–2, 148–9, 169–70, 185. *See also* authority relationships
workers' control 36, 38–9, 128, 158, 162–3, 175
world economy 103, 106, 110, 118–20, 125, 127–8, 134
Wright, E. O. 80–1, 95, 174, 182–4, 189–90, 202